I0147917

Historical Archaeology of the Irish Diaspora

Historical Archaeology of the Irish Diaspora

A Transnational Approach

Stephen A. Brighton

The University of Tennessee Press / Knoxville

First Edition.

The conclusion originally appeared in a different form as "Degrees of Alienation: The Material Evidence of Irish and Irish American Experience" in *Historical Archaeology* 42(4). Reprinted with permission.

The paper in this book meets the requirements of American National Standards Institute / National Information Standards Organization specification Z39.48-1992 (Permanence of Paper). It contains 30 percent post-consumer waste and is certified by the Forest Stewardship Council.

Library of Congress Cataloging-in-Publication Data

Brighton, Stephen A.
Historical archaeology of the Irish diaspora: a transnational approach / Stephen A. Brighton.
p. cm.
Includes bibliographical references and index.
ISBN-13: 978-1-57233-667-4 (hardcover: alk. paper)
ISBN-10: 1-57233-667-6 (hardcover: alk. paper)
1. Irish—United States—History—19th century.
2. Ireland—Emigration and immigration—History—19th century.
3. United States—Emigration and immigration—History—19th century.
4. Archaeology and history—United States.
5. Excavations (Archaeology)—United States.
6. Excavations (Archaeology)—New York (State)—New York.
7. Excavations (Archaeology)—New Jersey—Paterson.
8. Irish—Material culture.
9. National characteristics, Irish—History—19th century.
10. Ireland—History—Famine, 1845–1852.
I. Title.

E184.I6B84 2009
305.891'62073—dc22
2009010598

For Praveena and Ciarán

Contents

Illustrations

Figures

Tables

Acknowledgments

Thomas Wells deserves much praise and gratitude for his enthusiasm and dedication to make this book a reality. I would like to thank James Symonds and Paul Mullins for their reviews of the drafts; they made this a stronger book. The University of Maryland, Erve Chambers, and the Department of Anthropology deserve a special acknowledgment for giving me the time and guidance to complete this research. Specifically, I would like to express my appreciation to Mark Leone and Paul Shackel for reading various drafts and providing insightful comments and constructive critiques.

This book was inspired by Charles Orser and his unselfishness and generosity both professionally and personally. Our many discussions pushed me to become a better writer. I cannot express how much they meant to me. Of course, this book would not have existed if it were not for Mary Beaudry guiding my dissertation research. I would like to thank my entire committee: Mary Beaudry, Charles Orser, Kevin Kenny, and Kevin O'Neill. It has been my honor to learn from them.

Rebecca Yamin of John Milner Associates had faith in my abilities from the very beginning. Yamin was the first person to push me in the direction of giving public and professional presentations as well as publishing in peer-reviewed journals. I cannot thank her enough for introducing me to that aspect of historical archaeology. This research was also inspired by many conversations and debates with colleagues, including Thomas Barrett, Tadhg O'Keefe, Deb Rotman, Cheryl LaRoche, Thomas Killion, and David Gadsby.

While developing this book I had the ultimate luck in having as my wife and partner Praveena Gadam, who has continually forced me to challenge myself and see nothing but the very best in the world. We married during a most stressful period of my graduate career, at a time when I did not believe I could ever write. Her unquestioning love for me, sometimes more of a tough love, provided the belief in myself and the strength I needed to overcome all doubts. At the time of writing this book we had our son, Ciarán Stephen Krishna, and he witnessed my various levels of frustration and enlightenment. I hope that one day he understands me and his family by reading this book and comes to find an appreciation of his history not only in the United States but also in Ireland, Italy, and India.

Introduction

Time has an interesting way of distorting memories and romanticizing the struggles and injustices of the past. This is especially true of the experiences of the Irish diaspora. In the United States, over 40 million people claim Irish ancestry. Based on the number of websites and genealogical services available to Irish Americans, it is evident that people are interested in, yet ignorant of, their family's ethnic and social history. Throughout their journeys of self-discovery, most Irish Americans cling to an imagined Irish identity reinforced by popularized images of the "homeland" made up of quaint stone cottages, shamrocks, leprechauns, green fields, and songs such as "Danny Boy." Ironically, "Danny Boy," the seemingly Irish American theme song for all things Irish, was written by an upper-class Englishman for a mass audience and is not a traditional Irish folk ballad (McCourt 2003).

In reality, the romanticized images and sociocultural badges of Irish Americans today, once derogatory signs and symbols of an alienated foreign group, derive from a traumatic history of colonialism and, for the most part, forced dispersal dating back to the early part of the nineteenth century. In San Francisco, for example, t-shirts with slogans and images equating being Irish with drunkenness, a common stereotype, and excess were on sale prior to the 2007 St. Patrick's Day parade. Moreover, in 2003 the *Jeanie Johnston,* a replica of a nineteenth-century Famine ship, vessels ironically know as *coffin ships* because so many of their passenger died during the six-week crossing, sailed from Ireland to North America (Gordon 2003:46). In 2003, the passengers were mostly Irish Americans hoping to gain insights into what their ancestors experienced. The trip from Ireland to ports in the United States and Canada included all the amenities of a small cruise. The sterile environment on board, purported to be accurate, perpetuated ethnic and class-based myths that romanticize the true character of the Irish diasporic experience.

To be sure, individuals have their own personal beliefs as to what symbols represent, but when put in the broader social history of a national

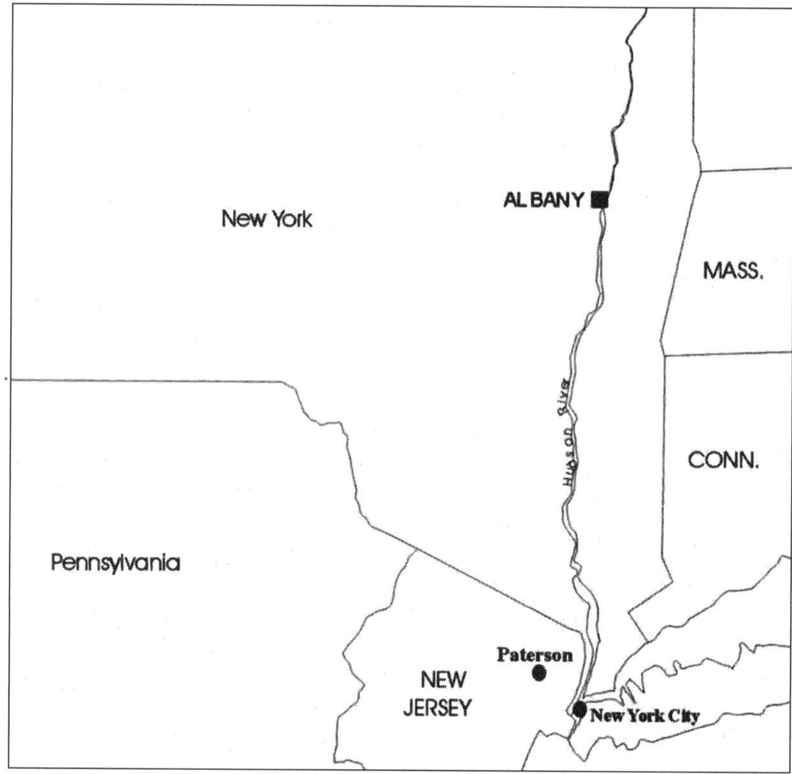

Figure 1. Map of New York and New Jersey showing the locations of Paterson and New York City.

(diasporic) identity, it becomes clear that these individual meanings form a group ideology with a long and interesting historical trajectory. This ideology forms part of the diasporic mentality in which the derogatory symbols have developed into what Gayatri Chakravorty Spivak (1988:205) refers to as "strategic essentialism," whereby marginalized groups use signifiers of their racialized identity for the purpose of contesting and disrupting dominant discourses that serve to exclude or alienate. The alienating symbols of Irish American history have been recovered as a source of empowerment reflecting the period of conflict, exclusion, and subordination and transforming it into something of a success story (the American dream).

The goal of this book is to locate the material development of that identity. This work marks the beginning of the process of bringing together all lines of evidence—archaeological, anthropological, and

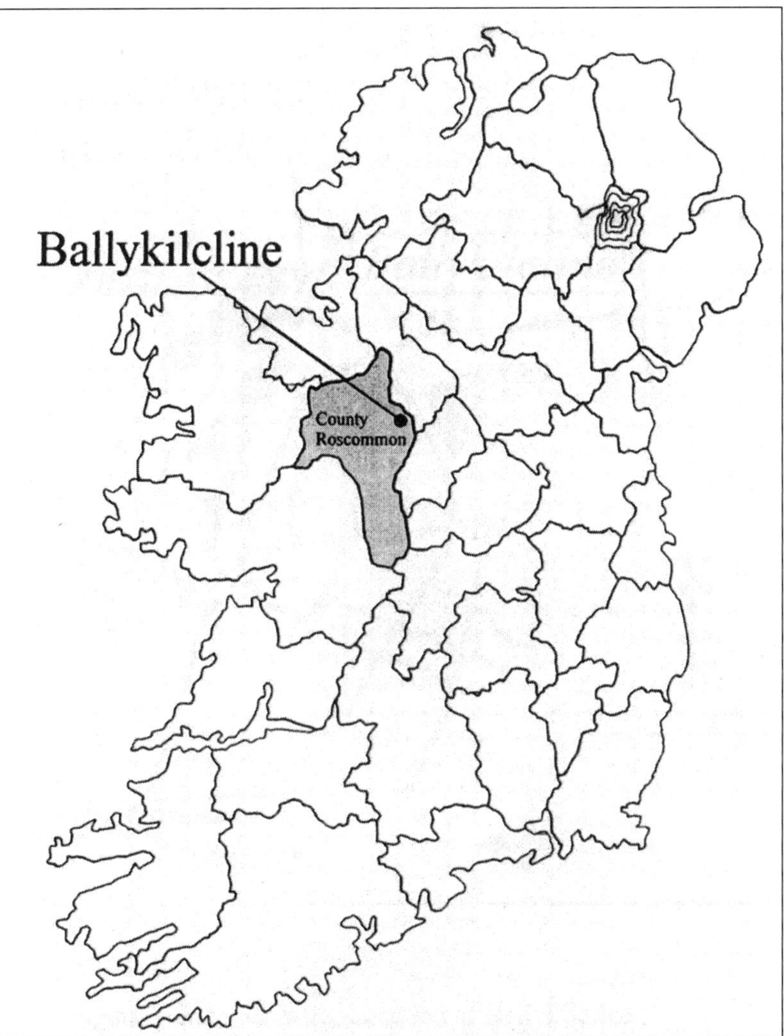

Figure 2. Map of Ireland showing the location of Ballykilcline, County Roscommon. (Courtesy of Charles Orser.)

historical—into a cohesive database to link the theoretical abstract and the tangible material evidence toward studying the processes of transnationalism and the collective formation of Irish and Irish American diasporic identities. The archaeologically recovered material used for this work is drawn from two sites in the urban northeastern United

States, recovered from two privy deposits associated with Irish immigrant tenements at the Five Points, Manhattan (ca. 1850–1870) and privy deposits from two single-family houses owned by Irish immigrant and Irish American families in the Dublin section of Paterson, New Jersey (ca. 1880–1910) (Figure 1). The artifacts from the U.S. sites are compared to those recovered from nineteenth-century sites in Ireland in order to illustrate a base for Irish material culture and therefore make sense of the data of recently arrived Irish immigrants—those who made up the rural poor in Ireland. The Irish data set consists of two pre-Famine cabin sites near the town of Strokestown, County Roscommon, Ireland. The stone cabins were occupied by the Nary family in the townland of Ballykilcline (1820–1848) (Figure 2).

The nineteenth century is one of the most dynamic periods in Irish and American history. The Famine period (also known as *An Ghorta Mor* or the Great Hunger) and several decades after marked the watershed for Irish dispersal and was the catalyst for the shaping of the modern world. In the United States, the first half of the nineteenth century was a period of substantial change, transition, and modernization. The arrival of the Irish in large numbers was part of the processes of creating the modern city in the United States (Chudacoff and Smith 2000:118)

To date, most scholars studying the Irish diaspora are social and economic historians, but little has been done to define or deconstruct the term *diaspora* and evaluate how it can be gainfully employed to understand the lived experiences of the Irish in both Ireland and the numerous new places of settlement. The enormous amount of literature spanning four hundred years of Irish migration demonstrates that there is no consensus as to how to categorize, organize, or even approach the subject of Irish dispersal worldwide. What is more problematic is that historians of Ireland and Irish dispersal debate whether this period of modern history should even be considered a diaspora. Kevin Kenny (2003:94), a historian of Irish America, argues that in order for the term *diaspora* to be of any analytical use to the historical analysis of Irish dispersal, a flexible typology is needed to account for diversity among the millions emigrating since the seventeenth century. Critically defining the term and using analytical typologies setting parameters for what constitutes a diaspora has allowed for a better understanding and illumination of the multiplicity of groups in the Irish diaspora.

The point of contention is grounded in contemporary social and political issues (Kennedy and Johnson 1997:34). To avoid issues that might have an adverse impact on the sociopolitical climate in Ireland, historians have focused only on economic forces to explain emigration, using the traditional push-pull factors affecting an undifferentiated ethnic group (Mokyr 1983; Ó Gráda 1988, 1994, 1995). The current academic climate has created obstacles to the development of any coherent discourse toward interpreting, quantifying, and qualifying this globally important period of Irish history.

In this study the analytical categories created in the interdisciplinary field of diaspora studies are studied and modified to understand the social history and material culture and to illustrate the different types of Irish factions comprising the Irish diaspora and their impact on the material record (Clifford 1994; Cohen 1997; Gilroy 1993; Safran 1991). The term *diaspora* is defined as a social condition and social process whereby identity is created and recreated through values of difference (Anthias 1998:565). It has long been synonymous with the historic dispersal of Jews. It was not until the 1960s that the term was used to refer to other dispersals, such as the forced movement of Africans during the Atlantic slave trade (Gilroy 1993; Shepperson 1966). Diaspora studies have expanded within the last decade to focus on the type of dispersal (Tölöyan 1996:3). The inclusion of all migrant groups is problematic because it glosses over the experiences that are for the most part unique to diasporic collectives.

The global movement of people does not necessarily define a diaspora. Jana Evans Braziel and Anita Mannur (2003:2–5) argue that diasporas are historically and culturally specific and form critical spaces within the new place of settlement. To establish an analytical discourse about discordant movement, therefore, one must understand the historical trajectory of the totality of the diaspora, including the historical moments detailing who travels, when, how, and under what circumstances. This approach captures the "embodiment of peoples and their distinctive historical experiences that is often a composite of many journeys to different parts of the globe, each with its own particularities" (Brah 1996:183; Braziel and Mannur 2003:3; Cohen 1997:2). The study of diasporas must include an understanding of the historical and contemporary elements in their "diachronic relationality" in that they are at once local and global networks of transnational identifications encompassing "imagined" and "encountered" communities that are bound together through a collective memory and rememory constituted within the crucible of the materiality of everyday life (Brah 1996:196–197). Thus theorizing *diaspora* must include a critical and reflexive application of the term when discussing international movement and networks.

A variety of groups exist within a diaspora. The different cohorts are based on social and economic positions in the homeland. The main diasporic types consist of *mobilized* (voluntary) and *proletarian* (involuntary) groups, and within this typology are a number of categories that distinguish various conditions for dispersal (Armstrong 1976). A *mobilized diaspora* represents a collective of the skilled and educated who choose to leave because of depressed economic conditions to seek capital gain elsewhere. In the new place of settlement, a mobilized group is quickly accepted and absorbed into the social structure because of its education and professional skills. Contrary to this, a *proletarian diaspora* consists of the unskilled who have been subjugated under the homeland's political and social conditions. This group is not well received in the place of settlement and must endure the social stigmas of alienation before gradually becoming incorporated into the new social structure.

Key to the definition of *diaspora* is the dispersal to and resettlement in one or more international locations. What is important about this is that sociocultural values, behaviors, and national allegiances to the homeland are not lost after resettlement; rather, they become infused gradually with new customs and loyalties (Meagher 1986a:4). In the case of this study, the Irish did not arrive as cultural blank slates quickly adopting new social values and material culture. They immigrated with entrenched social dispositions and ideologies reflected in objects and material signs. Understanding the material culture in Ireland expressing identities of the rural poor classes, those making up the Irish Diaspora throughout the nineteenth century, provides a basic comparable foundation to identifying the diachronic material transformations in the United States.

Echoing the argument put forth by Kenny, Ian Lilley (2004:293) posits that the full impact of the social theory of *diaspora* has yet to be felt in archaeology. The problem is that there is no defined analytical discourse exploring the history of and experiences in a diaspora and how these elements affect the material record. Archaeologists studying diasporic groups have not fully considered the effects that the social experiences of *diaspora* have on the material record (Lilley 2004:295).

Historical archaeology has the potential to be at the forefront of diaspora studies because it provides the most concrete illustration of how identities with a diasporic context are *operationalized*. Developments in the historical archaeology of the African diaspora and the study of generational process of transnationalism demonstrate the potential and importance of material culture to the study of diasporic groups. Insights have been gained by identifying similarities and differences between the material culture associated with Africans before being forced to leave and assemblages associated with enslaved Africans.

Initial transnational approaches to the archaeology of the African diaspora in the New World involved historical and anthropological studies of African culture. The studies were used to compare and contrast cultural reproduction and transformation in the United States (Armstrong and Fleischman 2003; Edwards-Ingram 2001; Farnsworth 1996; Ferguson 1992; Franklin 2001; Handler 1994, 1996, 1997; Handler and Lange 1978; Howson 1991; Meyers 1999; Orser 1996a, 1998a; Watters 1994; Wilkie and Farnsworth 1999). Jerome Handler (Handler and Lange 1978) was perhaps one of the first to make broad material links to enslaved Africans and cultural traditions in Africa through ideas of cultural retention in burial practices.

Leland Ferguson (1992) looks toward African material culture to interpret the presence of low-fired earthenware forms. By comparing the pottery style to pieces found in the Caribbean and America's South to correlates in Africa, he demonstrated the importance of establishing a material and transnational or global connection linking all locations involved with the African diaspora. Ferguson furthered the field by showing that historical archaeology can provide significant social and cultural data that is otherwise unrecorded in the historical literature. His research created avenues for others to follow in their study of undocumented elements of African identity, such as the complex belief systems and symbolism in African traditions and archeological materials such as glass beads, shells, copper, and iron (for examples, see Davidson 2004; Fennel 2000, 2003; Franklin 1996; Galle and Young 2004; Garman 1994; Jamieson 1995; Orser 1994, 1998a; Russell 1997; Stine et al. 1996; Weik 1997; Wilkie 1996, 1997).

At present, there is deep interest in the historical archaeology of African culture. Scholars believe that African American archaeology must be rooted in the study of African archaeology because it will provide invaluable information on production and meaning of African material culture prior to enslavement as well as on material changes resulting from European contact (DeCorse 1999:134; Posnansky 1999:36–37). An African material culture database is an important resource to aid in identifying multiplicities of African culture and its role in the fabrication of an African American world view (Lilley 2004:293; Orser 1998a:63–66).

The preliminary findings in Africa are beginning to be applied to American research questions. Archaeological projects focusing on spatial distributions and social systems in West Africa affected by the Atlantic slave trade have already begun to reveal interesting material parallels between artifacts made and used in West Africa and their American counterparts, such as pottery forms and decorative styles and symbolism on smoking pipes (DeCorse 1999, 2001; Hauser and DeCorse 2003; Ogundiran 2002; Pikirayi and Pwiti 1999; Stahl 2004). A transnational approach to the African diaspora answers old questions and asks new ones about the culture of enslaved Africans in the United States. The work has established a firm comparable material database to discern material patterns in the Caribbean, South America, and United States. The results demonstrate the importance of transnational material culture studies for interpreting the meaning of and changes to objects over time and space.

All historical archaeology of the African Diaspora has illustrated to various degrees that there is tangible evidence and information about cultural change and resilience and the creation of a new social and cultural identity through recovered ceramics, beads, smoking pipes, and architecture. The importance of historical archaeology to the African diaspora, as well as other diasporas, rests with its multidisciplinary and cross-disciplinary structure and its ability to bring together anthropology, history, folklore, sociology, thus providing unique insights not attainable through any one discipline alone (Orser 1998a:64–65).

This study creates an analytical discourse between diaspora theory in the social sciences and the practice of archaeology and material culture studies to explain the meaning of archaeologically recovered objects in the larger social structure of the experience of alienation from and gradual incorporation into American society, as well as a sustained social, economic, and political connection to Ireland extant within Irish diasporic communities. The sites chosen are good examples of different types of social relations and experiences of rural Irish and Irish immigrants struggling within a capitalist system, as well as of the development of new symbolism and material culture reflecting the social landscape of Irish Americans.

To attempt to bridge the gap among social theory, long transnational historical trajectories, and archaeological practice, there are basic principles underlying this research program. First, any social archaeological study of the modern world is a practice in understanding the impacts of a developing world system, industrialism, social stratification, institutional racialization, and capitalism. Inequalities and marginalization are compounded in a diasporic context and the degree of alienation or incorporation in the new place of settlement is in direct relation to social position in the homeland. Second, and more important to archaeologists, objects have value. Mass-produced goods have exchange values, and the commodification of objects is related to social value of the individual expressed through the ideology of material wealth and mass consumerism. Therefore it is possible to identify and track shifts in social and economic positions, that is to say, alienation from or incorporation into the marketplace, through changes in the material record.

The ultimate aim of this research is to demonstrate how experiences of the Irish proletarian diaspora shaped the material manifestation of Irish American identities in the late nineteenth century. The objects recovered from archaeological sites reflect the types of materials used in the daily lives of the men, women, and children of Ireland's rural poor and Irish immigrant communities not readily visible in historical documents. Although the agricultural poor in Ireland and working-class Irish immigrant households have been described in countless travelers' accounts, missionary reports, and historical literature, there is scant data regarding the daily lives of these people, and even less information about their material culture. The refined earthenware ceramic teacups, plates, and platters, glass tableware and medicinal bottles, and smoking pipes are used in conjunction with the social historical context to reconstruct these people's identity formation and the levels of alienation, transnationalism, and incorporation experienced affecting the emergence of an Irish American identity. Historians have argued that such identity formation was a very slow process in Irish immigrant communities in the United States, and it wasn't until the first Irish American generation matured, as early as the 1880s, that such an identity come into its own. The archaeological data in this book provide the physical evidence of this historical perspective through changes in the material record compared to that of contemporary non-Irish American-born households. This material shift strongly indicates the gradual exposure to new social behaviors.

For this study, the material culture from four sites is employed within a broad sociohistorical context in order to interpret the material formation of an Irish American identity. The study areas were chosen because each represents a specific time and place in Irish and Irish American history. The project area in Ireland is in the northeast corner of County Roscommon, which is the most eastern border of the province of Connacht. The two cabin sites are situated within one of the largest estates in the county and owned by the Mahon family. The project area is in the village of Ballykilcline and was once inhabited by the Nary family (1820–ca. 1847). The ordnance map of 1836 shows the location of two neighboring house sites belonging to Mark Nary and his sons, James, Luke, and Edward. From 1998 to 2002 archaeological surveys located and excavated these cabins and recovered 9,000 artifacts relating to the daily lives of this farming family.

To interpret the Irish experience in the United States, two sites have been selected. The sites provide evidence of the Irish American experience over time (ca. 1848–1910) pertaining not only to Irish immigrants but also to first-generation Irish Americans. The two privies in the rear courtyards of two tenements at the Five Points site (ca. 1848–1880) in Manhattan and two privies from two single-family houses from the Dublin site in Paterson, New Jersey (1880–1910) delineate the Irish experience in the New York metropolitan area. Comparisons among the sites provide valuable evidence of Irish American experience.

Interpreting the material manifestation of Irish identity in Ireland at this time is complex because of the lack of historical documentation of rural tenant farmers and landless laboring classes as well as the paucity of any archaeological data. The evidence used and the conclusions drawn are based solely on two stone cabins and a mud or sod cabin located within the lands of a single estate. This is somewhat problematic because the data from these sites cannot represent the entirety of the rural classes' lived experience. To ignore this fact would set a dangerous precedent for future work on Ireland's rural classes, branding them as an undifferentiated peasantry. The area under study in County Roscommon was located in one of the five areas of rural Ireland experiencing extreme poverty, disease, famine, and evictions in the nineteenth century. In fact, the sites were chosen because the data are associated with a tenant farming family living at or slightly above the subsistence level. It is not the purpose here to make a single interpretation for the entire rural population of Ireland; rather, I argue that the data provide an excellent example of the type of material culture existing at this time.

The fact that there is such a wide range of artifacts associated with rural Irish tenants and Irish immigrant communities has surprised many historians and archaeologists. Historical accounts of missionaries visiting the Irish immigrant communities in U.S. cities, as well as travelers' descriptions of rural Ireland, painted a bleak picture of material conditions. Observers failed to take note of objects such as decorated English-made refined earthenware, glass tumblers, wine glasses, and serving dishes, all of which survive as a testimony in the archaeological record.

To provide a meaningful interpretation of the archaeological data, I was selective about the classes of artifacts used in this study. The excavated data sets are too large to allow a full interpretation. As result, the data set chosen directly pertains to the diasporic experiences of identity formation, alienation, transnationalism, and incorporation and creates a pattern of meanings-in-practice through time and space. Meaning expounds action and is involved in forming a dialectical relationship between experience and expression. Establishing the historical context of the Irish diaspora provides the parameters for interpreting the meaning of continuities and changes in identities manifested in the material record.

Refined earthenware ceramic and glass vessels from Ireland provide the material foundation demonstrating the types of objects available to and owned by the rural poor classes in the Irish homeland. In comparison, the continuities and changes in vessel complexity and distribution of ceramic teaware, as well as ceramic and glass tableware and serving pieces between the sites in Ireland and the United States, offer insights into experiences of incorporation. Shifts in the types of vessels forms, for example, reflect a movement away from patterns of Irish consumer culture toward the formation of an Irish American identity and incorporation into American society.

The point of this comparison between Ireland and the United States is to locate not only the reproduction of a traditional sense of being Irish but also the gradual development of a material base expressing new social values and behaviors. The gradual acceptance of new consumer patterns and incorporation is indicative of practice put into action. The developing complexity of material culture in relation to eating and serving food is the evidence of learning and accepting new cultural patterns that replaced many of the traditional patterns (Mintz 1996). Historical archaeologists have long since correlated changes in traditional forms and decorative types with shifts in a group's sociocultural world view (Burley 1989, 2000; Cook et al. 1996; Fitts 1999; Hudgins 1999; Leone 1999; Mullins 1999a, 1999b; Shackle 1996, 1998; Steen 1999; Walker 2003; Wall 1994, 2001). Social change is defined here as a complex transgenerational process of combining cultural traits and traditions through contact, conflict, and negotiation of cultural distinctiveness resulting in new social values and behaviors without total assimilation or a loss of the past (Drummond 1980:34; Gundaker 2000:132; Hall 1992:310–314).

The experience of alienation is evidenced through the ratio between ethical and proprietary medical bottles. Ethical medicines came only from a doctor's prescription, whereas proprietary medicines were produced commercially as "cure-alls" and purchased without a doctor's prescription (Fike 1987:3–4). While all medicinal bottles can provide evidence of people's efforts to overcome unsanitary conditions and severe health problems, they also signal a degree of alienation from the U.S. healthcare system (Cabak et al. 1995; Ford 1994; Larsen 1994; Sullivan 1994; Veit 1996). A high percentage of ethical medicines indicates access to a physician, whereas commercial medicines suggest self-medication, and in the case of Irish immigrants, increasing alienation from American doctors, dispensaries, and charity hospitals (Kraut 1994, 1996). The choice to self-medicate with commercial medicines may not have arisen from choice or free will but may have been the last resort to avoid harsh judgment and criticism. In turn, an increase in use of ethical medicines by Irish and Irish American families toward the end of the nineteenth century can be seen as denoting shifting attitudes toward the Irish by American society.

The symbolism on the bowls of smoking pipes is steeped in ethnic and class politics. Symbolism on pipes has been examined in terms of cultural reproduction and ethnic identity, and researchers argue it is a public communication of an individual's personal ideologies, aspirations, and group and national affiliations (Cook 1989a, 1989b, 1997; Emerson 1994, 1999; Ferguson 1992; Fesler 2004; Hartnett 2004; Monroe and Malios 2004; Reckner 1999, 2000; Thomas and Thomas 2004). What is important about the decorative styles and symbolism on smoking pipes is not their obvious link to ethnicity but how their meaning changed over time and how they are situated within a specific historical context.

Irish and American symbolism in the pipe data present us with more than simple ethnic markers; it allows us to explore notions of retained social relations within a diasporic group struggling to maintain connections to the homeland as well as its struggles for freedom. Studied together within the localized historical context, the symbols express more than assimilation or static Irish nationalism, they reflect transnationalism and the blending of cultural metaphors to express loyalties both to homeland and the adopted country.

The approach in the following chapters is multidisciplinary in that it integrates archaeological data with social history, as well as social identity and diaspora studies from anthropology and sociology, to explore the material manifestation of Irish and Irish American identities. The nature of a diasporic identity is multifaceted, all at once subjective and constituted in and through culture, and structured on a frame of reference from shared cultural codes and a collective history (Brah 1996; Hall 1990). Incoming groups maintain various levels of cultural distinctiveness while struggling to be incorporated into the host society, thus creating a new sense of communal identity (Butler 2001; King 1998; Panossian 1998a, 1998b; Shukla 2001).

The theoretical framework I developed has far-reaching applications for historical archaeologists and historians. Broadly speaking, its purpose is to serve as a multidisciplinary model of how material culture can be used to interpret continuities and changes in social identity within a critical and analytical discourse of the term *diaspora.* I argue against the hunt for ethnic markers or simple class distinctions derived from sociocultural emblems of rank as sole determinants of identity. I do not neglect specific ethnic and class symbolism, but the relevance of such data rests in its location within the larger social and historical context of the Irish proletarian diaspora and the experiences of alienation, incorporation, and transnationalism.

Finally, it is important to reiterate that it is not the intent of this study to speak for the hundreds of thousands of Irish immigrants making up the Irish diaspora, nor the millions of Irish Americans descended from that historical reality. This is a regional study meant to illuminate localized histories and material culture over space and time to test the validity and relevance of historical archaeology as an important source of information. As more archaeological sites in the United States, Ireland, and elsewhere surface, the model generated should be tested and transformed based on differing groups forming the Irish diaspora and their various experiences with the new place of settlement and with other groups they encounter. Irish, Irish immigrant, and Irish American identities are not uniform, and the incorporation of the Irish into American society was not a simple process. The geographical location and historical period provide the all-important context of differentiation and diversity dictating the level of acceptance or exclusion. The following pages offer an avenue of exploration and a qualification of that theoretical perspective. Their intent is not to essentialize Irish or Irish American identity but to make a connection between the particular and the general histories as a framework for bridging the gaps that separate social theory, social history, and archaeological practice.

1
Archaeology of the Irish Diaspora

A formal historical archaeology of the Irish diaspora does not exist. In the United States, only a handful of published studies on sites relating to the Irish are available for analysis (for example, Baugher 1982; Cotz 1975; Cotz et al. 1980; De Cunzo 1982, 1983, 1987; Faulkner et al. 1978; McCarthy et al. 1995; McCarthy et al. 1996; Praetzellis and Stewart 2001; Yamin 1999, 2000a, 2000b). The point here is not to describe and deconstruct every site relating to Irish and Irish American communities but to illustrate by example sites in the northeastern United States that typify the established trends of archaeological theory and methods pertaining to nineteenth-century Irish immigrant and Irish American communities.

The trend in historical archaeology is the local or particularistic study of material culture and the study of the individual in everyday life. Archaeologists, and the social sciences in general, have eschewed meta-narratives and the longer historical trajectory of structuring social relations based on collective perceptions of ethnic, racial, gender, and class identities and the production of space that forms everyday life of the modern world (Orser 1996a:2007). The differences or similarities in material remains are argued to actively communicate internal diversity or similarity among multiethnic households expressing individual action and agency. In short, this school of thought espouses interpretations of the "individual human experience" (Yamin 1999:4). In doing so, an important part of collective social, political, and economic action and the history of alienation and struggle and their impact on material culture is missed.

The archaeology of Irish communities in the United States has focused on either ethnic or class identity. During the late 1970s and early 1980s the focus was on illustrating a traditional sense of ethnic identity through the presence or absence of ethnic markers. The work, inspired by anthropologists such as Fredrick Barth (1969), searched for cultural assemblages reflecting bounded and distinct ethnic identities. The theoretical approach was not designed to interpret Irish identity directly but to compare and differentiate among different ethnic groups in a community. The most common way to do this is through food remains and ceramic and glass vessels.

Lu Ann De Cunzo (1982, 1983, 1987) looked into residential life at the northern part of the Dublin section of Paterson, New Jersey. The area is comprised of ethnically mixed households, including English, Scottish, and Irish. Her focus centered on establishing a model for interpreting ethnicity using mass-produced, refined earthenware ceramics and glass tableware and bottles (De Cunzo 1983:4–7). Ethnicity was seen as being "an adaptation to the industrial, urban environment of Paterson" and De Cunzo theorized it was structured by residential and employment patterns and kinship manifested in consumption patterns (De Cunzo 1987:290). Distinct ethnic enclaves were indicative of bounded ethnic cohesion, and each ethnic group formed such communities to retain traditional cultural knowledge resistant to assimilation (De Cunzo 1982:17). In other words, ethnic identification rests with the acquisition of certain ceramic tea and tableware and alcohol bottles, as each group actively and freely chose to maintain traditional notions of identity (De Cunzo 1982:17). De Cunzo did detect slight differences from household to household, however, she admittedly failed to find any concrete physical manifestations of the social boundaries between ethnic groups. The differences did not occur in the table and tea forms of vessels but in the types of alcohol consumed; Irish households had a preference for whisky and beer, and the English-born households seem to consume wine and hard liquor. It is unclear that such localized studies of alcohol use through distribution of beverage containers in a small section of an urban multiethnic community is any indication of ethnic differences, but De Cunzo is successful in showing the complexities and contradictions of trying to discern ethnicity through mass-produced objects.

Drawing from De Cunzo's work, a study of Irish households in Philadelphia investigated ethnicity through comparisons of consumer patterns in the recovered ceramic table- and teaware. The study area focused on the Irish immigrant and Irish American households occupying the marginalized spaces of back courts and alleys. John McCarthy and his team (1995:70) argued that consumer patterns reflected ethnic economic networks and socioeconomic status and shed light on consumer behavior shaped by ethnicity.

Overall the research did not contain an in-depth interpretation of ethnicity. The approach presented something of an unproblematic ethnic quest for American middle-class status. The identification of specific decorative types and ceramics forms was argued to reflect middle-class emulation and assimilation into American culture (McCarthy et al. 1995:27). Ethnicity was argued to be degrees of affluence determined by the quality of ceramic vessels, leading to the conclusion that the Irish American community living in the cramped houses in the historically unsanitary back alleys and hidden rear courtyards lived comfortably yet modestly (McCarthy et al. 1995:70–73). Their contention rests with the idea of an uncomplicated social history of assimilation. It is a hard notion to reconcile given that Irish and Irish Americans were marginalized to this section of urban life.

Returning to the Dublin section of Paterson, Rebecca Yamin (1999) argued that ethnicity cannot be determined through material remains. Instead, the focus is on the material culture of class formation in an urbanized and industrialized community. In her study of the predominantly Irish community of Dublin's south end, Yamin (1999:155) posits that there are no indications of ethnic retention or acculturation identifiable in the material culture, and in fact it is very difficult to detect any ethnic expression in the objects under study. Although Yamin acknowledges a level of ethnicity based on the recovery of white clay smoking pipes with various Irish symbols and slogans, she argues that the symbols have more to do with the labor history of Paterson and the individual's everyday life and relationship to an increasing industrialized community (Yamin 1999:154).

The concept of ethnicity is considered to be epiphenomenal and independent of class identification. Yamin (1999:154) prefers to structure her study based on consumption patterns related to the economic standing of each household. Class relations centered on the relative quality and quantity (matching/nonmatching) of decorative ceramic vessels and cuts of meat acquired by homeowners and tenants (Yamin 1999:5–6). What is interesting about Yamin's study is that it argues against a simple notion of submitting to the desire to be middle class. Yamin (1999:161) argues that the material culture of Irish immigrant and Irish American tenants and homeowners does not suggest a desire to be upwardly mobile, nor does it express ethnic identity; rather, the objects represent the formation of individual expressions of a collective solidarity within the working-class community that took precedence over Irish heritage (Yamin 1999:161). Unfortunately, the interpretations negate both ethnicity and a real critical assessment of the role of being the ethnic "other" in the development of distinctions and the ideologies of mass consumerism and its impact on class formation. The particularistic focus rests with the individual household and is not held to the critical gaze of the broader social, economic, and political histories of diaspora, mass immigration, and diasporic social histories in industrialized American cities.

The point here is not to downplay the work that has been done. It is certain that class distinctions, conflicts, and solidarity are important factors in Dublin, as well as in the myriad Irish communities that formed. The ceramic and glass vessels and cuts of meat take on a level of importance relating to a collective identity in conjunction with Irish symbols on clay tobacco pipes found within the same stratagraphic context. As far as Yamin is concerned, and drawing from Paul Reckner (1999:147–153), the symbols are Irish, but their importance rests with class fractions and the expression of conflict and struggle within Paterson's labor movement. Reckner's hypothesis on smoking pipes and class struggle is extremely insightful and certainly advances the study of the working class through objects that otherwise would be relegated to static ethnic markers. He deftly illustrates the use and empowerment of these Irish symbols within the discourse of collective action and worker's rights. The key, however, is that they are ethnic symbols and relate to the formation of a transnational Irish American identity. What become lost in translation are the broader historical trajectories of an ethnic collective identity based on a shared history (real or imagined) stemming from reasons for leaving their homeland. More important, it is how these connections are maintained and applied to establish a collective memory used to negotiate their class status in the United States.

Current scholarly practice is to move away from delineating identity along either ethnic or class lines. In the ethnic enclave of the Five Points, Manhattan, for example, Yamin (2000a, 2000b) attempted to detail as many facets as possible of the lives of its immigrant inhabitants. Her aim was to construct the daily lives of the people living at the Five Points within the turmoil and struggle of being the foreign "other." The Five Points site is the most recent, and by the far the most extensive, excavation and historical treatment of immigrant life in the United States. The goal at the site was to give an alternative, more nuanced view of the nineteenth-century working poor, thus attacking the mythologizing ideologies of nineteenth-century reformers fostering mainstream American beliefs of the slum (Yamin 2000b:501–503).

The struggle was over creating a new model for understanding difference, continuity, and change that moved away from what was considered limiting models of acculturation and the dominant ideology thesis. The thousands of ceramic and glass vessels, tobacco pipes, and personal items recovered at the site were thought to represent more than a communication of an all-encompassing and all-controlling structure. As with Paterson, meaning was constructed on the idea that all people have agency and control over their lives. The objects acquired and discarded do not necessarily come ready packaged with meaning but are provided meaning by the individual or household under study. In this search for the individual the push was to illustrate that the people of the Five Points, mostly Irish, used mass-produced goods not to emulate the middle classes or to recreate or perpetuate traditional cultural practices but in active resistance to the alienating conditions and experiences of the being the foreign other (Yamin 2000b:6).

Yamin admits that there is a larger social structure of alienation, but unfortunately, her study does not examine the degree of alienation experienced by different ethnic groups at the Five Points. This presents a tough framework to understand Irish, or even class, identity and their larger collective experience. There is no discussion of the impact of alienation within the broader history of Irish immigration to the United States. Ultimately, ethnicity doesn't play a large role in the formation and reformation of class ideologies and class relations.

The Irish in Paterson, Philadelphia, and Manhattan were forced to negotiate their ethnic identity, which included being Catholic and unskilled, landless tenants in Ireland. This ethnic baggage was a prime reason for the Irish, as a group, to be racialized throughout the United States. Theirs is not simply a local history of rising up the social and economic hierarchy but a story of how a marginalized group negotiated and eventually bought into the ideology of mainstream American mass consumerism to display respectability and citizenship and through this reached a level of incorporation or at least tolerance.

A common thread in each of the studies presented here is the lack of any social historical information concerning what it meant to be either American or Irish. For instance, there is no real discussion for the reasons of leaving Ireland and the impact of that decision. The social, cultural, economic, and political history of Ireland is almost nonexistent. It seems at times that Irish immigrants arrived as cultural blank slates and their indoctrination into the material expression of civility and citizenship began at debarkation in Manhattan and Philadelphia.

It is apparent that seeing a traditional sense of Irish ethnicity, or ethnicity in general, is difficult at best. The studies discussed briefly here shifted their focus when they did not find ethnic markers and sought explanations through theories of class and socioeconomic status. In almost all cases ethnic and class identities were seen as independent variables. Mass-produced plates and teacups do not express ethnicity and in many cases do not guarantee to reveal class distinctions; however, the objects can indicate acceptance at varying levels of the ideology of modern capitalism. The importance of studying mass-produced material culture is not to illustrate assimilation, acculturation, or resistance but to unmask the ideologies of a modern capitalist society and how racialized groups negotiate their status and to track the slow processes acceptance in the United States.

To be sure, the studies are well done and very informative. The issue rests not with their ideas, outcomes, or structure, but with the scope of their research. The localized scope does not provide space to really delve into ethnic and class identity and struggle happening within the larger sociohistorical trajectory of the Irish diaspora. The missing comparable transnational database or other comparable sites in the United States limits the understanding of why people emigrated to the United States, under what conditions, and how that history has an impact on their position upon entering various urban regions in the United States. As I will argue in subsequent chapters, with the knowledge of the historical and material data from Ireland combined with a critical analysis and employment of diaspora theory there comes further understanding of collective experiences and the formation of Irish American communities.

In all fairness to the study of the Irish in the United States, there has been no real interest in examining the historical archaeology of Ireland's modern history, including the pre-Famine and Famine periods, until the late 1990s. Irish scholars long held that Ireland's modern history was the domain of historians and that material culture studies fell under the rubric of folk studies (Orser 2000:159–160). Irish archaeologists, since the emergence of Irish archaeology in the nineteenth century, have channeled their energies to the study of the prehistory of Ireland (Orser 1996b:82). The main reason, scholars argue, that this is so is due to the contested social and political struggles making up Ireland's modern history.

The prehistoric period is not without its struggles, but the monuments and material culture are a source of empowerment supporting issues of political factions, mainly nationalists, because they exemplify Ireland's extensive history before conquest and colonialism. Sites such as the Hill of Tara and New Grange represent indigenous Irish existence as far back as the second half of the first millennium B.C. The Hill of Tara has been an especially important landmark throughout the history of Irish struggles (McEwan 2003:27; Smith 1991:93). Daniel O'Connell, leader of the movement to repeal of the Act of Union in the first half of the nineteenth century, held outdoor meetings at the Hill of Tara to create a direct link to its rich history and instill a deep-seated sense of identity and nationalism in the Irish people (McEwan 2003:27–28).

Over the past 20 years historical archaeology, or postmedieval archaeology, has emerged in the scholarship, focusing on the early development of capitalism, colonialism, the conflict between them, and the everyday lives of indigenous Irish, English, Anglo-Irish, and Scottish Presbyterians (for example, see Brannon 1984, 1990; Delle 1999; Donnelly and Brannon 1998; Donnelly and Horning 2002; Klingelhofer 1992; Lacy 1979; O. Miller 1991). Postmedieval archaeologists are making great strides in studying the early development of capitalism and colonialism, however, these studies do not include the pre-Famine and Famine periods. On the surface of things, one could simply consider the laws and regulations in Ireland as the motivation for archaeological interest. As a working chronology defining postmedieval archaeology, sites dating before 1750 are considered relevant for study, thus excluding all histories leading to the famine. This was in part influenced by the Monuments Act of 1930 and its reworkings up to 2004, stating that archaeological relevance relates to monuments in existence prior to the eighteenth century.

The current level of inequality, of Ireland's archaeology of the recent past being considered anecdotal, serves only to limit the profession of archaeology as a whole. Historical archaeology or archaeology of the recent past is a multidisciplinary approach blending anthropological theory with the historical context, hopefully resulting in interpretations that provide meaningful insights that otherwise would not be gleamed from historical documents alone. Since the study period of modern world archaeology deals with the recent past, the findings and interpretations of archaeologists provide empowerment to descendent communities which allow them access to and engagement with their immediate history and heritage. Therefore, the political agenda behind the legal acts and archaeological relevance appears to be only part of the larger and more complex problem in Ireland. Public memory of the Famine continues to conjure up very strong emotions that many scholars wish to avoid. The lack of archaeological inquiry into the period surrounding the Famine is a direct reflection of the broader sociopolitical climate in Ireland. This has been the central theoretical argument of Irish historians.

Since the late 1990s —more specifically, up to and at the time of the 150th anniversary of the Famine, or at least the worst year, 1847—there has been renewed interest, albeit small, in the archaeology of the pre-Famine and Famine period. It was not until the 1990s that the Famine was considered an issue for serious academic study. Although a principal event in modern Irish history, historians tended to avoid scrutiny of its more controversial aspects, and that prevented a nuanced discourse on the Irish diaspora.

Broadly speaking, modern world archaeology has been ignored by many in archaeology as a discipline outside of the United States. The relevance of "modern era" archaeology, or that after 1700, has been questioned. This is especially true in the study of the rural Irish poor. Over a decade ago, Charles Orser (1996b) first asked two very important questions. First, can there be an archaeology of the Famine period? And second, why is archaeology not a part of Irish studies? The summer program conducted by the Centre for the Study of Irish Heritage, under his direction, continually demonstrates the former, but the latter has yet to be answered. The work conducted by the centre demonstrates the potential of Famine period archaeology. The main research aim of the centre's program, now in its fourteenth year, is to understand the material manifestations of class relations and the daily lives of those either undocumented or given little notice in the historical record yet most affected by colonialism, famine, and eviction, that is, Ireland's rural poor.

Orser's research program concerning Ireland's rural poor demonstrates the complexity of Irish social structure throughout the nineteenth century. In contrast, historians have argued that Irish landless poor were an undifferentiated peasantry devoid of any sense of material culture, and this facile notion carried over to the study of Irish identity in the United States. Their lines of evidence stem from the works of eighteenth- and nineteenth-century travelers to Ireland labeling the Irish poor as backward in their thinking and cultural ways and their lack of material culture as reflecting a lack of basic intelligence, self-respect, and inability to be part of the modern world. The perpetuation of assumed history of the rural Irish poor is exemplified by the inaccuracies and stereotypes presented by historian Robert Scally. In his 1995 book *The End of Hidden Ireland,* he describes the rural Irish as being unwashed, uncombed, ragged, and with scant material possessions. His work has been embraced by historians studying nineteenth-century Ireland as an accurate and insightful treatment of rural Irish life and is the guiding source for many current historical publications on the subject.

The historical archaeology of Ireland's rural poor, however, has shown that they were not simply an undifferentiated, communal peasantry. Contrary to historical evidence, Irish rural society was structured on a complex socioeconomic structure unto themselves that revolved around access to land and was expressed through the material culture.

What is perhaps more important to the archaeology of the Irish diaspora, the rural poor were, and have been since the eighteenth century, part of the larger globalized capitalist ideology. Unlike studies of the Irish in the United States, Orser's work (1996b, 1997, 1998b, 2000, 2001, 2004, 2007; Brighton and Orser 2006a; Hull and Brighton 2002; Orser and Hull 1998, 2001; Orser et al. 2000) has demonstrated that even landless tenants were indoctrinated into the ideology of modernity. The differing numbers of many imported items, such as transfer-printed refined earthenware from Staffordshire and Glasgow, reflect the ways in which the classes of the rural poor participated in and had knowledge of the larger global economy. Seemingly simple conclusions like these are critical because they directly challenge the view that Ireland's poor were not contributing to or taking part in the creation of the modern world, thus rendering them then and now as powerless actors in sociopolitical struggles. This knowledge of modern material culture, or mass consumption of commodities (nonessentials), changes the face of interpretation of those leaving Ireland during the diaspora.

Archaeological research in the modern history of Ireland is important for the formation of a new discourse challenging the assumed irrelevance of Ireland's material culture reflecting the developing social conditions of the recent past. This is one of the most dynamic periods in Irish history. Charles Orser has asked more of us as a profession by questioning the role of modern archaeology. His inquiries should remain as a constant reminder that we need to be reflexive and always seek out archaeology's relevance to understanding the past as well as the present. Orser's work has generated interest in both Ireland and the United States because it draws attention to the tangible contributions historical archaeology can make to facets of rural life that thus far have gone unrecorded.

As is the case in Ireland, there are volumes of historical treatments on Irish dispersal, but little is truly known historically about the scope of material culture in Irish immigrant communities or how Irish immigrants negotiated their position in the new places of settlement. The Irish did not arrive as cultural blank slates quickly adopting new social values and material culture. They immigrated with entrenched social dispositions, sociocultural values, behaviors, and allegiances, which were not lost after resettlement. Understanding the material culture in Ireland as expressing identities of the rural poor classes provides a basic comparable foundation to identifying the diachronic material transformations worldwide.

The archaeology of Ireland's recent history has a direct impact internationally. In the broader, or global, context, the nineteenth century is such a dynamic period, and this is especially so for the Irish, mostly rural poor, as they comprised the evicted populations that formed distinct communities worldwide, and all sites outside of Ireland should be placed on the broader scale of research in order to understand how the localized experiences are part of the Irish diaspora with different manifestations over space and time. The continuing results from Ireland are the foundation upon which historical archaeologists working on Irish immigrant and Irish American sites must build their own interpretations to find patterns and meaning in the archaeological data. While this work focuses on the Northeast, it provides the necessary methodology to develop a database for understanding the meaning and formation of Irish immigrant and Irish American identities.

The point is not only to locate the reproduction of a traditional sense of being Irish but also, and more important, to track the slow processes of the material manifestations of being indoctrinated into new American social values and behaviors. The gradual acceptance of new consumer patterns and incorporation is indicative of practice put into action. Social change is defined here as a complex transgenerational process of combining cultural traits and traditions through contact, conflict, and negotiation of cultural distinctiveness resulting in new social values and behaviors without total assimilation or a loss of the past.

The next chapter details the importance of diaspora studies to the interpretation of the multiplicities of Irish identity and experience in the United States. Historical archaeology of the Irish diaspora has the potential of being at the forefront because we as a discipline can illustrate how various discarded objects, used in day-to-day realities, reflect the larger social processes of identity formation and the myriad of conflicts, negotiations, and resolutions of the social processes entangled in the ideological concepts of citizenship, modernity, and respectability. To date there has been no overarching theory quantifying or qualifying the Irish diaspora. In archaeology much needs to be done to define and deconstruct the term *diaspora* and how material culture reflects the long historical trajectory of varied social, political, and economic relations and the formation and reformation of identities in making Irish America.

The purpose is to begin a dialogue moving from site-specific interpretations to a broader narrative shedding light on the important role of material culture reflecting the varied social relations of conflict and negotiation leading to the formation of Irish American identities. In the case of the Irish diaspora, there are different levels of access and limitations to social and economic advantages and benefits in American society. This reality needs to be highlighted because it accentuates the fluidity of racial categorizations and social constructs of differentiation of seemingly the same "ethnic" and "racial" groups. This governs the fields within which each group moves through and lives out their collective daily lives. As a result, social and economic success or failure is predicated by and reflected through the types of material goods.

Critically defining the Irish diaspora through the understanding of contemporary diasporic theory and utilizing the analytical typologies from these theoretical positions establishes the necessary parameters for a better understanding and illumination of the experiences of the Irish collectives in both Ireland and the United States. Over the past decade, historians have done this to varying degrees of success. What we must put into our practice are the chronological and spatial frameworks, failures, and successes of these historians to illuminate the material manifestations reflecting the varied social relations.

For the complex and contradictory study of the Irish diaspora, more needs to be deconstructed and transformed into an archaeology of diaspora that allows for a deeper understanding of the impact of racialization and alienation creating social and economic inequalities as evidenced by marginalized landscapes and types of material culture. Important to the interpretation of the material culture, regardless of group or time period, is the specific reasons for departure. This convergence of various threads of social relations and differentiation is reflected in the types of material culture. The point and the relevancy of archaeology in this venture is not to link the ethnic/national/religious group to a single monolithic description, as that approach actually adheres to nineteenth-century racialized philosophy, but to highlight differences in the degrees of alienation and incorporation into the modern world, capitalism, and the inequalities resulting from the social, political, and economic climate. The importance of our studies must rest with a critical social archaeology of diaspora. The mute and mundane daily objects need to be situated within the larger historical realities scaffolding social relations between Irish immigrants (of various class and cultural identities), Irish Americans, and the larger non-Irish, American society.

2
Defining Diaspora and Identity Formation

The word *diaspora* comes from the Greek preposition *dia* (over) and the verb *speiro* (to sow) and defines the movement, migration, and colonization of a group or groups of people (Cohen 1997:2). *Diaspora* took its more traditional and somber meaning when it was used to refer to the dispersal of the Jewish people from the eighth to sixth centuries B.C. It identifies a relational network produced by dispersal, forced in varying degrees, or a reluctant scattering. Factors such as famine, war, enslavement, ethnic cleansing, conquest, and political repression are integral to and a dominant influence upon diasporas. Such factors give the term a sense of urgency beyond simple movement. In essence it is "flight following violence," social, economic, or political, rather than necessarily freely chosen displacement (Gilroy 1997:318). The level of trauma resulting in dispersal has an impact on the formation of a collective consciousness of remembrance and commemoration and a sense of attachment to the homeland.

Prior to the 1960s, *diaspora* referred exclusively to displacements chronicled in Jewish and Christian histories of religion. Scholars studying other groups employed different terms, such as *exile* and *overseas communities* (Tölöyan 1996:3). In his 1966 study of the dispersion of sub-Saharan Africans through the colonial slave trade, George Shepperson was one of the earliest scholars to use the word in a non-Jewish context (Baumann 1997:378). Once Shepperson operationalized the term in this new sense, it was employed cautiously outside the context of Jewish history. It was not until the late 1970s that social scientists began to acknowledge that other migrant groups experienced diasporas (McCaffrey 1997; Armstrong 1976).

Recently there has been a renewed interest in diaspora studies. It is developing into a dynamic field of inquiry of large-scale group movements as a societal process signifying transnationality and the struggles of a displaced group to define its social position as a distinct community. The term *diaspora* has become an analytical category establishing interpretive frameworks for studying the economic, political, and cultural modalities of historically specific forms of migrancy and their relation within subjective social relations of identity (Anthias 1998:557; Brah 1996:16; Clifford 1994:308; Kearney 1995:548, 559; Tölöyan 1996:3–6). Scholars have only begun to study the transnational consciousness created within a diaspora group (Bhabha 1994; Butler 2001; Chow 1993; Cohen 1997; Drzewiecka 2002; Gilroy 1993; Kearney 1995; Shukla 2001). The upsurge of diaspora studies was the impetus for the journal *Diaspora*, created by Khachig Tölöyan in 1991.

No diaspora is a monolith. There can be different groups within a diaspora. The differences between individuals rest on the experiences of and reasons for leaving the homeland (Fortier 1998; Panagakos 1998; Panossian 1998b). Analytical categories and typologies have been created and refined to enable us to understand diversity within a diasporic community (Armstrong 1976; Butler 2001; Cohen 1997; Safran 1991). John Armstrong (1976) developed two broad categories of diasporic groups, *mobilized* and *proletarian*. These analytical categories reflect differences in social, economic, and political positions of a community and how they are received in the host land.

A *mobilized diaspora* is made up of individuals who start with social and economic capital and therefore cultural and material advantages and opportunities in both the home and host lands. The group is composed of technically skilled individuals who begin on a lower socioeconomic level in the new society but do so with ready skills to create opportunities to be upwardly mobile (Armstrong 1976:397). Armstrong (1976:393–394) has noted that those within a mobilized diaspora have "a sophistication in calculating social and economic advantages" so they can quickly identify with the dominant culture, and because they are technically skilled they are looked upon favorably and not as a threat to the existing socioeconomic structure. Because the collective is permitted to negotiate and establish its upward positions they are in turn willing to accommodate to the dominant social structure. Therefore, they become quickly incorporated into mainstream of society (Armstrong 1976:396).

In contrast to this cohort, a *proletarian diaspora* is composed of individuals without ready capital who remain at and are forced to remain at the lower end of the socioeconomic spectrum. In the homeland, this group represents the subordinate indigenous population. Social values based on differentiation legitimize their social condition and their economic status is perceived to be a direct result of their inferiority; consequently, their occupational roles come to define their sociocultural positions. This social and economic fact is the cornerstone for the constraints preventing them from attaining any advantages and opportunities for advancement in both the places of origin and resettlement (Armstrong 1976:406).

In order to further the analytical diasporic discourse, Kim Butler (2001), Robin Cohen (1997), and William Safran (1991) provide a further nuance to the broad categories of dispersal examined by Armstrong through typologies defining characteristics of a diaspora group that take into consideration the reasons for dispersal and the social relations in the place of settlement. The aim is to establish a theoretical perspective to qualify and compare diaspora contexts spatially and temporally. Multiplicity in the term *diaspora* reflects the possibilities of a population experiencing many different "diasporas" within the same historical event or over the long historical trajectory of that diasporic experience. Cohen's typology includes the diaspora categories "Imperial," "Trade," "Voluntary," "Victim," and "Labor" (Cohen 1997:xii, 2). The latter two types have more definition in that they include indentured servants, slaves, forced emigrants, and exiles.

Voluntary emigration and migration is associated with both a *mobilized* and *proletarian diaspora*. In either case, a group moves because of deteriorating conditions in the place of origin. What makes this type of movement part of a mobilized or proletarian diaspora depends on the overall technical skill level and social positions of the diasporic group in the homeland prior to departing (Cohen 1997:66–67).

Emigration and migration are similar in that both terms reflect a voluntary separation from the homeland. While migration is temporary, emigration is a more definitive form of separation as it represents a permanent relocation of a group or individual to a single locale (Cohen 1997). Reasons for departing include increasingly intolerable social and economic conditions. Emigration must fit within the history of a larger diaspora or else it simply refers to the movement of a select group of individuals to a single locale. It must be part of a larger social network of individuals in more than two locations (Butler 2001:202). Emigration does not always represent large-scale movement. Cohen (1997:57) refers to this mostly as part of the "Trade and Imperial Diaspora," in which volunteers are part of the colonial expansion forming trade networks and gain economic opportunities through activities such as land speculation and commercial trade. Labor diasporas, in which a group of individuals migrate away from the homeland at specific times of the year in search of employment, also fit within this category. Individuals of either type leave as individuals or small pockets of people, with the result that intergroup relations are not as strong in the place of settlement as in the case of large-scale migration and may take an extended period of time to develop.

Voluntary deportation implies a choice to leave the homeland in the face of intolerable conditions with the possibility of returning (Butler 2001:201). This cohort, to varying degrees, is placed under "Victim Diaspora." The term *voluntary exile* is misleading because it implies that people exercise agency in decisions to leave. Can one voluntarily be thrown out of one's home or country? It becomes a complicated scenario when there is an imputation of free will, yet exile is the viable choice when the sole alternative is to remain in an exploited and subordinate social and economic position. A diasporic mentality based on a shared experience of injustice formulates quickly with this diasporic type.

Forced deportation refers to involuntary expulsion from the homeland. Unlike indentured servitude or slavery, in such cases there is always the possibility of and hope for a return to the homeland (Cohen 1997). Exiles generally experience inferior conditions in the host land. As a result, the collective develops an oppositional relationship with the established population in the place of settlement (Butler 2001:203).

Captivity refers to enslavement or indentured servitude through deliberate forced removal of people from their homeland to serve as labor for colonial implementation elsewhere and resides firmly in the "Victim Diaspora" typology. It is forced and involuntary, and at times extremely violent. As long as people are considered captives, whether slaves or indentured servants, they are forcefully prevented from having any connection to or returning to the homeland (Butler 2001:200).

Captivity always falls under the category of *proletarian diaspora.* While enslavement is beyond the control of the individual or group, indentured servitude represents a limited choice arising out of a desire to escape intolerable social and economic conditions in the place of origin. The case of nineteenth-century India and the British Empire illustrates the lack of real choice for the colonized, unskilled proletarian population.

By 1830 India was forced into the international labor market. After the abolition of slavery in British Empire, British colonial governments in the Caribbean, Indian Ocean, and Pacific turned to their colony in India to provide cheap labor (Shukla 2001:555). The intolerable economic conditions in India in areas such as Bihar, Bengal, and Uttar Pradesh were the impetus for the poorer classes to sell their labor. Contracts for indenture were lengthy, usually being no less than ten years. Individuals who signed on as indentured servants did so only because the work meant at least rations, dwelling, and a daily wage, something not readily available to all in British colonial India. Brij Lal (1996:169) argues that the emergence of Indian indentured servitude represented a new system of slavery and exploitation and dehumanization.

Exile can be forced or voluntary and is part of the Victim Diaspora. It can involve either mobilized or proletarian diasporic groups. The conditions of being forced from the homeland have a strong effect on the degree of resistance to or incorporation into the social structure of the new locale.

As seen through either mobilized or proletarian diasporas there is more to the social historical context than just victimization. Although all cohorts leaving the homeland represent an international scattering of two or more locations, what is important is to contextualize the differences in the dispersal—those who left voluntarily and those who were expelled, exiled, or otherwise forced out. Individuals making up the mobilized aspect of a diaspora leave the homeland for profit or better opportunities and represent what can be considered the voluntary cohorts. They are active agents in the expansion of empire and colonization elsewhere, as they in turn became part of the machine that created diasporas and unlike the collectives forming the proletarian diaspora experience less alienation in place of settlement in relation to the amount of social and economic capital they have entering the new place of settlement (Butler 2001:195). The typologies are time sensitive and reflect the time or the process of time in the period of incorporation in the new place of settlement. Those of the mobilized groups adapt quickly the new environment, unlike those who form the ranks of the unskilled or slaves as they experience slow processes of incorporation and therefore for most of the first generation remain partly segregated from the larger society. The refinement of the social, historical, and economic context of a particular group through these analytical typologies allows for the classification of diverse class, ethnic, and religious factions within the totality of a diaspora.

In this context, a proletarian diasporic identity differs from an immigrant identity, and certainly from a mobilized diasporic identity, because being in this category of diaspora means a permanent loss and the diffusion of a large number of people who maintain strong collective communities away from the original homeland (Bhabha 1994; Chow

1993). Departing the homeland is a collective experience and involuntary because of social, economic, or political conditions. The events are traumatic and form the necessary element for the shared memory of the "great historic injustice that binds the group together" (Cohen 1997:23). Additionally, diasporic groups establish bonds around a collective memory of displacement and violent loss; they cannot be "cured" by assimilation, forced or otherwise, into the social structure of the new place of settlement (Clifford 1994:307).

In the case of proletarian diasporic collectives, dispersal is often resulting from the effects of colonialism, colonization being the process whereby a foreign group establishes arbitrary power over an indigenous group. Native people are considered separate from and subordinate to the ruling power; their position is established and maintained through relations of racism and racialization based on values of differentiation (Ruane 1992:294–295). The process effectively distorts all forms of the native social structure. The grounds for dispersal from the homeland within a colonial context are classified by "degrees of violation" that include captivity, exile, emigration, or migration (either forced or voluntary).

Sandhya Shukla (2001:554–555), studying the history and impact of the Indian diaspora, part of the larger South Asian diaspora, argues that the international movement of all classes of Indians was the result of British imperialism. Furthermore, Shukla (2001:555) contends that the Indian diaspora, spanning from 1835 to 1920, comprised diverse groups leaving India, each group having a level of choice and compulsion. There were those who were compelled to become indentured servants and field workers because of social and political conditions (proletarian), while others departed mainly to seize economic opportunity and advancement (mobilized).

Stigmas and stereotypes are social values that inhibit the incorporation of proletarian collectives to the host land. The consequence of stigmas is a widening of the social gap between the dominant society and the diasporic group (Armstrong 1976:406). In such contexts, social relations are squarely rooted in a dominant-versus-subordinate dialectic in which the proletarian diasporic group is forced to negotiate their sociocultural identity with that designated by the dominant society—the inferior "foreign other." Although most incoming groups begin at or near the lower end of society, proletarian collectives are continually racialized and spatially marginalized and therefore experience slow economic and cultural advancement (Shukla 2001:37).

Social Relations in the New Place of Settlement

Identity formation within a diaspora cannot be fully understood without expounding on the social relations constructed in the place of resettlement. In this context the formation of social identity is based on the type, category, and cohesion of the diasporic group, which in turn affects the degree of alienation and incorporation. This process of fitting in to the new location is tempered by the level of transnationalism and retention of social values of and continuing interests in the homeland.

The social glue binding the diasporic community together is a common historical experience constructed upon ethnic or national myths and ties to a geographic place (Vertovec 1997:278–279). The mentality of a diasporic collective is formed in large part from created memories and "imaginative histories" (Said 1991:55). Indian ethnic communities such as "Little India" in Southall, England, and Jackson Heights in Queens, New York, have formed around an increased sense of place and nationalism as well as renewed ideas of tradition, culture, and religion (Shukla 2001). Movements that blend religion and nationalism, such as Hindutva, have reestablished the connection between the Indian diasporic group and India through created histories and myths combining stories of religion, culture, and nationalism (Shukla 2001:563).

In any diaspora there is always a "sentimental pathos" toward the symbols of the homeland. A common feature of all diasporas is the real or putative ancestral home, and that provides the core for a collective commitment to its maintenance, restoration, safety, and prosperity—even to its creation (Conner 1986:16; Cohen 1997:105–106). There is a perpetual transnational connection that is emotional, economic, and cultural and is manifested through a range of social organizations and institutions. Connection to the homeland arises from the overriding sense of guilt for forsaking those who remained. This culminates in an overcompensation of identity expressed through traditional rituals and ethnic symbolism (Anthias 1998:565). In her study of Cuban Americans in Miami, Marie Garcia (1996) focuses on the cultural variations between generations belonging to the first wave of Cuban immigrants (1959–1962) and those of today. She (1996:84) illustrates the romantic notions of how preserving the language, manner of speaking, social organizations, and material culture belonging to the pre-Castro period is part of the expression of being *cubanidad* (Cuban). Garcia points out, however, that in the eyes of postrevolutionary Cuban immigrants, *cubanidad* sociocultural manners, materials, and symbols do not represent Cuba today but rather *la Cuba de ayer* (the Cuba of yesterday).

The cultural "re-turn" to the homeland, whether actual or imagined, is critical to the development of social identities in the host land because it anchors the community by a shared connection (Vertovec 1997; Tölöyan 1991, 1996). Over time the relationship with the distant homeland becomes increasingly romanticized yet remains a large part of the new identity. Ties to the homeland may include sentimental expressions through ballads, poems, social clubs, letters and news from home, as well as material and physical connections such as sending or raising money for a common cause (Drzewiecka 2002; King 1998; Panossian 1998a, 1998b; Safran 1991). Maintained social and cultural attachments provide the group a sense of roots as they challenge the social norms encountered in the host land (Clifford 1994:308).

Alienation is a common experience among proletarian diasporic groups in the new place of settlement. Through contact and conflict with the native population, immigrant factions are segregated and classified as the foreign other—strangers, foreigners, aliens (Cohen 1994:192–195; Cohen 1997:106; Vertovec 1997:278–279). Natives evoke real or imagined images to express their distinctive social identities. Social boundaries constructed between immigrant and host societies move beyond an us-versus-them opposition to a dominant-versus-subordinate discourse in which the term *native* is synonymous with domination (Brah 1996:190).

Alienation is not necessarily altogether negative. A diasporic group uses its social position strategically to gain a voice in social and political relations. Because the community is made distinct by hostile responses, it can use its minority status to mobilize and solidify group consciousness (Safran 1991:83–84; Butler 2001:190). As the homeland of such groups is seen as a point of exclusion from the dominant society, the actions of recreating the homeland in the new place can serve as a bonding mechanism and empower that community in negotiation of and struggle with their minoritized space in the new place of settlement (Cohen 1997:106). Diaspora is an aspect of collective life with reinforced interests in primordial ethnicities. Appeals to a distant homeland and the experience of expulsion serve to romanticize and authenticate cultural group politics in the host land (Drzewiecka 2002:15–16).

Individuals in a diasporic group can be powerful actors in manipulating and creating collective associations in both places (Vertovec 1997:279). Jolanta Drzewiecka (2002:18) categorizes this as an identity game legitimating a group's *in between* social position in two different national contexts whereby the diasporic community is careful to claim its current citizenship as a primary identification in its activities on behalf of the homeland. On the surface of social relations, to gain a new social position and become incorporated into the new social structure, a diasporic group must dismiss all reasons for possible accusations of betrayal to their new nationality (Safran 1991; Cohen 1997). It must attempt to balance subjective positions of "citizen" and "immigrant" wrapped within complex relations between "home" and "diaspora" (Mankekar 1994:364). Drzewiecka demonstrates this by the shifting discourses of Polish American diasporic identities.

The basis of the Polish American diasporic mentality is the reproduction of a collective historical experience of being exiles. After World War II, Polish Americans formed ethnic organizations to take part in the struggles dealing with such issues as the Holocaust in Poland and the fall of communism (Drzewiecka 2002:17). The Polish-American Congress, the largest Polish American organization, created a charter with a section called the "American Agenda" for the purpose of educating Polish Americans on how to become better American citizens. The organization has another charter, the "Polish Agenda," directing Polish Americans to become better informed about sociopolitical issues affecting the people of Poland (Drzewiecka 2002:5). According to Drzewiecka (2002:10), Polish Americans remain entrenched in and outspoken on Polish social and political affairs, but they do so as "Americans of Polish ancestry" imbued with the common democratic values of the American people.

Diaspora and Social Identity

Diasporic groups create and maintain bonds and common social identity around varying degrees of a collective memory of displacement and violent loss. The process of dispersal and impetus for it forms the necessary elements to create a shared memory of the "great historic injustice that binds the group together" (Cohen 1997:23). The process of social identity formation consists of a process of constant reevaluation of what group membership means as immigrants collectively forge new social relations and identity in the place of settlement (Fortier 1998; Panagakos 1998; Panossian 1998a, 1998b).

Studying identity formation among diasporic groups is an analytical discourse in understanding the social processes of differentiation. Difference is constituted within the interstices of sociopolitical and economic relations, which are historically situated and employed in regimes of power where "modes of differentiation" such as class, race, gender, and ethnicity are instituted in terms of "structured formations" (Brah 1996:15, 117–118; Radhakrishnan 2003:119–123). Esteem values and modes of behavior are central to how people are perceived and placed in the social strata, and this affects life's chances. In society, social values are most likely dictated by the dominant group; therefore, discussions about culture and identity must be understood within the context of power relations among different groups (Brah 1996:19). This process is not a pre-given reality but is itself a cultural construction and formed into an ideology that presents itself as reality (Gilroy 2003:50–51). The experiences gained on both sides of the social boundary form the basis for collective histories of dominance and subordination and the foundation for social identity.

Social identity is a social construct that is fluid and historically situated. It is multifaceted, context specific, and subjective. Social identity is given meaning through social relations created by a frame of reference of shared cultural codes and collective history (Brah 1996:21, 47; Hall 1990:223; Radhakrishnan 2003:119). It is a concept of "self-knowledge" defined by belonging to a group (or groups) that provides a sense of place in the world and the material and emotional significance attached to that membership (Ashmore et al. 2001; Comaroff and Comaroff 1992; Tajfel 1981; Woodward 1997). Through experience, individuals learn to classify differences as a fundamental tool for contending with the social environment (Payne 2000:2; Bhabha 1994:51).

Experience is gained through social interaction and constructs what is considered reality. It is a resource of knowledge affecting the imagery of social boundaries (Brah 1996:11). It can be "true" or "false" and evaluated as justified or illegitimate in relation to the subject and his or her world (Mohanty 2000:32). Experience is the cognitive raw material in which social identities are constructed in order to make sense of the world and define and reshape our values (Barth 2000:31; Mohanty 2000:43).

In a diaspora, social identity is always in the process of being created and recreated. It never really "is" but is perpetually in "production" as a manner of constantly "retelling the past" (Hall 1990). Social identity is constructed through diverse narratives and myths drawn from specific patterns that are embedded in historically situated social relations of power, exploitation, and oppression (Bhabha 1994; Gans 1995). Although the formation and process of a diasporic identity changes, it assumes specific patterns within the processes of alienation and incorporation. Patterns are more apparent at the social boundaries between groups and take the form of *authentic* markers (Barth 1969, 1994, 2000). The recognition of authentic markers constitutes a powerful element in creating and maintaining social identity (Bhabha 1994; Comaroff and Comaroff 1992). Diaspora identities are operationalized during contact and conflict and appeal to a collective experience, history, and shared economic positions. Authentic markers are created to express a cohesive group and conjure up collective memories as well as to express new symbolism of social and national belonging (Hall 1990:224).

In the Indian diaspora, laborers and indentured servants forged new identities in their places of settlement. They formed a new kind of Indian society blending the cultural materials and behaviors of both places, which resulted in a distinct community. Scholars have argued that participants in the Indian diaspora are considered more individualistic, more pragmatic, and more egalitarian than Indians in the homeland, while they are proud of their culture and heritage of being Indian (Lal 1996:169). Through their shared history of conflict, alienation, and uprootedness, Indians throughout the world have formed a strong sense of a transnational connection and affinity with India that is communicated through preserved patterns and markers of the Hindu religion (Lal 1996:181).

As an analytical paradigm, diaspora encompass the totality of considerations of who travels, when, how, and why; under what social, cultural, and economic conditions they travel; and what regimes of power inscribe the formation of a particular diaspora. Although most studies focus on the mournful experiences of exile, flight, and expulsion, Khachig Tölöyan (1996:8) argues for more detailed studies defining groups as being legitimately in a diasporic context, and the ways in which social identities are formed and recreated in new places of settlement, while retaining links to the places of origin. Therefore, to interpret the diaspora experience successfully, one must incorporate the history of movement and interpret how this affected social relations both within the diasporic group and among those in the new place of settlement. Although there is variability in the types of groups within diasporic communities, the group is always perceived to be homogenous by the people of the host land. At the new place of settlement there is an environment of marginalization whereby social values are placed on distinctions between the incoming and host groups (Anthias 1998). The immigrant group is deconstructed, and its varying physical and social attributes are publicly labeled as subordinate and inferior within the sociocultural framework of dominant society.

The term *diaspora* is highly contested and fraught with emotion. The very word conjures tragedy and the victimization of a large number of people. The case of Ireland is no exception. Nevertheless, many scholars question the legitimacy of calling Ireland's history of emigration (forced or voluntary) a diaspora. The main reason for not employing the term resides with the fact that the term brings with it strong emotions, especially in the context of the Famine. The following chapter examines the extensive history of the Irish diaspora and the types of dispersal experienced. Identifying the type of diasporic group is vital to understanding and interpreting patterns and authentic markers of a diasporic identity in the archaeological record. Material culture does not reflect diasporic groups or social identity automatically but is constantly assigned meaning where people create space for it in a particular context. Its meaning derives from the understanding of the social world based on daily experiences and is profoundly embedded in the differentiations of social relations between the Irish diasporic community and native-born Americans. Understanding the social positions of those swept up in the Irish diaspora and the degrees of experienced alienation, incorporation, and transnationalism will shed light on how material culture was used in the creation of an Irish American identity.

3
The Irish Diaspora? Creating an Analytical Discourse

The title of this chapter is posed as a question because researching the enormous amount of literature spanning 400 years of Irish migration demonstrates that there is no consensus as to how to categorize, organize, or even approach the subject of Irish dispersal worldwide. What is needed is an overarching theoretical framework bringing together the complex history of Irish colonialism and the international movement of diverse religious and economic groups. Social theory defining *diaspora* through the development of diasporic categories and typologies demonstrates the potential for creating an analytical discourse toward interpreting the material culture and social history of multiple groups and their experiences within the totality of a diaspora. Employing the categories of mobilized diasporas and proletarian diasporas, as well as applying the different group typologies within each diasporic category, furthers our understanding of the Irish experiences of colonialism, social, economic, and religious inequality, extreme poverty, and the amount of agency or choice various groups had in deciding whether to stay or leave Ireland.

Making the Irish Diaspora

Irish historians debate whether the Irish dispersal should be considered a diaspora. Arguments stem from how Irish history should be interpreted in the present because it is profoundly embedded in contemporary social and political issues (Kennedy and Johnson 1997:34). Alan O'Day (1996:197) argues that because Irish history is complicated by modern troubles, historians are prevented from developing an overarching methodology to research what is arguably a diaspora. Instead, Irish historians look to economic forces to explain emigration, using the traditional push-pull factors affecting an undifferentiated peasantry (Mokyr 1983; Ó Gráda 1988, 1994, 1995). In doing so, they avoid controversial topics that have an enormous impact on the social and political understandings of Irish history.

The idea of an undifferentiated Irish peasantry has a strong influence on how the Irish are studied in the United States. Historians of Irish immigration approach the subject with an unproblematic perspective of assimilation with similar economic and religious groups (Belchem 1995). Oscar Handlin was one of the first, and most influential, historians to present the Irish in this manner. In *Boston's Irish, 1790–1865: A Study in Acculturation* (1949), Handlin characterized the Irish as a homogenous ethnic group labeled as culturally conservative and superstitious. Handlin's format became the model to be followed or questioned by later historians of Irish immigrant history (Brown 1966; Degler 1984; Fanning 2000; Jones 1960; Kraut 1982; Levine 1966; McCaffrey 1997; Shannon 1963; Sowell 1981; Towey 1986).

Since Handlin's work, most historical studies have taken a regional focus to explain the Irish experience in America (Brewer 1987; Clark 1973; Erie 1988; Greeley 1973; McCaffrey 1997; Meagher 1986a, 1986b, 1986c). Kerby Miller's book *Emigrants and Exiles: Ireland and the Irish Exodus to North America* (1985), however, was the first to provide an in-depth transnational study of the Irish diaspora that deconstructed the causes of the push-pull factors in Ireland and America. Miller's influence has recreated the study of Irish immigration, and today historians are looking into more complex issues of racism, discrimination, and prejudice in America (Bodnar 1985; Ignatiev 1995; Kenny 1998; Meagher 1986a, 1986b, 2001; Takaki 1979). Miller's work illustrates the need for a more nuanced transnational study acknowledging sociocultural diversity in the Irish population emigrating in concert with the concept of lived experiences of colonialism and marginalization through time and space. Ireland's current social and political issues and entanglements have prevented this type of research.

Approaches to Irish History

It cannot be denied that there are more people with Irish ancestry living worldwide than in Ireland. The historical reasons for this have been fused with political debates in Ireland between nationalists and unionists (Cullen 1995:168; Hutton and Stewart 1991:1–2). Interpretations of historical events have hit ethnic and/or religious nerves, leading many scholars to avoid studies of certain subjects considered to be a hindrance to solving contemporary issues. This was especially true during the height of the "troubles" in Ireland in the 1960s and 1970s. Unionists regarded popular Irish history to be the catalyst for renewed militant nationalism (Bradshaw 1989:342). To counter this, a group of Irish historians developed a theoretical and methodological paradigm called the "new history" of Ireland. The new approach was considered completely objective and avoided topics considered part of the destructive processes of politicizing history (Fanning 1988; Foster 1988).

In theory, the "new" approach to Irish history was intended to be value free and based on a systematic application of the scientific method. Revisionist historians argued that contemporary studies are steeped in popular (nationalist) mythology (Brady 1994:24; Edwards 1994:56; Moody 1994:86). The agenda was to dislodge the popular and politically charged Irish nationalist history, which was considered to lack objective historical truth. The emotive aspect of historical research into the Great Famine was seen as a prime example of the myth making of a national history.

Revisionist historians argue that the causes of the Great Famine and the effects it had on the social and political structure of Ireland were greatly exaggerated by contemporary writers, such as journalist-historian John Mitchel (O'Farrell 1982). Mitchel's descriptive and inflammatory works, such as the *Jail Journal of Five Years in British Prisons* (1854) and *The Last Conquest of Ireland (Perhaps)* (1861), influenced how the Famine was presented and interpreted up through the twentieth century (Davis 2000b:16; Ó Ciosáin 2001:107). Mitchel was one of the first writers of the Famine to purposely draw emotion from readers by implying that it was a fortunate accident that Britain used to rid Ireland of its surplus population (Mitchell 1861:112, 119; Morash 2000:42–44, 47). The intent of the new history was to remove blame from historical research and replace it with an emotionless and factual approach derived from the "cold light of history" (Akenson 1994; Boyce and O'Day 1996; Connolly 1996; Curtain 1996; Davis 2000b; Foster 1988; Moody 1994; O'Sullivan 1997a, 2000).

Two influential writers of the new history are Raymond Crotty (1966) and Louis Cullen (1969). Crotty (1966) posits that poverty and famine were not caused by an oppressive social structure but by the failure of the Irish to adapt to changing economic trends. He argued against the perpetuation of studies detailing widespread chronic poverty and underdevelopment because it overshadowed the facts of the long wave of spectacular economic expansion and prosperity throughout Ireland's history (Crotty 1966). Similarly, Cullen (1969) purposely focused on Ireland's economic history to distinguish his work from the popular histories that stressed the "emotionally perceived" injustices of the seventeenth-century confiscations and Protestant ascendancy. Both historians insisted that studying the failures of the Ireland's economy was key to interpreting Irish history.

The revisionists' clinical approach sterilized the impact of catastrophic events of conquest and colonialism. Two of the most outspoken critics of the new history are Brendan Bradshaw (1989) and Desmond Fennel (1988). Their biggest critique is of the revisionist history's claims to be value free and its refusal to consider the traumas experienced in Irish history (Bradshaw 1989:337; Fennel 1988:22). To Bradshaw and Fennel, interpretations are never completely objective and are always based on some form of judgment or moral interpretation. Revisionist histories are heavily Anglocentric in their interpretations and dismiss oral and other popular histories as "myths," not historical facts (Ó Tuathaigh 1994:308). According to Fennel (1988:22–25), such myths are actually practical moral convictions concerning "a nation's right to freedom, acknowledging the wrongness of its being subject to another nation, and the rightness of resisting and rebelling against such oppression." Furthermore, Seamus Deane (1994:234) calls revisionist thinking a form of "pseudo-scientific orthodoxy" that is tailored to match the prevailing political climate.

Bradshaw (1989) has created three analytical categories illustrating the inadequacies of revisionist history: evasion, normalization, and neglect. These terms emphasize how revisionist history ignores traumatic details of conquest and longstanding patterns of oppression and violence (Bradshaw 1989:338–339). According to Bradshaw, Ciaran Brady and Raymond Gillespie's (1986) edited volume *Natives and Newcomers: Essays on the Making of Irish Colonial Society, 1534–1641* evades much of the history of violence, such as the suppression of the Kildare rebellion (1534–1535) and the Cromwellian massacres at Drogheda and Wexford (1649), during the establishment of English presence in Ireland as part of the central element of Irish history. Through evasion, then, the revisionist historians deliberately overlook aspects of Irish history that are fraught with negative sentiment and lead directly to historical events such as the Famine and the worldwide dispersal of much of the Irish population up to the twentieth century.

Normalization refers to the act of making social processes of colonization and famine part of the natural continuum of the creation of modern Ireland. Revisionist history has consistently normalized many of the highly charged sociopolitical relations associated with Ireland's history of colonization. For instance, Raymond Gillespie's 1985 *Colonial Ulster: The Settlement of East Ulster* and Michael MacCarthy-Morrogh's 1986 *The Munster Plantation: English Migration to Southern Ireland, 1538–1641* trace the developments of land confiscations and the implementation of the plantation system but represent these processes as a natural part of the larger pattern of British movement and settlement.

Neglect commonly refers to the revisionist tendency to downplay the importance of the Great Famine because it looms so largely in Irish consciousness as both a historical event and a touchstone of national identity. The first academic study of the Famine did not appear until the 1950s (Edwards and Williams 1956). Topics of the Famine were not visited again for thirty years. Irish scholars such as Mary E. Daly (1986), Joel Mokyr (1983), and Cormac Ó Gráda (1988, 1995) renewed interest in understanding the causes of the nationwide potato failure. Such scholars attempted to balance their interpretations between popular history and revisionist methodology (Bradshaw 1989). Today, research remains closer to the revisionist camp in which blame is diffused between the "reckless Irish" and "the unevenness of the benefits of the Industrial Revolution" (Ó Gráda 1988:1–3).

It was not until the 1990s that the Great Famine was considered an issue for serious academic study. Although a principal event in modern Irish history, historians tend to avoid scrutiny of its more controversial aspects (Kinealy 1995:xv). This makes any study of the Famine period of the Irish diaspora difficult because previous research does not discuss or deconstruct the root social causes of the Famine. For many Irish historians the aim is to reconcile the dichotomy between what is considered nationalist history and revisionism and look for a middle ground in which people figure in the scope of history but avoid issues such as laying blame to a single source (Daly 1996:85). Cormac Ó Gráda (1994) refers to this as a "paradox within Irish historiography" because the methodology downplays any controversial aspects of the Famine that could have an impact in contemporary politics.

The middle-ground approach continues to be problematic in the study of the Irish diaspora because revisionist history has infiltrated the study and influenced its focus. Until very recently, the term *diaspora* was not widely used in Irish history because it connotes victimization and suffering at the hands of the British government (Belchem 1995). Recently it has been employed in various books and edited volumes, but none in a definitive and critical way as most believe that fully developing Irish migration under the paradigm of diaspora studies contributes to the sentiment of "oppression history" because it focuses on the "wrongs" of British policy (Cullen 1995:168–169, 186; O'Sullivan 2000:1–2). Consequently, many scholars use an overarching theoretical approach from descriptive studies of migration.

In *Patterns of Migration,* Patrick O'Sullivan (1997a:xviii–xx) insists that the study of Irish migration as a diaspora is a simple approach seeking to categorize the Irish as a disadvantaged group under an oppression, compensation, and contribution continuum. C. J. Houston and W. J. Smyth (1993:338; emphasis added) state:

> In recent years the evocative term, diaspora, has been employed, thereby linking in metaphor the dispersal of the Irish with that of the Jews. The concept of diaspora, with its emphasis upon the displacement of people from their home and connotations of exile, is a compelling but limited description of the Irish experience. Certainly poverty, hunger, force and desperation drove hundreds of thousands out of Ireland, but many more exited *voluntarily,* motivated by a perception of future loss of social status and drawn by opportunities in colonies abroad.

This quotation epitomizes the revisionist perspective. First, it quickly dismisses any historical or material connection with the Jewish Diaspora and its inherent definition of victimization. Second, revisionists dismiss the notion of the Irish as victims, claiming that emigration resulted from agency, with the Irish being rational actors.

Since the term *diaspora* is emotionally freighted, historians studying Irish dispersal have used other terms having fewer political implications. Colorful phrases such as "the great migration," "vast outward flow," and "voluntary flight" have been used, and each phrase connotes choice or agency (O'Gallagher 2000; Ó Grada 1988; O'Sullivan and Lucking 2000).

Alternatively, the descriptive term *exile* has been used in understanding Famine emigrants. Lynn Hollen Lees (1979) eschewed the term *diaspora,* replacing it with *exile* in studies associated with the Famine period. She was not the first to use the term *exile* in an Irish context. Florence Gibson (1951) declared that the Irish regarded themselves as homesick exiles. Unfortunately, neither study provides any in-depth interpretation of what the word meant to the Irish nor how can it be related to the larger sense of Irish history. Referring back to Kerby Miller's (1985) seminal work, he employed the term *exile* and attempted to link it with the Irish (Catholic) diasporic mentality. He argued for the importance of Ireland's push factors (intolerable social, economic, and political conditions), which forced the Irish to leave Ireland. Miller's analysis broke new ground because he demonstrated the vast and complex nature of the Irish diaspora.

Donald Akenson (1994, 1997, 2000), Piaras Mac Éinrí (2000), Patrick O'Sullivan (1997a, 1997b, 2000), and Robert Scally (1995:272–273) denounce the term *exile.* They argue that exile was a myth created in the late nineteenth century as a rallying point to organize the Irish in America. Instead they call for the use of the term *migration studies.*

Migration studies focus on internal, external, and return migration. These studies set themselves apart from topics of immigration and emigration because they are seen to reflect only international movement, whereas migration represents a broader interpretation encompassing both international and national movement (Jackson 1986). O'Sullivan (1997a:xvii; 1997b:13–15; 2000:13) argues for Everett S. Lee's (1966) approach based on an individual's reactions to positive and negative factors. He (1966:56) argues that those choosing to leave because of positive (pull) factors are "highly educated persons" who hold professional and managerial positions because of the possibility of better offers elsewhere. In contrast to this, those leaving because of minus (push) factors are "negatively selected" and are "*persons who have failed economically* or *socially.* . . . [It is] more likely to be the uneducated or the *disturbed* who are forced to migrate" (emphasis added). Irish scholars using such an approach do so because it removes all indications of blame by naturalizing a subjective conception of class structures. In the context of the Irish diaspora, it is a perfect fit for moderate and revisionist historians who wish to promote the fallacy that the intolerable conditions experienced by Ireland's majority were of their own making.

Theoretical advancement in the study of the Irish diaspora remains relatively undistinguished because scholars have not moved past the debate over the use of terms such as *diaspora* and *migration.* Although there is a vast amount of published research, little has been accomplished to advance our understanding of the dynamics of the Irish experience of dispersal. Dismissal of the analytical paradigm of diaspora studies has created a one-dimensional history of Irish emigration that glosses over specific events that have formed the shared history of displacement and identity in the host land. Therefore, the study of the Irish diaspora should seek to identify the diverse composition of groups enmeshed in webs of social relations.

If It Happened, When?

It is not surprising that historians cannot agree on the approach to the Irish diaspora. A serious interest in the topic did not emerge until the beginning of the 1990s. The impetus for studying Irish emigration began with the impending 150th anniversary of the Great Famine and the speech of then-president of Ireland Mary Robinson in 1995 (Davis 2000b:15). For the first time, the president spoke publicly about the extreme importance of the larger transnational historical processes linking Ireland and those of Irish descent worldwide. Since then, the debate has continued over not only how to study the processes creating an international descendent community but also how to define them.

The Famine period (1845–1852) is thought by many to represent the watershed for Irish dispersal (Erie 1988; Kinealy 1995; McCaffrey 1992; 1997; Meagher 2001; Miller 1985; Ó Gráda 1988, 1989; O'Sullivan 1997a, 1997b, 2000; Scally 1995). At that time, between 1 and 1.5 million people were compelled to leave because of large-scale evictions, famine, and disease (Kinealy 1995:297). The Famine marks the largest global dispersal within the totality of the Irish diaspora and established a cohesive international network of Irish communities.

Cormac Ó Gráda (1988:48) contends that Irish dispersal in this period can be properly called a diaspora because people who emigrated because of the Famine differed both in numbers and social position from emigrants in other periods. Those leaving were the poor from rural areas from the western and southwestern counties (Ó Gráda 1988:48). What is more, he points to the poor conditions and mortality rate suffered by immigrants during the crossing as a marker that differentiates this dispersal from any other (Mokyr 1983:267–268).

Graham Davis (2000a, 2000b) and others (Neal 2000; O'Gallagher 2000) suggest that the Irish diaspora began at the close of the Napoleonic War in 1815. Postwar economic downturns in combination with a dramatic increase in population fostered a climate for mass emigration. This movement was worldwide and established emigrant networks that facilitated later movement from all counties in Ireland (Davis 2000a:21). Davis (2000b:22) argues that this period is usually ignored because most historians focus their attention on the larger numbers leaving during the Famine period.

For some, the beginning of the seventeenth century marked the commencement of the Irish diaspora. English colonialism directly caused emigration and had a lasting effect on the policies and events leading to immigration in the nineteenth century (Archdeacon 1983; Bradshaw 1989; Cullen 1995; Dickson 1966; Fitzgerald 1997; McGurk 1997; Miller 1985; Miller et al. 2003; O'Callaghan 2000; O'Day 1996; O'Grady 1973). Ireland's emigration history begins with the initial processes of the English plantation system, land confiscations, and violent resistance (Fennell 1988). By midcentury Ireland was the largest supplier of white servants to the West Indies, including Montserrat, Nevis, St. Christopher's, and parts of North America (Beckles 1990; O'Callaghan 2000).

The type of emigration differed along the lines of social position and religion. Sean O'Callaghan (2000:55–64) suggests that Catholics were forced to leave Ireland as part of England's developing plantation system. Catholic-owned lands were confiscated and the tenants were forcibly removed to the rocky and barren lands west of the Shannon River or transported to sugar plantations in the West Indies as indentured servants. According to O'Callaghan (2000:77–88) over 50,000 Irish men, women, and children were transported to Barbados between 1652 and 1659 as part of the establishment of the "the white slave trade."

The largest group leaving Ireland was the Irish Protestants. Many were "Scots-Irish" living in areas of Ulster considered Dissenters in the eyes of the Church of England (McCauley 2000:44; Miller et al. 2003:4–5; O'Grady 1973:20–21). Religious intolerance forced many to leave as they were barred from holding public office and forced to work within the guidelines of an oppressive system (Walsh 1996:50).

This broad overview illustrates the many problems inherent in studying the Irish diaspora. No consensus exists as to whether there was a diaspora, and if so, when it happened. The problem rests in how Irish history is interpreted and presented. Many historians wish to normalize modern Irish history. This approach has resulted in a somewhat sterile interpretation, the analytical potential of which has not yet been fully realized. For this to happen scholars must place the social context of the Irish diaspora within analytical categories and typologies drawn from the social sciences.

An Analytical Discourse

The Irish diaspora began in the seventeenth century and spanned 400 years of colonization, racialization, and involuntary movement. To capture the dynamics and complexities of an extensive diasporic history, the following pages divide the Irish diaspora into diasporic categories and typologies to establish a diachronic framework of dispersal. It is necessary to establish the historical parameters for the study of the Irish diaspora. Major events such as colonialism and the Penal Laws, for example, ultimately led to mass evictions and emigration. Fernand Braudel (1980:28) contends that an event represents a momentary "cause" and "effect" that becomes "wedded, either freely or not, to a whole chain of events, of underlying realities which are then, it seems, impossible to separate." The events making up modern Irish history are interconnected moments over the longer duration of time (Braudel 1972:651; 1980:29).

The first years of the seventeenth century marked the establishment of English rule and Protestant ascendancy in modern Irish history. The development of plantations in Ulster and Munster represented the beginnings of English rule in Ireland (Noonan 1998). The policy for establishing English strongholds beyond Dublin was designed to eradicate traditional Gaelic culture and force the native Irish population to assimilate into the English social structure.

Land confiscations were a major part of the plantation system. As a colony, the Irish Catholic majority (850,000) was forced to be subordinate to the Protestant minority (160,000) (Barnard 1973:31–33). The oppressive colonial regime led to the failed Catholic uprising in 1641, a rebellion that lasted ten years and is remembered for the brutality on both sides (Noonan 1998; Ohlmeyer 1999). England's reaction to the uprising was violent and devastating. Oliver Cromwell and the English army arrived to "reconquer" Ireland. He accomplished this by forcibly transplanting indigenous Irish to Connacht under the Act of Resettlement (1652) (Barnard 1973:31, 39; Canny 1973:592–595; Miller et al. 2003:13). The fertile lands were in turn granted to English soldiers, adventurers, and imported Scottish Presbyterians. The English handed over nearly seven million acres, or almost half of Ireland, to more than 2,000 incoming Protestant settlers (Bottigheimer 1967:12–13; Hill 1993:29).

Cromwell's concept of transportation did not end west of the Shannon. Irish Catholics considered rebels were forcibly transported as indentured servants to burgeoning colonies in the West Indies (Beckles 1990; Fogelman 1998; Houston and Smyth 1993; O'Callaghan 2000; Ohlmeyer 1999). This marked the first large-scale international movement.

The defeat of the Irish Catholic army at the Battle of the Boyne in 1688 signified the end of any Catholic collective power in Ireland. Remnants of traditional Irish identity were also undermined (O'Mahony and Delanty 1998:38). The Protestant victory brought with it more land confiscations. As a result, Catholic landownership fell from 20 to

14 percent, and the introduction of the Penal Laws decreased Catholic landownership to 5 percent (Hachey et al. 1989:27–30).

The Penal Laws ensured Protestant ascendancy. The laws subdued the Irish Catholic population by removing any control of and power over Irish affairs (Wilson 1998:15). They barred all Catholics from economic and political affairs. They prohibited Catholics from purchasing or leasing land for more than 31 years, and any profits gained from leased land could not exceed the annual rent by more than one-third. Fathers could not bequeath land to sons at their discretion but only at the time of death. Furthermore, the land had to be divided equally among heirs, thereby fragmenting large holdings into small subdivided plots. Alternatively, if a son converted to the Anglican Church, he could immediately claim ownership of the entire holding. Catholics could not vote, hold office, serve in militias, enter into any white-collar professions, engage in commerce, carry a sword or possess a gun, own a horse worth more than five pounds, or be educated in a Catholic institution (Miller 1985:22). The laws were instilled in conjunction with the last major land confiscations and played a key role in reducing the majority of the Irish Catholic population to a state of poverty (Connolly 1996:23; Harris 1999:5).

By the end of the eighteenth century, Ireland was in control of the Protestant minority. The Act of Union firmly positioned Ireland as a subordinate colony in the British Empire (Whelan 1996:139). It abolished the Irish Parliament and with it Ireland's ability to act on the developing agricultural crises (Kennedy and Johnson 1997:55, 57; Mokyr 1983:281). Economic advancement as a result of the act was uneven. At least one-third of the population was pushed into extreme poverty.

Ireland was thrust into the global market. Competition with English manufacturers forced much of Ireland's industry to consolidate in areas such as Belfast and Dublin. As labor opportunities shrank in the industrial sector, many moved to rural areas to compete for work. The overpopulation of rural areas reduced the demand for rural labor, causing a large section of the population to be financially dependent on agricultural employment controlled by the minority of landowners. Landowners became focused on obtaining profits through commercial agriculture that made laborers redundant (Canny 1982:91–104; Donnelly 1975:62–63; Guinnane 1994:304; Young 1996:667). The Act of Union created sharp class distinctions that ultimately contributed to what Christine Kinealy (1995:6, 1999:42–43) refers to as "the horrific events of the Famine."

The Great Famine is well documented. What is not so widely known is that several potato failures occurred throughout the eighteenth and early nineteenth centuries, each providing impetus for Irish emigration.

From the beginning of the nineteenth century to the eve of the Great Famine more than 1.5 million Irish left Ireland (Ó Gráda 1995:7). The great dispersal of Irish began at the end of the Napoleonic War in 1815 (McTernan 1992:2–3). Throughout this time there was a constant and continual outward flow to North America, mainly to Canada.

England's industrial revolution had an adverse effect on Ireland's economy. Agricultural practices changed from a traditional subsistence base to a profit-oriented, capitalist venture (O'Neill 1984). The poorest people suffered as a result because the new agricultural regimes eliminated the demand for home industries (Cullen 1969:96; Miller 1985:206). The rate of rural unemployment continued to increase as the nineteenth century progressed.

The introduction of new technology and machines made rural labor redundant in the linen textile regions of Ulster and adjoining regions of northern Connacht and northern Leinster. Increasingly, textile workers earned less for their labor as cheaper mass-produced clothing flooded the market (Donnelly 2001; Fitzpatrick 1984; Miller 1985). Outside the "linen triangle" comprising Belfast, Dungannon, and Lurgan, the cottage industry of spinning and weaving declined from 1810 onward (Ó Gráda 1995:20–21).

Those compelled to leave Ireland during the first decades of the nineteenth century were mostly skilled workers and strong farmers. Emigrants departing because of economic downturns were for the most part Protestant, either Anglicans or Presbyterians from counties inside Ulster such as Armagh and Fermanagh, with smaller numbers from the adjoining counties of Sligo, Leitrim, Longford, and Louth (Young 1996:668). Emigrants from Ireland averaged approximately 20,000 annually, and they left Ireland either as family groups or as individuals with established kin networks in North America (Houston and Smyth 1993:343, 346, 348). Economic depressions left the rural poor more susceptible to potato failure throughout the first half of the nineteenth century.

Numerous potato famines occurred between 1800 and 1845. These events were localized, however, and did not affect the entire country. The major famines occurred in 1800, 1802, 1812, 1816–1819, 1821–1822, and 1830–1831 (Beckett 1980:336; Donnelly 2001:9; Hachey et al. 1989:55; Ó Gráda 1995:15; Wood-Martin 1890:65). The most severe were between 1800–1801 and 1816–1819. The mortality rate was approximately 50,000–60,000, and most of the deaths were attributable to disease, not starvation (Kinealy 1995:27). Cholera and typhus, also known as "black fever," struck during the 1801–1802 and 1816–1819 potato failures. W. G. Wood-Martin (1890:65) notes, "Famine and pestilence may be said to be almost synonymous expressions. Thus we learn that in 1816 and 1817 smallpox made fearful inroads among the population, whilst numbers died of malignant fever." Diseases such as typhus struck predominantly in poorer areas because of failing sanitary conditions (McTernan 1992:3).

Prior to the Great Famine, the most dramatic failure of the potato crop happened between 1831 and 1842. In the midst of the distress, cholera was epidemic. Eighteen thirty-two became known as the "cholera year" (Ó Gráda 1995:13). Again Wood-Martin (1890:69) provides an example of the conditions during this period, by quoting a medical survey of County Sligo: "According to the testimony of the medical profession, cases of fever were daily increasing in number and malignancy as evidenced by the numbers in the fever hospital but the prospect was indeed gloomy if contagion began its ravages among the poor at a period when, from inability to pay for separate dwellings, four or five families were crowded together in hovels, compared with which many a stable might be viewed as a mansion."

Emigration increased exponentially during this period. An Irish newspaper referred to the vast numbers of people leaving as a "national mania" (Houston and Smyth 1993:346). The distinguishing feature of this phase of the Irish diaspora was that its emigrants represented an increasingly diverse section of Irish society that was divided by social position and religion. By the 1830s, the majority of people leaving Ireland were Catholics from the rural poor classes of small farmers, cottiers, and landless tenants. The rural poor, once immobilized by poverty, could now emigrate because of competitive prices offered by new shipping companies catering to the massive outward flow (Adams 1967:102–127; Miller 1985:194–195; Mokyr and Ó Gráda 1984:482).

The nationwide failure of the potato crop between 1845 and 1850 was more catastrophic than other previous failures and was immeasurable compared to potato failures in other European countries, because it occurred repeatedly over successive years (Beckett 1980:336; Donnelly 2001:41; Kinealy 1997:16; Mokyr 1980:430, 433). It is not my purpose here to detail the voluminous literature documenting the Famine but to briefly to discuss the events that had greatest impact on the classes making up the Irish proletarian diaspora: the rural poor.

Population in Ireland nearly tripled in the first half of the nineteenth century. By 1850 the population density in the West was three times as high as in the South and Southeast of Ireland (Daultrey et al. 1981; Davis

2000b). The majority of rural Irish were dependent on the potato as the sole means of subsistence. Growing potatoes was also advantageous in the crop rotation system. The crop cleanses the soil and prevents leaching without reducing the earth's nitrogen content. Landowners took advantage of that fact and made profits by renting out heavily manured plots or conacres in exchange for bonded labor (Connell 1962a; Hoffman and Mokyr 1983; Ó Gráda 1988). Potato fields accounted for approximately one-third of all tilled land (approximately 2 million acres) in Ireland (Ó Gráda 1995:17). According to Davis (2000b:23), a minimum of 15 acres of potato land was needed to sustain a family. On the eve of the Famine, the majority of landholdings were between 10 and 15 acres, although an increasing number of people were renting holdings of fewer than 10 acres (Bourke 1993:78; O'Sullivan 2000:4).

The fungus *Phytophtera infestans* was the direct cause of the Famine. The blight first affected crops in 1845 and quickly spread throughout the countryside. The most affected were rural tenants and laborers who depended upon the potato as their only means of subsistence (Ó Gráda 1995:32–33). When the blight returned in 1846, the potato harvest countrywide was less than half a ton per acre. This yield stands in contrast to the average of 6 tons per acre during normal years (Donnelly 2001:57). No one knows the overall death toll caused by the Famine. Historians have estimated that between one and three million people died during this period (Geary 1997:308; Houston and Smyth 1993:348; McCauley 2000:46; Mokyr 1980:433; Mokyr and Ó Gráda 1984:484–486). It was nearly impossible to track every death throughout the country because the weekly mortality rate grew to such large numbers. For example, the records from Cork estimated that 300 people were moving to the city from rural areas daily, and that approximately 500 were dying on a weekly basis. In Cork City 20,000 people died in 1847 alone (Davis 2000b:28; Donnelly 1975:87).

Starvation was not the only cause of death. Disease was epidemic. Ireland's medical system was inadequate to handle the large number of cases. Fever sheds were constructed outside hospital grounds to provide a minimum of relief to those flooding already crowded hospitals (Ó Cathaoir 1997:231). Cholera spread quickly; between 1848 and 1850 it was responsible for the deaths of at least 34,426 people (Beckett 1980:342–343; Geary 1997:308–309; Kinealy 1995:122–123; Mokyr 1980:437). Dysentery and typhus were also rampant, attacking primarily the young (those under 10) and the old (> 60 years of age) (Geary 1997:344).

During the Famine more than two-thirds of the population lived below the poverty level and were in desperate need of governmental relief (Hetton and Williamson 1993:575). The only public assistance developed for handling large numbers of people was the Poor Law of 1838. The law brought all existing agencies of poor relief under the jurisdiction of a single institution—the workhouse. Poverty was deemed a moral failure of the individual, with the exception of the indigent, widows, and the elderly. Therefore, if an individual was destitute and did not match the criteria above, he/she was labeled lazy and idle (Beckett 1980:338; McLoughlin 1997:66; Neal 1997:333; Ó Cathaoir 1997:222). The fundamental principle of workhouse aid was to make the poor relief so unattractive that it would represent the final alternative for those seeking help.

In 1845, 130 workhouses existed in Ireland. In 1847 the number tripled. There were more than 115,000 inmates annually seeking refuge in the workhouses during the Famine, which was more than they were designed to accommodate (Kinealy 1995:24–25; Ó Gráda 1995:24–25). For example, the workhouse in Fermoy, County Cork, could handle 800 people but had a population of 1,800. Disease spread quickly as the sick were mixed with the healthy. In the first three months of 1847 more than 2,294 people died in the Fermoy workhouse (Donnelly 2001:103).

The second year of the Famine brought new guidelines to control the increase demand by the poor. Relief was granted in exchange for labor on public work projects under the Public Works Act of 1846. The funding for the work was placed squarely on the shoulders of local sources. Projects included building roads and hedge walls as well as making improvements on estates (Neal 1997:335). Because of a non-intervention policy, many landowners capitalized on the misfortunes of the poor. Landowners paid "starvation wages" insufficient to maintain a family even during normal conditions much less during a food crisis (Ó Gráda 1995:47).

The public works scheme became more advantageous to landowners with the passing of the Quarter-Acre Clause. The clause was a provision of the Poor Law Amendment Act of June 1847 and was intended to be a deterrent against the "deceptions and impositions practiced by the poor" (Donnelly 2001:110; Ó Cathaoir 1997:230). To qualify for public assistance, tenants had to surrender all but a quarter-acre of land. Landowners forced tenants to quit their claim to their entire holdings in order to make way for the more profitable pastoral market (Coleman 1999; Scally 1995). Approximately 65,412 families were forcibly evicted from their homes over the course of the Famine period (Davis 2000b:27–28; Donnelly 2001:140). Clearances were nationwide and forced a massive torrent of homeless Irish into the workhouses.

Assisted emigration was for many the only alternative for escaping the horrors of the workhouse. Britain amended the Irish Poor Law in 1847 to allow guardians of the workhouses to rid themselves of unwanted inmates by providing passage to North America (Kinealy 1995:312; McLoughlin 1997:66–68; Ó Cathaoir 1997:232–233). Landowners, in lieu of paying the high cost of maintaining tenants on public works and poor relief, found it cheaper to provide the basic cost of travel. Between 1846 and 1855 landowners cleared tenants off their estates and shipped them to North America.

Transportation on prison ships was another form of assisted emigration. Crime rates rose exponentially during the Famine period. Prior to this time, the crime rate was approximately 20,000 crimes reported annually; it soared to 31,209 in 1847, increased to 38,522 in 1848, and finally peaked at 41,989 in 1849 (Ó Gráda 1995:36). The majority of crimes were nonviolent. The offences, a reflection of the desperate times experienced by the rural laboring classes, included stealing food such as grains and livestock. People caught stealing were automatically shipped to Australia to serve a sentence of between 7 to 15 years (Donnelly 1975:88). The events forming the modern history of Ireland illustrates the impact of colonialism, conflict, and the social, political, and economic processes that led to and caused the Irish diaspora. That history makes it clear that not all leaving Ireland were part of the proletarian collective; rather, Irish left the homeland under diverse conditions and circumstances. To further the analytical discourse of the Irish diaspora, different groups need to be placed within the categories and typologies of diaspora studies in order to have any impact on the social historical or archaeological understanding of the Irish experience in new places of settlement.

Defining Group Dispersal to America

There are two broad diasporic types comprising the Irish diaspora. The typology is a reflection of the shared experiences and social positions of a collective group at the time of leaving Ireland and reveals broad yet significant, patterns of diasporic identities. Those compelled to leave to find independence and better opportunities for economic and social advancement were either part of the middle and wealthier classes in

Ireland (the mobilized diaspora) or part of the rural poor classes (the proletarian diaspora), who sold their labor as indentured servants during times of economic and colonial expansion or were evicted during the Famine. The type of diasporic group is based not only on social class but also on religious affiliation. Although a minority of unskilled and lower-class Protestants and upper-class and skilled Catholics emigrated, the numbers of either group were too small to affect the balance of this interpretation.

Voluntary Emigration and the Mobilized Diaspora, 1650–ca. 1820

Between 1607 and 1820 the majority of Irish emigrants were middle-class Presbyterian Scots-Irish or Anglo-Irish. This group included skilled professionals, artisans, and middling farmers (Miller 1985:133). Initially, large-scale emigration of Irish Protestants was mainly to Canada, but by the eighteenth century more people were emigrating to America (Doyle 1981; Marshall 1979; McCauley 2000; Stewart 1977).

During this period, religious intolerance was a shared experience not only among Irish immigrants but also for many Americans. Scholars argue that Irish Protestant immigrants were quickly considered part of American society, especially during the American Revolutionary War because they were the most ardent supporters of colonial grievance against the home government (Watt 1988). Moreover, the Scots-Irish adhered to the American social structure by declaring themselves a distinct group fundamentally different from Irish Catholics, whom they argued were socially inferior (Doyle 1981; Leyburn 1962; McCauley 2000; Miller 2000).

By the beginning of the nineteenth century, Protestant Irish immigrants were still in the majority. The province of Ulster supplied the majority of emigrants, at least half of the total mobilized diasporic group (Clark and Donnelly 1983; Donnelly 2001; Houston and Smyth 1993; Young 1996). People emigrated because they could afford to do so. In an 1825 survey conducted by the House of Commons on the economic state of Ireland, Col. John Irwin of Tanregoe, County Sligo, commented that Protestants were much more inclined to leave Ireland because they "have the means of going" (House of Commons 1825:10).

Religion was an important factor in being able to leave pre-Famine Ireland. In Ireland, religion dictated social, economic, and political power. The Penal Laws established a caste system to the detriment of

Irish Catholics in both Ireland and America (Miller 2000:142). Irish Protestants were not perceived as a threat to American society because they brought with them skills of the professional classes and, perhaps more important, ready capital (McCauley 2000:50). Irish Protestants were thus accepted and began life in America on a much different social and economic level than Irish Catholics.

Indentured Servitude and the Proletarian Diaspora, ca. 1650–1775

As Protestants were leaving Ireland of their own volition, Catholics were compelled to emigrate. For indentured servants, their destination was either the West Indies or North America (Fogleman 1998; Goodfriend 1997; Houston and Smyth 1993; O'Callaghan 2000) (Table 2). Hilary Beckles (1990:507) provides an interesting view of the violent nature of Catholic emigration, quoting Cromwell's reports after the Battle of Drogheda: "The Enemy were about 3,000. They made stout resistance . . . [but those who] escaped with their lives . . . are in safe custody for the Barbados."

Indentured servitude in the West Indies and North America was presented to the Irish poor as the only choice for economic opportunity. The terms and conditions were seemingly straightforward. They were promised the cost of passage, food, clothing, and shelter in return for a maximum of seven years' contracted labor. The contract also guaranteed they would be granted a plot of land at the end of their tenure (Beckles 1990:506). By selling their labor, Irish Catholics hoped eventually to gain social and economic upward mobility.

Life as an indentured servant was grim. The social relations between plantation owners in the West Indies and North America and indentured servants were at best strained. Irish Catholics were seen as a constant enemy to English landowners and naturally subversive (Beckles 1990; Fogleman 1998; Puckrein 1984; Shepard 1977). In order to maintain the social hierarchy, indentured servants were kept in slave-like conditions, working in undesirable occupations that offered no opportunity to gains skills or the means of becoming upwardly mobile (Beckles 1986; Shepard 1977).

Involuntary Emigration and the Proletarian Diaspora, ca. 1820–1900

Indentured servitude to North America ended at the close of the eighteenth century, at which time it was replaced by involuntary emigration.

The first major movement of Catholics was from the southern and western areas of Ireland (Houston and Smyth 1993:343).

By 1830, diaspora demographics had changed rapidly to unskilled individuals, who could only offer their manual labor for capital. More than 60 percent of the total number of Irish emigrants were Catholic from rural areas (McCaffrey 1997:65; Miller 1985:196–198). Many were forced to quit their lands, predominantly through evictions, and arrived at U.S. ports destitute (Diner 1983; Gilje 1997; Goodfriend 1997; Hershkowitz 1997; McLoughlin 1997).

New policies emerged in the nineteenth century regarding immigrants in America. The implementation of the Alien and Sedition Act in 1796 validated American policy to racialize the Irish Catholics as a single culture of social inferiors. Because the Irish proletarian diaspora was largely made up of uneducated and unskilled small farmers and landless laborers, they were considered valueless. Economic depressions in the 1820s and 1830s fostered anti-Irish sentiment (Davis 1925:768). Social boundaries were delineated, thereby furthering the void between the Irish Catholic and the American Protestant working classes. Irish Catholic men were barred from the more lucrative working-class occupations, such as in the carting, shipbuilding, carpentry, cabinet making, and baking industries (Anbinder 2001:114; Stott 1990:112). During the decades following the Famine, thousands of Irish immigrants from poor and rural sections of Ireland landed in America's port cities. At this time, more Irish women immigrated to North America than in any other period (Diner 1983; McLoughlin 1997; Miller et al. 1997). According to Dympna McLoughlin (1997), over 50,000 pauper women were expelled from the workhouses and shipped to North America between 1840 and 1870 (Diner 1983; Kraut 1982:85; Murphy 2000; Wilentz 1984:123).

The Irish diaspora was not monolithic. Over the course of its history it was made up of different types of people comprising all classes and religions (Armstrong 1976). In broad terms, religion dictated access to social and economic capital. Protestants, whether Anglican or Presbyterian, had more opportunities in Ireland and America. Catholics were among the poorest in both countries. Whether part of the mobilized or proletarian diaspora, those leaving Ireland established communities drawn from shared experiences and history. They blended Irish sociocultural patterns and behaviors with those learned in America. Some accommodated to the American social structure more quickly than others.

The seventeenth century marks the beginning of modern Irish history, as well as the rise of the Irish diaspora. It was a period of conflict and struggle between traditional and capitalistic structures and of the subordination of the former through the hegemonic discourse of colonialism. The social structure created unequal relations of power based on social differentiation. Whether Irish historians choose to refute or ignore this truism is irrelevant.

Ireland's modern history is embroiled in the events of the present. The focus on historical interpretations is guided in part by subjective and political views. Historians searching for a common ground have been tentative in delving into events that have modern-day political implications. The debate over interpreting and presenting modern Irish history has prevented the development of an analytical discourse to locate identifiable patterns and diversity in the Irish diaspora. What is needed is to untangle, for the moment, this history of the Irish diaspora and its connections to contemporary political issues. The impact of the types of factions leaving Ireland has a direct impact on their experiences in the United States. Therefore, it is necessary to highlight both the local and broader historical context to move closer to an understanding of the continuities and transformations in the material record.

4
The Social History and Archaeology of Pre-Famine Rural Ireland

Understanding the social context in which those forced to emigrate lived is the basis of studying diasporic groups. At the heart of the Irish diaspora lie the processes of capitalism. In nineteenth-century Ireland, social worth was placed on differences in ownership and access to land. Land is central to any study of pre-Famine rural Ireland. It dictated social position based on a complex web of socioeconomic relations with a stratified social structure centered on access to and control of the land (Beames 1978; Guinnane 1997; Quinlan 1998). Table 1 illustrates this point.

Members of the landowning class were at the top of the socioeconomic structure and controlled most of the rural Irish landscape. Anglo-Irish families owned the majority of the large estates. Many were descended from ranking English and Anglo-Irish officers and soldiers who had been granted large tracts of land after Cromwell's "reconquest" of Ireland.

Table. 1. Number of Land Holdings in 1845.

Size of holding	Number	Percentage
Less than or equal to an acre	135,314	15.0
Above 1 acre and not exceeding 5 acres	181,950	19.0
Above 5 acres and not exceeding 10 acres	187,909	20.0
Above 10 acres and not exceeding 20 acres	187,582	20.0
Above 20 acres and not exceeding 50 acres	141,819	16.0
Above 50 acres	70,441	6.0
Unclassified	30,433	4.0
Total	935,448	100.0

Source: Bourke 1993:380; Kennedy et al. 1999:162.

The Anglo-Irish gentry were completely entrenched and controlled the economic and social structure at the turn of the nineteenth century (Quinlan 1998:252). Their estates ranged from hundreds to thousands of acres (Hughes 1987:105, 109). The oppressive structure of tenancy employed by the landed class curtailed any accumulation of capital by others, and the system was legitimized by English rule (Marx and Engels 1972:122–129).

Their large estates were subdivided and leased to the farming class. The farming class consisted of commercial farmers and graziers earning a profit from their produce (Coleman 1999:18–19; Hoppen 1999:40–41; Hull 2004:82). Those in the farming class formed Ireland's middle class and earned annual rents, paid directly to the estate, by subdividing sections of their holdings and leasing them to the rural poor, the majority of the population (Beames 1978:83; Fitzpatrick 1980:68; Miller 1985:46; Quinlan 1998:254).

The majority of the population, the rural poor classes, held the least amount of land. The rural poor included different socioeconomic class fractions of small farmers, cottiers, and landless laborers, but all were subsistence-level farmers and laborers. The differences reside in the amount of access to land and whether farming could provide income and subsistence for the household, or whether individuals had to sell their labor to the estate or to other farms during harvest season. In total, the rural poor accounted for 692,755 holdings out of a total of 935,448 holdings, about 74 percent of the country's holdings. As a group, leases were at the discretion (at-will) of the farming class, and at the discretion of the landlord a holding could be auctioned off without warning (Quinlan 1998:253).

In the unequal and class-based social structure, evictions and land clearances were usually the result of tenants making substantial improvements to their holdings. Improvements included such things as reclaiming wasteland by draining fields in order to make them productive for their own crops and livestock (Marx and Engels 1972:62). Distinctions between the classes were based on the amount of land rented and the degree to which individuals were forced to sell their labor to survive (Clark 1982; Johnson 1990:264; Langan-Egan 1999:53; Shanin 1987).

Small farmers practiced full-time subsistence-based agriculture. Farming typically consisted of two crops. The first was the potato, the staple of the family's diet, and the second was corn, which was sold at market. The proceeds from corn would be used to meet the annual rent (Miller 1985:50–51). The cottier was a part-time subsistence-level farmer and laborer. Leases for land ranged from one to five acres; the holding included a single-room cabin. Potatoes were grown in a small plot for food, and some, perhaps, were sold at market. More times than not the annual rent could not be met through a cottier's own agricultural pursuits, and many were forced to become laborers for the farming classes (Clark and Donnelly 1983:27). Lastly, the full-time laboring class was at the lowest social and economic position in Ireland. This group had no real access to land and lived at the mercy of the landlord. In exchange for their labor they received a very small plot of land, usually considered to be the worst available, and a single-room cabin. The average plot ranged from under an acre to no more than five acres. The land was used to grow potatoes exclusively for the family's subsistence (Foster 1846:388–389). Laborers generally lived in clusters forming communities known throughout Ireland as "bog villages" (Donnelly 2001:5) (Figure 3). Thomas Crofton Croker (1824:61) describes a bog village:

> The cabins of the peasantry are most deplorable; and the state of filth in which the owners live, inconceivable to an Englishman who has not traveled in Ireland. Twenty of those hovels sometimes succeed each other without a chimney; and invariably a stagnant black puddle is seen close to the door, appointed receiver-general of all kinds of filth, stream from which issue in every direction, on generally entering at the cabin door and trickling down over its mud floor.

Figure 3. Bog village in Ireland. (*Illustrated London News,* February 7, 1880.)

To be a landless laborer was to live in a state of perpetual bondage. Marilyn Silverman (2001:130) states that

> it was the farmer whom s/he met everyday, who provided largely seasonal and not permanent work, and who insisted, if the work were permanent, that the laborer live in a 'tied cottage' from which s/he would be evicted if the job did not work out. It was farmer who directly exploited his/her labor, who did not moderate the wage nexus and dearth through charity, and who asserted a social and ideological superiority despite daily interaction.

Low wages and exorbitant rent kept the laboring class in a constant position of subordination. Thomas Doolan (1847:16–17) observed the dire situation of the laborer and the conacre system:

> The laborer in Ireland received from sixpence to eightpence per day, nominally; that is to say, although he may work from six in the morning till six in the evening, this is the amount that he is promised, but as to the laborer receiving his wages in ready money, that is very rarely the case. The laborer who is employed by the farmer rents of him a cottage, or, more properly speaking, a hut, for which he may pay from two to three pounds per annum. Supposing his family to consist of a wife and six children, it would require half an acre of potatoes for their support; for which half-acre, not including the cost of its cultivation, he is charged at the rate of from eight to ten guineas per acre. Now, presuming this laborer to have constant work at eightpence a-day all the year round (which is a very unlikely case), the amount at the rate of remuneration for the year would be about ten pounds. The rent of his cottage is about two pounds' his half-acre, together with cost of cultivation, about seven pounds ten shillings; so that, even on the supposition of his having employment throughout the year, there would only remain at its close ten shillings to clothe himself and his family.

Table 2 details the average income and expenditure of a typical laboring tenant household. Wages varied from county to county but on average were 6 pence for short days and 7 to 8 pence for long days; during the harvest season, wages were usually as high as 11 pence (Comber 1985:26; Inglis 1835:24–25).

Employment for this class of rural poor was not consistent. Strong farmers and graziers only needed a labor force during harvest season and on market days. This averaged approximately four months out of the year. Long stretches of unemployment were known as "the lean times" and occurred from November to March (Comber 1985). During the lean times, laborers were forced to migrate and seek temporary employ-

Table 2. Average Income and Expenditures of the Laborer Class.

Source of income	Income (in pounds)[1]	Source of expenditure	Expenditure (in pounds)[2]
Sale of eggs	4.00.0	Rent	1.10.0
Sale of pigs	1.10.0	County cess	.02.6
Sale of bullock	1.10.0	Church	.05.0
Migratory labor	10.00.0	Meal and flour	4.04.0
		Groceries	3.15.0
		Tobacco	2.12.0
		Clothes	3.10.0
		Household	1.10.0
Total	17.00.0		17.08.6

Source: Johnson 1967:98.
Notes: [1]Income refers to sale of items in column 1.
[2]Expenditure refers to cost of rent, etc., in column 3.

ment in places such as England and Scotland (Almquist 1979:715; Boyle 1983:315; Johnson 1967:97–98; Langan-Egan 1999:130–131; Miller 1985:34–35).

Credit from the farming class was an option in times of economic distress. Credit arrangements were unfavorable to the rural poor because interest rates were extremely high and placed the laborer further in debt (Comber 1985:109; Scally 1995:84–85). Other options for credit were the "gombeen men" (*gaimbín* in Irish), or brokers, and the "scullogues" (*scollóga* in Irish), or moneylenders (O'Neill 1984:69–72). Ironically, many of these men were agents working for the estate or the farming classes. In any case, the rates for credit, whether directly from the landlord or a broker, went beyond market prices and pushed poorer classes further into poverty (Miller 1985:34; Langan-Egan 1999:49).

During seasonal downturns, women and children resorted to begging to make the annual rent. This was considered the most demeaning way of gaining income (Coleman 1999:19; Langan-Egan 1999:21, 48; Scally 1995:35, 124, 212). Begging was a last resort and done only when a family's cabin and plot of land was "in hold" because of an already outstanding debt.

Housing was another signifier of the social and class hierarchy in Ireland. It is easy to differentiate between estate manors and less stately strong farmer and grazier housing. The variations among middling farmers and the rural poor classes, however, are more difficult to distinguish.

Vernacular building traditions sometimes masked the socioeconomic differences among class fractions. Kevin Whelan (1999:137) argues that middling farmer housing was the same as that of the small farmer. In his travels, Alexis de Tocqueville (1958:158) was baffled by the apparent lack of durability in the middling farmers' cabins when he noticed that most of their housing consisted of mud walls and thatched roofs, similar to that of poorer class.

By 1841, Irish housing fell into one of four tiers. Quality and durability affected the values placed on dwellings, based on building materials (e.g., stone vs. mud), the number of rooms, and other architectural elements, including roofing material, windows, and gable-end hearths (Aalen et al. 1997; Donnelly 2001; Gailey 1984; Mokyr and Ó Gráda 1984) (Table 3). The majority of rural housing throughout the first half of the nineteenth century was of the 4th tier. In the western counties, 4th-tier dwellings comprised approximately 80 percent of all housing (Kennedy et al. 1999:76).

Building materials varied regionally, so what people used to build their houses was based on access to material. Cabin walls were either stone, mud, or turf. Stone cabins were constructed with roughly dressed fieldstones either dry laid or mortared with clay or limestone, but stone was not widely used until after the Famine (Aalen 1997:146, 154; Kennedy et al. 1999:76). In most areas, mud or turf provided the most expedient and cheapest building material. Mud walls were made from a composite

Table 3. 1841 Census Categories of Irish Housing.

Housing class	Material	Class	Number	Percentage
4th Tier	Mud cabin with cottiers and one room and byre end	Landless laborers	480,000	36.3
3rd Tier	Mud or stone with 2 to 4 rooms with windows and probable byre end	Middling and small farmers	535,000	40.4
2nd Tier	Stone farm house 5 to 9 rooms with windows	Graziers and strong farmers	265,000	20.0
1st Tier	Listed as all those houses of better description	Landlords	43,000	3.3
Total			1,323,000	100.0

Source: Keating 1996:11–12; Kennedy et al. 1999:76–78.

of wet clay and rushes built up and trimmed with a spade. The cabins sometimes rested on basal stone courses (Aalen 1997:155). In *Famine Echoes* (1995:28–30), Cathal Póirtéir quotes pre-Famine memories about constructing mud walls by "scooping the earth from the center of the ditch leaving the shell at the sides stand in the shape of walls that could be roofed over with sticks and heath."

Thatch was the most common roofing material, but slate often replaced it by midcentury (Gailey 1987:95). Arthur Young (1780:25–26) describes thatched roofs:

> The roofs of the cabins are rafters, raised from the tops of the mud walls, and the covering varies; some are thatched with straw, potato stalks, or with heath, others only covered with sods of turf, and weeds sprouting from every part, gives them the appearance of a weedy dung hill, especially when the cabin is not built with regular walls, but supported on one, or perhaps both sides by the banks of a broad ditch, the roof then seems a hillock, upon which perhaps the pig grazes.

A single-storied structure based on a rectangular plan was the common layout for 3rd- and 4th-tier housing. Cabins ranged from 15 to 20 feet in length, 10 to 20 feet in width, and 6 to 8 feet in height (Langan-Egan 1999:25–26). The number of rooms determined a cabin's length. Most dwellings were just tall enough to allow a person to stand up. Arthur Young (1780:25–26) observed that "these [walls] are rarely about 7 feet high, and not always above 5 or 6; they are about 2 feet thick."

Cabin entrances and windows, if present, were positioned on the long walls. Although windows or small window openings were common, glass was rare. Most cabins had a small opening to let light in and smoke from the hearth out (Langan-Egan 1999:26). Hely Dutton (1824) described such cabins in County Galway:

> There is scarcely a cottage that has not a step down into in and a dunghill uniformly near the door. To the bad effects of a damp situation may be added the want of ventilation, which in general is confined to that between doors; for if there is a hole in the wall with a pane of glass fixed in it, it is the most they possess; as to the window that opens, that is a luxury possessed by very few except show cottages.

The hearth was traditionally located on the clay floor away from the cabin's entrance. It formed the central focus of the cabin. Prior to the prevalence of gable-end stone hearths and chimney flues after the Famine, in this arrangement smoke from the fire would escape through the entranceway, a small window, or a small hole in the thatched roof (Aalen

1999:149–151; Langan-Egan 1999:26). Arthur Young (1780:25–26) described a traditional cabin with a hearth on the floor, noting that it had

> only a door, which lets in light instead of a window, and should let the smoak [*sic*] out instead of a chimney, but they had rather keep it in: these 2 conveniences they hold so cheap, that I have seen them both stopped up in stone cottages, built by improving landlords; the smoak warms them, but certainly is as injurious to their eyes as it is to the complexions of the women, which in general in the cabins of Ireland has a near resemblance to that of smoaked ham.

Housing livestock in the cabin was a common practice among the rural poor classes. At night animals such as pigs, goslings, and cows were kept in the byre end, which was often separated from the living quarters by a light wooden partition (Gailey 1987:95). Animals, especially pigs, were vital to the subsistence of the family. Pigs were considered the "gentleman who paid the rent," as they were never eaten by the family but raised and sold at market to meet the annual rent (Hull 2004:65). The importance of the pig to the rural poor, and to the disgust of travelers, was remarked on by Thomas Croker (1824:103): "I recollect once trying to convince a man that he might with very little trouble improve the state of his cabin by building a shed for his pig and banishing him to the chimney corner, but he coolly answered, 'Sure then and who has a better right to be in it? Isn't he the man of the house? And isn't it he that will pay the rent?'" The animals were brought in at night to prevent them from being harmed or stolen, as they provided much-needed supplemental income to the family.

Family was most important in combating the hardships of poverty. The household was structured first and foremost as a labor source (Connell 1962b:521; O'Neill 1984:125–128). To supplement the income of the male figurehead, women and children took a variety of cottage industries, such as spinning and butter production (Connolly 2001:45; Hull 2004:85–86).

Labor among married women and unmarried daughters was divided into three broad categories: maintaining the household, producing goods for sale through cottage industries, and working in the labor market outside the household. Unmarried daughters could work either as laborers or domestic servants (Guinnane 1997:54). Throughout the late eighteenth century and up to the time of the Famine, the domestic service sector was an ever-growing sphere of employment. Domestic service was considered a very respectable vocation, and it appealed to single women from rural poor classes (Fitzpatrick 1987:164–165; Langan-Egan 1999:19–20).

The care of the household was the primary responsibility of married women. Tasks included child bearing and rearing, cooking, cleaning, mending clothes, and hundreds of other daily chores that kept the family functioning as a productive unit. Although a married woman's duties were not reported as employment in contemporary histories or census data, her role was perhaps the most important in the family unit and ensured the family's survival.

Women were also responsible for the immediate area outside the house, including the potato field. It was common for women to dig the potato beds as well as to plant and harvest the potatoes. Women also were in direct charge of any animals the family owned, including cows, pigs, sheep, and chickens—and the products derived from them (Fitzpatrick 1987:166–168; Guinnane 1997:54; Langan-Egan 1999:21). In addition to ensuring that the household functioned properly, women were active in cottage industries, including the linen and textile industries (Almquist 1979:700). Flax in particular was a useful crop to grow on small pieces of ground. Spinning wheels were omnipresent in the rural Irish households of Connacht. Henry Inglis (1835:27) recalled, "I went into, and looked into hundreds of cabins; and there was scarcely one, in which I did not see the females busily engaged in spinning." Women earned more money from spinning than from selling products derived from the livestock and the garden (Almquist 1979:702).

The Famine marked the end of cottage industry. Since the 1820s Ireland had been flooded with cheap, mass-produced clothing from England. By 1841 the textile and linen industry in Ireland had declined, and the removal of this necessary income proved fatal to the rural poor (Langan-Egan 1999:9–10; 18). In the western counties of Mayo, Sligo, Donegal, and Roscommon, the poor were most affected by the Famine

Table 4. Changes in Land Distribution of Holdings in Ireland before and after Evictions.

Year	1 acre or less	1–5 acres	5–15 acres	Over 15 acres
1845	135,314	181,950	311,133	276,618
1847	73,016	139,041	269,534	321,434
1851	37,728	88,083	191,854	290,404
Percentage of change, 1845-1851	-72.1	-51.6	-38.3	+5.0

Source: Donnelly 2001:161.

and, in particular, this loss of income for basic survival (Almquist 1979:709; Mokyr and Ó Gráda 1988:212).

As a result of the potato failure, disease, death, and economic distress, landlords began to forcibly evict their tenants. Landowners were able to consolidate their estates for more profitable commercial farming by clearing the land of what they considered a redundant population (Jones 1999:90; O'Neill 1984:38). Table 4 demonstrates the dramatic decrease of the landless farming population between 1845 and 1851.

Policies such as the Gregory Clause facilitated mass evictions. This clause mandated that poverty-stricken families could not seek poor relief if they possessed rented lands of at least a quarter-acre (Donnelly 2001:110; Kineally 1995:190; Miller 1985:287; Silverman 2001:78). Many tenants were thrown off their holdings, but most refused to enter the workhouses. They often lived day to day in poorly built huts or "sheelings" along the roadsides (Donnelly 2001:113; Kineally 1995:243; Miller 1985:288). It is estimated that 500,000 individuals of the poorer classes were evicted between 1849 and 1854, resulting in the abandonment of at least 200,000 smallholdings (Póirtéir 1995:229).

Evictions were violent. Landlords and their hired agents used extreme physical force to remove people and completely destroy their cabins (Donnelly 2001:114). Police and British soldiers often accompanied the bailiffs carrying out the evictions. Because of the violence they used in burning the roof and leveling the cabin walls, the bailiffs became known as the "crowbar brigade" (Donnelly 2001:114; Póirtéir 1995:231). Counties such as Clare, Kerry, Galway, Mayo, and Roscommon had the highest rate of evictions in Ireland (Kennedy et al. 1999).

County Roscommon is considered part of the "heartland of Ireland." It is located in the eastern end of Connacht, just west of the country's center. The county comprises six baronies and half-baronies, including Boyle, Roscommon, Ballintobber (north and south), Athlone, the half-barony of Ballymoe, and the half-barony Moyncarne (Coleman 1999:7). The county's four major estates were the Lorton estate with 29,242 acres, Lord de Freyne estate with 25,436 acres, Mount Sandford estate with 24,410 acres, and Mahon estate with 26, 980 acres (Coleman 1999:8, 53; Scally 1995:25).

In 1688 lands of County Roscommon were confiscated from the indigenous Irish and divided in to large estates. Nicholas Mahon, an Anglo-Irish officer serving under Oliver Cromwell, was granted a large parcel of land in the northeast corner of County Roscommon. Over time, his estate grew to be one of the largest in the county (Scally 1995:274).

Native Irish townlands such as Ballykilcline were subsumed under the Mahon estate.

Ballykilcline was a townland located in the northeastern corner of County Roscommon and 4.97 miles (8 km) northeast of Strokestown (Figure 4). Historically, Ballykilcline was made up of four quarters named Kiltullyvary (church hill townland), Bungarif (rough bottom or end), Aghamore (great or large field), and Barravally (high or hill townland) (Orser 1998b:1–2). There were four traditional Irish land divisions, the first and largest being the *baile* (Scally 1995:3). The remaining and lesser divisions include a quarter, a cartron, and a gnive. The townland was located in the parish of Kilglass in the barony of Ballintober North and consisted of sixty square miles containing a population of 19,370 individuals, averaging 323 people per square mile, mostly in area unsuitable for commercial grazing (Scally 1995:18, 41). Third- and 4th-tier housing (1,622 in the 3rd tier, and 1,498 in the 4th) dominated the landscape and greatly outnumbered the larger and more durable dwellings (6 in the 1st tier and 241 in the 2nd).

Ballykilcline was part of an area leased for 41 years to the Mahon estate from Charles, Viscount Dillon of Costelloe, in 1793 (Scally

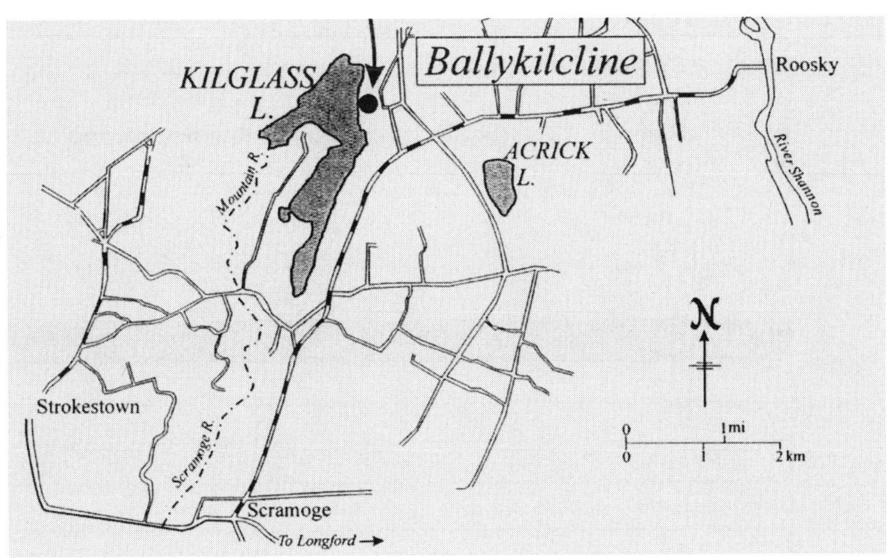

Figure 4. Location of Ballykilcline in County Roscommon. (Courtesy of Charles Orser.)

1995:25). The townland spread 620 statute acres or in Irish measurement 371 acres, 2 roods, and 30 perches. The exact population total varied over the decades prior to the Famine, but its maximum was 526 individuals; prior to the clearances the lowest population was 470. On average Ballykilcline included 500 individuals forming 100 families (Scally 1995:4).

Ballykilcline contained hilly and boggy areas. The land was not considered to be the richest arable land, nor was it thought to be suitable for grazing (Scally 1995:23). The area could provide enough land for subsistence farming (Table 5). The tenants of Ballykilcline had short-term or "at-will" leases and no legal claim to the land. On average the tenants were contracted to pay 14 shillings an acre (Scally 1995:28).

Because it was grazing country, the arable land was uninhabited. Parcels of bog or wasteland, however, had the majority of the population (Freeman 1957:256). By the first half of the nineteenth century, the county ranked highest in its population of impoverished. It also ranked among the highest in leased holdings averaging less than an acre (2,500 and above) and second for holdings under five acres (7,000 to less than 9,000). Because the majority of the population was poor, the dominant housing types were 3rd and 4th tier.

During the Famine, County Roscommon had one of the highest eviction rates during the Famine. As a result the county lost 1,650,330 people, or 30 percent of its total population between 1841 and 1851 (Coleman 1999:53). The tenants at the Mahon estate, including the Nary family, were among those evicted.

The early history of the Narys is unknown, except that they settled at Ballykilcline by 1820 (Scally 1995:80). The Brassington and Gale

Table 5. Individual Holdings at Ballykilcline, 1836.

Acreage	Number of holdings	Percentage
< 2	11	13.9
2–10	49	62.0
10–30	19	24.1
30–60	0	0
Total	79	100.0

Source: Orser 2004:218.

map shows the location of the Nary property (Figure 5). The two cabins in the quarters of Kiltullyvary and Bungariff are listed as belonging to Mark Nary and his sons, James, Luke, and Edward (Hull and Brighton 2002:1). The Nary family lived in Ballykilcline until they were forcibly evicted sometime between September 1847 and April 1848. The rents of all tenants had been in arrears since 1834 (Scally 1995:105–129).

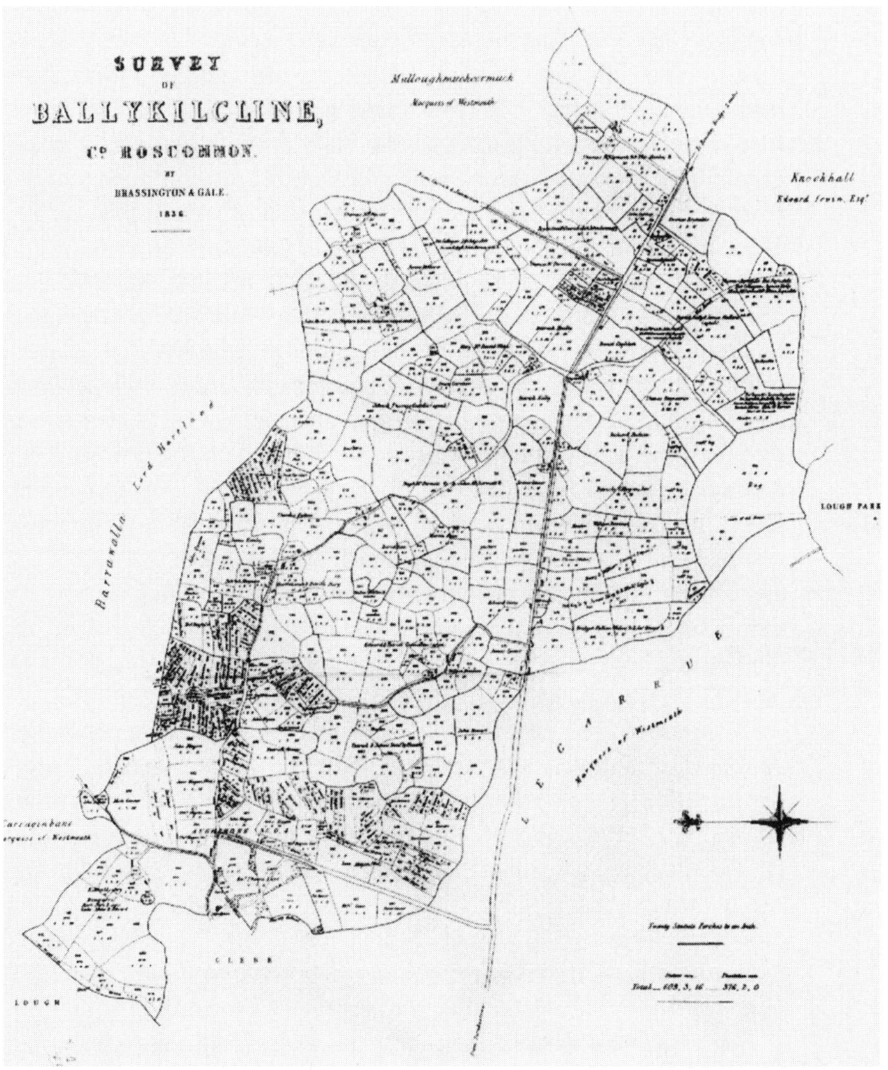

Figure 5. Brassington and Gale 1836 survey map of the holdings at Ballykilcline. The Nary holdings are in the lower left corner.

The Nary family unit had a holding size totaling approximately 44 acres, the third largest tenant holdings in Ballykilcline. The largest belonged to the McDermott family, who held 49.75 acres (four holders), and the Donnellan family, with 48.30 (two holders) (Orser 2004:219). This is in direct contrast to the cottiers and laborers in the townland, such as the Coyle family, who held 4.89 acres (two holders); the Toolan family, with 1.22 acres (one holder); the Pellegren and Ginty families, each with .50 acres (one holder); and the Mahon family, the smallest, with only .41 acres (one holder) (Orser 2004:219).

The Nary holdings were divided over six fields and six family members. Individually, each family member's holdings averaged seven acres. It is unclear at this time whether the Nary family represents a group of middling or small farmers. Taken as a whole, the land rented by the Nary family would place them in the social class of middling farmer. They are documented as paying rent directly to the crown and not to a strong farmer or grazier. This is problematic because even middling farmers were thought to pay rent to landowner. Furthermore, there are no known records stating that the Nary family members hired laborers. It is possible that the work was done through the large family network, and they had no apparent need for outside employment. The question that needs to be asked is "does it matter?" Based on the historical evidence of economic downturns experienced by the middling farmer after 1815, this class did not fare much better than small farmers, therefore it is really of no consequence here which label is put to them since it is evident that the Nary family, represented by the two cabin sites, was a family living just above the subsistence level and were cleared off the land as quickly and as violently as any other member of Ireland's rural poor.

The process of ridding what was considered the redundant population consisted of removing the tenants in "batches" beginning in the spring of 1847 (Scally 1995:108). In the parish of Kilglass alone, 150 families consisting of approximately 800 to 900 people were cleared from the land (Coleman 1999:51–52). The fate of many evictees is unknown. Many probably left Ireland. If they survived the Atlantic crossing, they most likely ended up in Canada or the United States. The Nary family, like many other Ballykilcline families, emigrated to America; they eventually settled in LaSalle County, Illinois (Orser 2004:229).

Ballykilcline ceased to exist after the 1847–1848 mass clearances. The evictions were on record as being swift and violent. Individuals and households had minutes to gather belongings to take with them, and most objects were broken during the struggle or left behind. The cabins of the evicted tenants were demolished completely then leveled, and the larger cut stone were removed by non-evicted tenants and the larger rent paying farmers to construct boundary walls and other projects in the area. What remained were the buried remains of mud and stone cabins and the fragments of the objects of daily life belonging to the landless tenants of Ballykilcline, like the Narys.

The Archaeology of Ballykilcline

From 1998 to 2002 two stone cabins belonging to the Nary family in an unplowed flat pasture were excavated. It is unknown which Nary family members lived in which cabin, therefore the cabins were designated simply as "north cabin" and "south cabin." The first two field seasons focused the southern cabin (n = 51 excavation units), with limited testing in the area of the north cabin (n = 20 excavation units) (Orser 1998b; Orser et al. 2000). The north cabin was investigated exclusively during the 2001 and 2002 seasons (n = 50 excavation units) (Orser and Hull 2001; Hull and Brighton 2002). In total, 121 units (south cabin = 51, north cabin = 70) were excavated and 9,000 artifacts were recovered.

The excavations exposed architectural debris and other structural remains, such as interior and exterior drains, pathways, and cobble and hard-packed floor surfaces. The cabins were 3rd-tier housing. The fact that the Brassington and Gale map includes them reflects the structures' durable nature, and the archaeological remains confirm that. Subsurface wall remnants of both cabins consisted of mortared fieldstones. Neither cabin had a gable-ended chimney with the hearths placed directly on the clay floor (Hull and Brighton 2002:10) (Figure 6).

The eviction process—burning the roof and toppling the walls—is clearly visible at Ballykilcline. A stone scatter three courses deep just north of the north cabin's packed stone foundation reflects the wall collapse from the outside (Hull and Brighton 2002:11; Orser and Hull 2001:12). At the south cabin, excavations revealed a cobble surface just outside the remains of the cabin walls. The scatter of small, cobble-like stones has been interpreted as the remnants of wall stones leveled, the larger stones having been taken away to prevent to tenants from returning to the dwelling (Orser et al. 2000:24, 30). Soil layers consisting of black to yellow-brown silty soil intermixed with specks of charcoal are indicative of roof burning. The artifacts recovered from the Nary cabins provides a glimpse into the daily lives of the landless tenants at Ballykilcline.

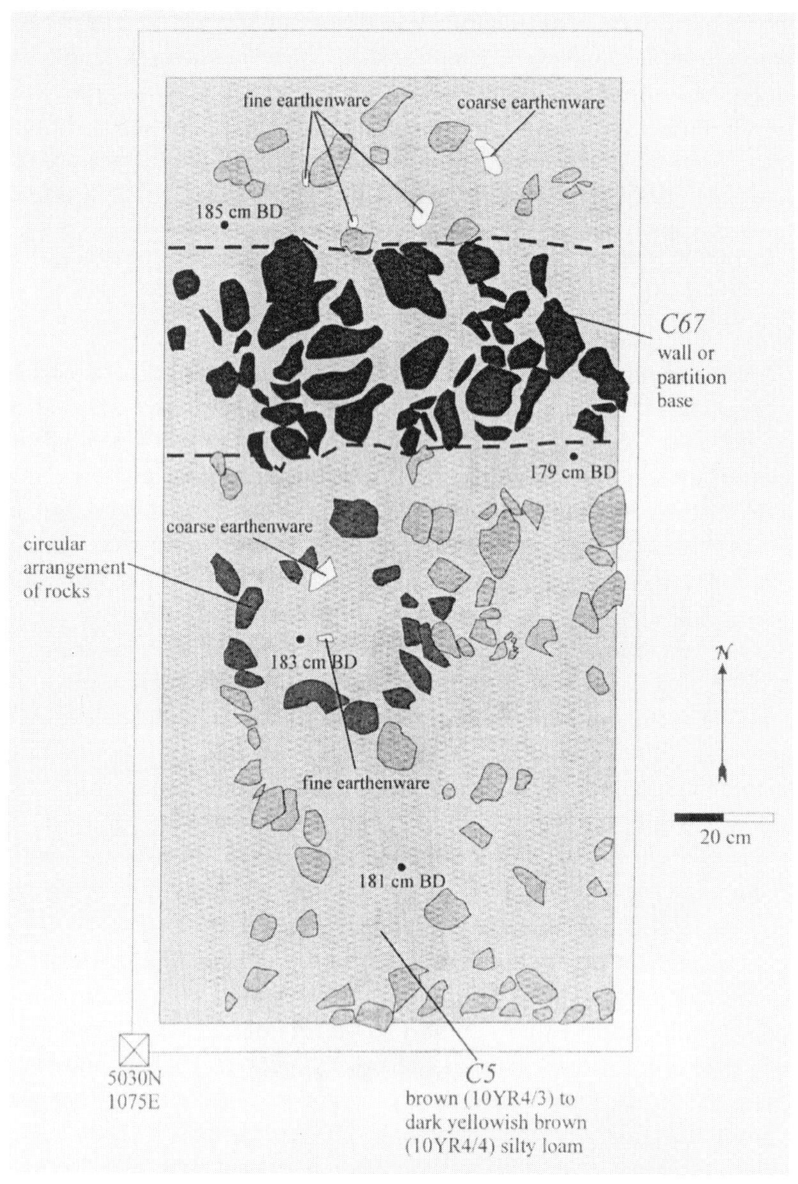

Figure 6. Plan view of the north cabin at Ballykilcline showing wall base and stone hearth pit. (Courtesy of Charles Orser.)

Figure 7. Polychrome teaware from the north cabin, Ballykilcline. (Courtesy of Charles Orser.)

North Cabin

In the north cabin there are a total of 65 refined earthenware vessels representing the Tableware (n = 30), Serving (n = 1), and Teaware (n = 33) categories, with a single vessel in the Serving category (Appendix A). The date range for the assemblage is 1810–1836, corresponding to the occupation period of the Nary family and the time leading up to the eviction. The single serving vessel is a blue transfer-printed serving platter in the Willow pattern and matches the 6 transfer-printed plates. The remaining tableware consists mostly of blue shell-edged plates (n = 20) and 5 undecorated soup plates (n = 5). The shell-edged plates are decorated with an even scalloped rim with either curved or straight lines, a motif used about 1810 to 1830. Four plates have molded sprigs in conjunction with the shell-edged design, dating their manufacture to approximately 1820 to 1835, and 3 are soup plates.

The 33 tea-related vessels are decorated with painted floral patterns or transfer-printed chinoiserie patterns, and the assemblage ranges in date from 1816 to 1836. The floral patterns on the teacups and saucers do not match. The polychrome vessels, two cups and a saucer, share a common but nonmatching polychrome floral pattern of stylized flowers and vines (Figure 7). The blue painted teacups and saucers have nonmatching floral designs consisting of large stylized tulips. Twelve blue transfer-printed teacups and saucers make up the decorative tea forms. Four vessels (2 cups and 2 saucers) are decorated with the same chinoiserie pattern, consisting of a pagoda and willow tree.

A total of 7 glass vessels were recovered from the north cabin area. Most of the vessels are olive green beverage bottles, most likely alcohol related. Three relate to the functional categories under study. A wine glass (stemware) is the only vessel in the tableware category. A portion of the stem was recovered and includes a small portion of the undecorated bowl and glass foot. The medicine bottles (n = 2) are aqua colored and square bodied. The rim finish is similar to that of medicinal bottles with a flat lip ledge. The lack of an embossment suggests that the bottles were of the ethical variety.

Twenty-eight clay smoking pipes were recovered from the north cabin. Most of the pipes have no markings. The exception is a pipe

Figure 8. Pipe bowl fragment with the letters PEAL. The complete stamp would have been REPEAL. (Courtesy of Charles Orser.)

bowl with the partial stamped slogan REPEAL on the bowl (Figure 8). The stamped slogan refers to the Repeal movement, protesting Ireland's forced entrance into the British Empire through the Act of Union in 1800 and illustrates the collective political action in the Ballykilcline townland.

South Cabin

Thirty refined earthenware ceramic vessels make up the south cabin ceramic assemblage. The majority of refined earthenware vessels are in the Tableware (n = 12) , Serving (n = 1), and Teaware (n = 17) categories (Appendix A). The presence of a variety of colored transfer-printed vessels suggests a date range between 1820 and 1836. Most of the 12 tableware ceramic vessels are shell-edged dinner plates (n = 8), represented by rim sherds in both blue (n = 6) and green (n = 2). The assemblage contains two types of shell-edged decoration. A single green and 5 blue shell-edged plates have even scalloped rims with curved lines (1810–1835), and another plate has a scalloped rim and straight lines (1820–1835). The remaining tableware consists of 3 transfer-printed dinner plates in the Willow pattern. The serving dish is elaborate in comparison to the vessel types found both in the north and south cabins. It is a deep-sided serving dish with a blue transfer-printed pattern titled The Bridge of Lucano (1810–1831) (Coysch and Henrywood 1982:55–56; Williams 1978:204) (Figure 9). The pattern depicts a rural scene of a four-arched bridge, behind which is the ruin of a round tower. Three large birds fly overhead, and in the foreground two cows graze. Spode first produced the pattern in 1810, but by the 1820s it was being copied by numerous Staffordshire potters (Coysch and Henrywood 1982:56).

Over half of the ceramics from the south cabin were tea related forms (n = 17) consisting mostly of transfer-printed teacups and saucers (n = 12). Five vessels are blue transfer-printed in chinoiserie patterns; 4 of the 5 have the same pattern, matching vessels from the north cabin. Three vessels, 2 teacups and 1 saucer, are decorated with the black transfer-printed Staffordshire pattern Arabian (1834–1843) (Williams 1978:188) (Figure 10). Painted vessels (n = 5) consist of either blue (1815–1830) or polychrome floral patterns (1800–1835). The blue floral painted vessels consist of a matching pearlware teacup and saucer. The varying polychrome floral patterns on two teacups and a saucer are similar but do not match.

Eleven glass vessels make up this artifact type. Most are dark olive green alcohol bottles and lamp glass. The single tableware vessel

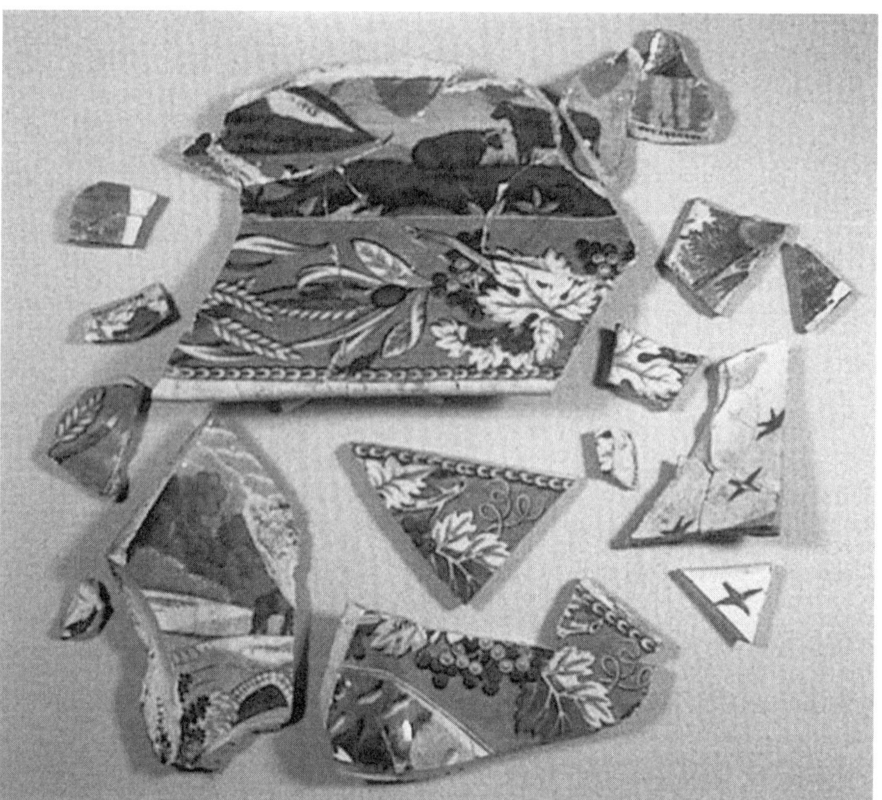

Figure 9. The recovered sherds of the serving dish decorated with the transfer-printed pattern Bridge of Lucano. (Courtesy of Charles Orser.)

fragment is from a stem of a plain wine glass or goblet. The piece is similar to the stemware recovered from the north cabin.

Although there are numerous white ball clay stem fragments, only 2 clay pipes can be definitely counted as distinct pipes. Neither the fragments nor the pipes were molded or stamped with any slogans or symbols.

Establishing the historical and archaeological context of the Irish diaspora provides the parameters for interpreting the meaning of continuities and changes in practices and values occurring over time. Historical accounts alone do not provide a satisfactory account for experiences within the Irish proletarian diaspora, nor do they explain the meaning of objects left behind and owned by the people who persevered against

Figure 10. Teaware sherds in the Staffordshire transfer-printed pattern Arabian. (Courtesy of Charles Orser.)

the conditions of colonialism, eviction, and poverty. The goal of historical archaeology is to blend the historical context and the archaeological evidence to provide meaningful insights that would not be informative from either data set alone. The archaeological history of the Irish proletarian diaspora covers one of the most dynamic periods in Ireland and America. It reveals the daily lives of men, women, and children of Ireland's rural poor and Irish immigrant communities in dismal living conditions that were documented by the middle and upper classes who failed to acknowledge the meaning of the objects in forming a cultural tradition. Although there are many historical accounts and descriptions of the Irish experience both home and abroad, little if anything is known historically about how these people used objects to construct their lives. The archaeological data provides an important perspective because it offers a physical manifestation of their experiences.

A proletarian diaspora is made up of individuals positioned to begin and remain at the lower end of the socioeconomic spectrum, where their occupational roles come to define their sociocultural positions. The consequences are a widening of the social and economic gap between the dominant or controlling population and the subordinate group (Armstrong 1976:406). This social and economic fact is the cornerstone for the constraints that prevent poor classes from taking advantage of opportunities and skills for advancement. In diaspora theory, the reasons for dispersal rest on intolerable social and economic conditions, and the lower classes are considered inferior and racialized as a single culture.

Conditions were intolerable for the rural poor of the Irish proletarian diaspora. The last stroke came not only with the Famine but also with the massive clearances. The process was set into motion long before the Famine. By 1815, capitalism and large-scale commercial agriculture widened the gap between the landed and the landless. This is exemplified through the experiences of the rural poor at Ballykilcline and Mulliviltrin.

The social stigmas created in Ireland followed Irish immigrants to America. Upon their arrival, the rural poor, now forming the Irish proletarian diaspora, were positioned at the lowest end of American society. The next chapter details the social history of negotiation and conflict of the mid-nineteenth-century rural poor as they become immigrants. It examines their experience of alienation and transnationalism as well as the transformation of that identity with the first-generation American-born and their quest for incorporation.

5
The Irish Proletarian Diaspora in America

Nineteenth-century America, for all its rebellion and conflict with England, remained English in language, institutions, tastes, religion, and prejudices, and this was apparent with the arrival of late-eighteenth-century Irish immigrants (McCaffrey 1997:85). The United Irishmen, political exiles from Ireland after the failed rebellion of 1798, became vilified as the "wild Irish" on arriving in the postcolonial American cities of Boston, New York, Philadelphia, and Baltimore. Such radicals were feared because of their quickness to organize politically ("One of 'Em" 1925:793). Irish radicals were able to drum up voters quickly from Irish and German immigrant communities to support Thomas Jefferson against Alexander Hamilton and the Federalist Party.

Alexander Hamilton and the Federalist Party pushed for a strong central government that would dictate the ways of U.S. business, market, and trade. But the establishment of a strong central government dictating trade and commerce was at the expense of the poor and working class. The expanding wealthy classes, who gained their wealth and power through international trade, supported Hamilton (Burrows and Wallace 1999). In postcolonial America, merchants were free to experience and exploit free trade and to profit from the expanding international market. Merchants saw the perfect opportunity to cash in on the trade with both France and England and to import cheap manufactured goods at the expense of American and immigrant working classes (Wilentz 1984:63).

Contrary to this view was Thomas Jefferson's economic platform. Jefferson opposed all capitalist notions. The Federalist Party accused Jefferson and the Democratic Party of attempting to stem the natural order and development of civil society (Wilentz 1984). Enlightened thinking established that the "natural order" of things and people was founded on inequality; social hierarchy was nature's way of maintaining happiness (Herzog 1998). Anything against the emerging controlling mainstream, therefore, was subversive to the natural order of human relations—creating revolution, chaos, and starting an era of possible degeneration of human and civil society (Fry 1925:736–737).

American political and class tensions revolved around the events of the French Revolution. During its early stages, most if not all Americans sided with the French proletariat. This remained so until Hamilton and the Federalist Party raised grave concerns about the proletariat making violent demands to seize control of the government (Burrows and Wallace 1999). Such overtures illustrated the dangers of upsetting the natural order of civility by placing too much power in the hands of the lower classes. This rhetoric supported the Federalist view of creating a strong central government in order to check such civil disobedience (Chickering 1925 [1848]:763; United States Twenty-Fifth Congress 1925:738). The Federalist Party further argued that there was potential for similar conflict in America.

The strong political potential of Irish radicals in the United States substantiated the possible threat to the newly created American way of life. Their increasing numbers perpetuated an environment of trepidation and mistrust of all things Irish (Fry 1925:733–734; Address to the Delegates of the Native American National Convention [1845] 1925:745–746). The idea of invasion from within the United States seemed very real and eminent when the United Irishmen organized local militia groups in various U.S. cities.

Violent uprising had been a reality for most Americans since 1786–1787, when the failed uprising in Springfield, Massachusetts, known as Shays's Rebellion arose over the heated debate between ideologies of centralized political power and a state's right to govern its own people. Soon after the uprising was quelled, Irish radicals appeared in American cities, unknowingly adding to the tensions and rumors of America's uncertain future (Levin 1925:755–757). In order to curtail any threats from Irish political activities, the Federalist Party began a campaign of slander and propaganda painting all Irish immigrants as inherently anti-American (O'Grady 1973; McCaffrey 1997).

From the success of this campaign came the 1798 Alien and Sedition Act. The purpose of this law was to restrict the flow of immigration to the United States and to extend the time of naturalization and citizenship. The main goal was to extend an immigrant's required residency period for qualifying for citizenship from 4 years to 15 years. It also required new citizens to "abjure and renounce all allegiance and subjection to all and every foreign King, prince, potentate, and state in all matters ecclesiastical as well as civil" (Hershkowitz 1997:14).

Newly arrived Irish were the focus of the anti-immigrant campaign. Federalist John Otis claimed that the restrictions were "to prevent wild hordes of Irish upsetting the tranquility of this country" (Wilson 1998:48). One such Irish radical was John Daly Burk. Burk, leader of the United Irishmen chapter in New York City, who in 1797 fled Dublin for New York City, where he wrote several anti-administration and pro-Irish rebellion articles in his newspaper the *Time Piece*. Federalists called to have him arrested, and it is believed that his case was the impetus behind the passing of the Alien and Sedition Act (Burrows and Wallace 1999:328).

The beginning of the nineteenth century marked a new era in American domestic politics. While Protestant immigration decreased, the number of semi- and unskilled Irish Catholics increased. The economic depressions in 1820s and 1830s fostered anti-Irish sentiment. Irish immigrants were made the scapegoats for America's financial troubles (Davis 1925:768). Lines were drawn dividing the Irish from the American-born working classes. The Irish were excluded from several occupations, including the carting business and shipbuilding trades (Stott 1990:112). In New York City, for example, better paid occupations such as cabinet making and baking were held exclusively by white native Americans (Anbinder 2001:114).

Prejudice in the United States was directed toward Irish Catholics. In 1806 the first Roman Catholic church in New York, St. Peter's, was built, but it was burned downed by a group of working-class Protestant Americans soon after its completion. At the same time, similar violence occurred against Catholics in Philadelphia and Boston (Gallman 2000; Ignatiev 1995). In 1834, an American mob set fire to a convent in Charlestown, Massachusetts (O'Connor 1995:46–47).

By 1830 most American-born Protestants associated being Catholic with a single-minded allegiance to the pope, which was considered a serious threat to the American way of life. Irish Catholics were thought to be part of the priest-controlled machine (Lord 1925:807; United States Twenty-Fifth Congress [1838] 1925:738). American Protestant newspapers such as the *Protestant* (1830) and the *American Protestant Vindicator and Defender of Civil and Religious Liberty Against the Inroads of Popery* (1834) printed articles about a possible papal plot to overthrow all non-Catholic governments in Europe and America. As a result, American-born workers revived the late-eighteenth-century activity of Pope's Day Festivities, during which processions, commonly known as Paddy Processions, paraded through Irish neighborhoods with straw effigies of the pope and St. Patrick (Burrows and Wallace 1999:401). These marches served to heighten tensions between Irish immigrants and Americans. The "wild Irish" stereotype reemerged and was used to reinforce the notion that all Irish Catholics were barbarous. This stereotype remained with the Irish in America throughout the nineteenth century, providing a firm foundation for establishing the social and political obstacles the Irish of the Famine were forced to negotiate.

The Irish immigrants of the Famine period were placed at the lowest rungs of America's social and economic ladder. By the mid-nineteenth century Irish immigrants made up 87 percent of America's urban unskilled work force, and newly arrived Irish were advised by their established compatriots to "do everything that they [i.e., native and other immigrant workers] do, no matter how degrading, and do it for less than they can afford to do it" (Mooney 1850:69). The United States' unskilled labor force was composed almost exclusively of Irish men, both single and married. Employment varied according to region. Common occupations included laborer, porter, huckster, paver, stevedore, and unskilled and semiskilled factory operative in textile towns and steel and iron factories (Dublin 1979; Mitchell 1986; Vinyard 1976). Outside the large urban areas, Irish males found employment in the anthracite mines of Pennsylvania and Montana as miners, pumpmen, or blacksmiths (Emmons 1989; Kenny 1998). There was enough work for the thousands of Irish men coming to America, but the down sides were long hours and seasonal variability. As with the "lean times" in Ireland, unskilled laborers experienced unemployment two to three months out of the year (Stott 1990:112).

Women, whether married or single, comprised more than half of the total population of the Irish proletarian diaspora. As with their male counterparts, employment for women was low paying and highly competitive and the hours were long. Married women rarely worked outside the home. After marriage their primary role was to care for the family and to manage the household finances. Married women took on additional occupations in the home, such as laundress, boardinghouse keeper, or piece-worker for the garment industry.

Piece-work was the most common form of employment for single and married Irish women. It was a sought-after and highly competitive occupation. Dresses, trousers, shirts, collars, lace fringes, and cloaks were the garments most often produced in the home, and in order for this work to generate any kind of income, women worked extremely long hours for very low wages (Diner 1983:78). On average, women were paid as low as seven cents a day; at best they earned a dollar a week (Stott 1990:115). The work done in apartments for relatively low wages and long hours became known as the "sweated trades" (Kraut 1982:85; Anbinder 2001:129).

The "sweated trades," or "sweating," was a concept that evolved from the introduction and success of mass-produced goods such as cheap, ready-made clothing. The term "sweater" was given to the clothing contractor who, in an effort to underbid all other clothing competition, constantly reduced the women's already low wages while demanding an increase in finished goods (Wilentz 1984:123). Clothing manufacturers had busy seasons, usually in the fall and spring, when the demand had to be met. The slow season, the winter and summer months, was a hard time for immigrant working-class families (Diner 1983). To counteract seasonal variations to the family income, women rented space in already-crowded apartments to boarders (Walter 2001:57).

Most single Irish women had better employment opportunities in the United States. Young and single women were recruited for employment in the burgeoning mills in Massachusetts. By midcentury, there was a great demand for female labor, and the influx of Irish women filled the United States' labor needs (Walter 2001:51). For two decades Irish women were the majority in the textile mills in Paterson, New Jersey, and Lowell, Massachusetts, and the carpet mills in Philadelphia attracted Irish women moving out of New York and Boston (Clark 1986; Diner 1983; Dublin 1979; Mitchell 1986).

Domestic service is probably the most popularly known occupation for single Irish women. In fact, Irish maids were so numerous that the stereotype of "Bridget" the bumbling, simple-minded, and ignorant Irish servant appeared as a constant character in American literature, media, and plays (Burchell 1980; Diner 1983; Murphy 2000). The stereotype's origins developed from common, but dangerous and at times fatal, mishaps during the course of employment. Irish women hired as domestic servants were unfamiliar with lighting kitchen stoves and kerosene oil, and often they were severely burned, maimed, or killed from fires and explosions (Murphy 2000:156–158). The U.S. media placed blame on the Irish race's natural state of ignorance rather than on the servants' inexperience with new technology.

Anti-Irish sentiment toward Irish women also derived from the ideology that occupations such as domestic servant were far beneath the wholesome and genteel American girl. Catherine Beecher and Harriet B. Stowe (1994 [1869]:39–40) noted that American girls were "reluctant to engage in domestic work and it stems from pride, and that caste has the strongest hold of any on the human mind; and so long as servitude places a woman in the lowest and most despised rank, no consideration of health and no pecuniary offers will draw American women into it, if they can escape it." A position as a domestic servant, however, meant steady employment and room and board. Unlike dressmakers and sewers, live-in servants were not subject to economic depressions or seasonal variations. More important, a single woman could earn on average two to three dollars a week without the added expense of maintaining a family or paying rent (Diner 1983:71; Walter 2001:55).

By midcentury, and with the emergence of the modern industrialized cities in the United States, the Irish were marginalized to less than desirable areas of those cities. These areas quickly became some of the first American slums. The Irish formed distinct neighborhoods such as the Kerry Patch in St. Louis, Missouri, Dublin Gulch and Corktown in Butte, Montana, and Limerick Alley in Troy, New York (Emmons 1989; Meagher 1986c, 2001; Towey 1986). Rather than acknowledge the racialized space the Irish were forced to inhabit, U.S. newspapers labeled the Famine Irish as "culturally conservative" with a strong need to "clan together content to live together in filth and disorder" (Miller 1985:326). Kerby Miller (1985:134) has argued that the Irish in the mid-nineteenth century were in "a transition between traditional and modern patterns of thinking and behaving" and dependent on communal support and the bond of family that conflicted with American social behaviors of individualism and competition. Although social traditions of Irish communalism may have been one reason the Famine Irish banded together, the alienating social structure created and enforced by the American public was more likely than not the major factor (Gallman 2000:10–11).

Many American Protestant politicians and media perpetuated the idea that the large influx of Famine Irish as a social plague, a "cultural tumor eating away at America's heart and soul," and an invasion of the American way of life (Gallman 2000:13; McCaffery 1997:93; "One of 'Em" 1925:792; *Putnam's Monthly* 1925:796; Thernstrom 1964:58; Vinyard 1976:205) (Figure 11). As a result, many Irish immigrants faced difficult obstacles obtaining vocational callings and accumulating material and financial wealth. American idealism centered on the notions that not all individuals inherently possessed the ability to prosper and succeed in life and that failure resulted from an individual's inadequacy and immorality (Weber 1976; Herzog 1998:36). Americans viewed virtue and intelligence as unequally distributed and wealth as the outward sign of one's virtue and intelligence (Weber 1976).

Irish immigrants were racialized as a group because they were deemed naturally inferior, chiefly because of the social and economic deprivations they had suffered in Ireland. An extract from an 1848 report by the Massachusetts Senate (1925:584) made clear the perceived status of the Famine Irish:

> In the commencement and earliest years of the government, those who came here were generally persons of education, of pecuniary means, industry, and character [Irish mobilized diaspora]. In coming, they added to the intelligence and wealth of the community; while, as producers, they assisted in developing resources of the country. Those now pouring in upon us, in masses of thousands upon thousands, are wholly of another kind in morals and intellect, and, through ignorance and degradation from systematic oppression of bad rulers at home, neither add to the intelligence nor wealth of this comparatively new country. As a body, they are consumers, and not producers to an extent equaling their own physical wants [proletarian diaspora].

Figure 11. Cartoon by Thomas Nast depicting the invasion of the Irish Catholics, 1850s. Bishops are emerging from the sea as sea monsters in the foreground, the Vatican is in the background flying the Celtic harp flag (*upper left corner*), the American school is in ruins (*back center*), and Irish immigrants from within are taking Americans to the gallows (*upper right corner*). (Coffey and Golway 1997:57.)

In 1835, A. H. Everett (1925:444–445) observed that the living conditions of the rural poor in Ireland accounted for their low social positions in America:

> It is the Irishman, and all who, like the Irishman, have been destined to contend with the ceaseless and disorganizing extractions of provincial vassalage. That Ireland is overwhelmed with a beggarly and redundant population; that its millions are starving amidst of plenty, and seem to live only to bring into the world millions as miserable and distracted as themselves, is a matter of common observation, not only to all who have visited the country itself, but to all that have compared it with other states, even in the lowest stage of civilization, and under circumstances generally supposed the most adverse to human improvement. There is no instance on record of so great an inundation of inhabitants breaking into any country, barbarous or civilized, not even when the Goths and Vandals overwhelmed the Roman Empire.

In the United States during the last half of the nineteenth century, to be poor, unemployed, and living in overcrowded tenements was thought by most Americans to be the fault of the individual. The state of poverty, or being poor, was believed to be linked to levels of depravity and a "self-inflicted moral failing" (Ward 1989:43, 55, 63). Members of the American wealthy and middle classes argued that poverty was the fault of the individual because as "citizens of a free and happy land, [there] are no insuperable barriers to the highest moral and social elevation of each and all" (Ladies of the Mission 1854:292).

There were exceptions to this rule. The poor were classified as being either worthy or unworthy of public assistance. Those deemed the "deserving poor" or those whose predicaments leading to poverty were beyond their control included old maids, widows with young children, and invalids. The remaining contingent of poor, the "undeserving, the deviant, the degraded," consisted of able-bodied men and women, many of them immigrants (Gallman 2000:49). Reformers argued that it was the increase in unskilled immigrants to urban areas that disrupted the "moral order" and that those living among them in the poorer areas were degraded as a result of the more deviant among them (Ward 1989:43).

The classifications of "deserving" and "undeserving" poor were created solely through moral and value judgments of social differences (Gans 1995:1). Labels such as "undeserving poor" bring with them a series of stereotypes and stigmas. The connotation of being "undeserving" unjustly categorizes people as morally corrupt, willfully rejecting the values system of mainstream society (Gans 1995:13). Labels that stigmatize communities create social and financial limitations in accessing better jobs and the education needed to escape the confines of poverty.

Irish Catholics were considered the primary cause of poverty in the United States. In *American Notes* ([1842] 1985:88–90), Charles Dickens's description of poverty and the fast-paced growth of urbanism shocked middle-class readers, alarming them about the poverty and disease at their doorstep. Although Dickens's agenda was to express to the middle and wealthier classes his belief that the physical environment of cities bred poverty and the degradation of humanity, he also help instill fear and paranoia among the middle class through his metaphors equating poverty with danger:

> The coarse and bloated faces at the doors have counterparts at home. Debauchery has made the very houses prematurely old. See how the rotten beams are tumbling down, and how the patched and broken windows seem to scowl dimly like eyes that have been hurt in drunken frays. . . . Other ruins loom large upon the eye, as though the world of vice and misery had nothing else to show; hideous tenements which take their name from robbery and murder: all that is loathsome, drooping and decayed is here!

Exacerbating this perceived threat, American politicians and the media created a campaign that dehumanized Irish Catholic immigrants by depicting them as nonwhite and animal-like. Such imagery aimed to illustrate the danger the Irish posed to Americans and to legitimize Protestant control over them as a group (Baum 1978:973–974; Chickering 1925 [1848]:762; Gorn 1987:394; Holt 1973:324; Knobel 1986:134–135; McCaffery 1997:101). Popular opinion on the cause and spread of disease, however, blamed the poor, specifically, Irish immigrants. In Philadelphia and New York, for example, typhus was commonly referred to as "Irish fever" (Gallman 2000:87).

Equated with poverty and immorality was disease. Obtaining proper health care, visiting a doctor, and being confident in receiving more than the bare minimum level of medical care were luxuries few immigrants could afford. For the majority of the Irish immigrant population the only avenue was public assistance. In times of outbreaks and epidemics, they were forced to rely on public dispensaries, where free medicines and medical advice was given out, and privately run charity hospitals.

Charity hospitals and dispensaries provided a service to the poor on the basis of a patient's worthiness (Gallman 2000:86–87; Mohl 1971:241–259; Prunty 1998:26–27; Rosner 1982:22; Ward 1989:28–31). Those who ran dispensaries, and the medical personnel at charitable hospitals, often accused the overwhelming number of people seeking care and medicines of cheating the American health-care system. American physicians argued that most who considered themselves "respectable" should have some money to pay for their own health care (Rosenberg 1987:52). They considered excessive drinking as the root cause of the spread of disease and considered intemperance a natural way of life for Irish Catholic immigrants (Kraut 1994:33; 1996:154). Physicians thus established criteria to expel those considered unworthy (i.e., unemployed, contagious, or otherwise undesirable) (Rosner 1982:21–22). In most urban areas, the American medical community considered Irish neighborhoods unworthy of medical care because "personal habits seemed quite as important as locality, in determining an attack of the complaint. For the most part, the temperate, the moral, the well conditioned, escaped; whilst the imprudent, the vicious and the poorly fed, succumbed to its insidious influence" (Boston City Document No. 66 1925:593–596).

During this era of anti-Irish and anti-Catholic sentiment, a political group or secret society, the Order of the Star Spangled Banner, emerged. By the 1850s it had become the Know-Nothing Party (Gallman 2000:14; Gorn 1987:394; McCaffery 1997:101). Its platform focused initially on issues of slavery but shifted after the entry of the Famine Irish (Baum 1978:959). The goals of the Know-Nothing Party were to restrict and control immigration by lengthening residency qualifications for naturalization and by excluding all foreign-born residents from public office. The latter policy ensured that political and economical power remained in the hands of American Protestants (Address of the Delegates [1845] 1925:745–746; Baum 1978:973–974; Fry 1925:736; Knobel 1986:134–135).

The Know-Nothing Party dominated politics in Boston, New York, and Pennsylvania between 1854 and 1859 (Baum 1978:960). In Pittsburgh, Pennsylvania, the elected mayor's sobriquet was the "People's and Anti-Catholic Candidate" (Holt 1973:313). In Michigan, the Know-Nothing Party produced a pamphlet titled *Wide Awake! Romanism: Its Aims and Tendencies* expressing the party's sentiments:

> We aim to Americanize America. None but native Americans to office. A pure *American* Common School System. War to the hilt, on Romanism. The advocacy of a sound, healthy, and safe nationality. More stringent and effective Emigration Laws. In short—the elevation, education, rights, happiness of the people. (Vinyard 1976:224)

In reaction to political and social events in Ireland, but more important in the United States, several Irish social and political organizations formed by midcentury and fostered the diasporic bonds of a common history and struggle. The cohesion created by these organizations aided in negotiating Irish immigrant social positions in mainstream American society. More important, they were a place for Irish immigrants to reconnect with Ireland, providing news of and debate on socioeconomic issues. Many Irish organizations were social clubs that provided news from home and employment and housing opportunities in American cities. They had names like the Hibernian Society and Sons of the Emerald Isle. Other organizations had more of a militant stance appearance, and some resembled Ireland's secret societies. These militant organizations were named after Irish military figures, for example, the Shields Guard, Meagher's Guard, Hibernian Rifles, and Sarsfield Rifle Guard (Burchell 1980:96–97; Gallman 2000:201).

Most prominent among the militant organizations was the American wing of the Irish Republican Brotherhood, the Fenian Brotherhood. In both Ireland and the United States, the Fenian Brotherhood was an oath-bound group. Its goal was the liberation of Ireland through armed force (Comerford 1985; de Nie 2001; Golway 2000; Rafferty 1999). The Fenians supplied arms and money to the brotherhood in Ireland, and after the American Civil War they provided Irish and Irish American veteran soldiers to take part in the rebellion (de Nie 2001:215).

At the outbreak of the American Civil War, the Fenian Brotherhood recruited Irish to fight for both the Union and Confederacy. The Irish saw it as something of a "sacred duty of every Irishman at home and abroad to prepare himself to fight the battle of his country [Ireland] and kindred when and how he may" (Spann 1996:194). At the same time, many in the Irish immigrant community thought that fighting in the war would prove Irish loyalty to America (Golway 2000:139). Those who participated in the fighting believed that they would go off to war an Irish exile and return an American citizen (Maguire 1968:552; Miller 1985:360).

Irish brigades formed quickly across the country. Regardless of which side the Irish fought for, the common symbols of the United Irishmen and the Fenian Brotherhood were present on the flags of Irish brigades. Irish symbols included the Celtic harp, shamrocks, and the sunburst. Regiments included the Montgomery Guards of Georgia, the Tenth Tennessee Volunteers, the 116th Pennsylvania, the 28th Massachusetts, and the 88th, 63rd, and 69th of New York. Their symbols often were displayed alongside American symbols such as the eagle and the Stars and Stripes. Throughout the war banners lining the streets of New York and Washington, DC, were entwined with the Stars and Stripes and the green flags of Ireland (Golway 2000; Spann 1996).

At war's end the Fenian Brotherhood and the Irish Republican Brotherhood were intent on uniting the Irish veterans to disrupt the British Empire in North America. Two failed invasions of Canada in 1866 and 1870 were the end result. Aside from the dismal failures of these military actions, the attempted invasions stirred dormant fears of a pope-led Irish Catholic uprising in the United States. The American-born public denounced the Fenian Brotherhood. More important, the American Catholic Church also publicly cut all ties to the organization.

The final nail in the coffin for Irish American militant secret societies in the eyes of American politicians and media was the 1884 Dynamite Campaign in England. The group claimed responsibility for bombings in Whitehall, Victoria Station, Scotland Yard, and the Tower of London (Skerret 1986:127, 130). Afterward, the stereotype of the inherently violent and brutish Irish reemerged in the American media. To stem the fears of the America public and secure a tenuous citizenship, Irish immigrants and first-generation Irish Americans formed nonviolent organizations. Their transnational agenda meshed American and Irish social, economic, and political issues in a nonviolent platform (Emmons 1989:45; Foner 1980:156; Meagher 2001:178–179; Vinyard 1976:303–304).

By the 1880s, first-generation Irish Americans outnumbered Irish immigrants. The new generation of Irish Americans learned the history of the outrages of land tenancy and the Famine in Ireland, as well as the Irish role in building America. Such history instilled a strong romantic pathos toward Irish and American heritage (Brown 1966; Meagher 2001). An Irish visitor to the United States noted, "I have met men of the second generation, sons of Irish parents, American in voice and appearance, who have never set foot on Irish soil, with as ardent affection for Ireland as any native born rebel" (Foner 1980:153). Charles Stewart Parnell, Irish nationalist leader in the late nineteenth century, remarked that Irish Americans are "even more Irish than the Irish themselves in the true spirit of patriotism" (Emmons 1989:185).

True to the diasporic discourse in transnationalism, Irish American nationalism rested on the Irish proving their American patriotism through the lens of freeing Ireland from the British Empire. Michael Davitt remarked, "You want to be honored among the elements that constitute this nation [America]. . . . You want to be regarded with the respect due you; that you may thus be looked on, aid us in Ireland to remove the stain of degradation from your birth . . . and [you] will get the respect you deserve" (Brown 1966:24). Newspapers such as the *Times* recognized this fact, stating that "as the Irish are exalted they [Irish Americans] are exalted also and as their race is crushed and defeated they are humiliated" (Meagher 2001:193).

From this view point, issues of tenant rights in Ireland were linked to the evils of American capitalists. The Irish landlords, also known as "land robbers," were compared to the rampant exploitation of workers by America's wealthy industrialists, railroad barons, and bank owners. It was argued that America's robber barons controlled a system that constituted "unfair aggrandizement of natural resources which God intended to be shared by all" (Bodnar 1985:90; Foner 1980:158). The popular rise of and a peaceful commitment to Irish nationalism through the shared heritage of being American citizens marked the first real steps by the Irish toward incorporation into American society.

The notion of assimilation cannot adequately account for the experience of the Irish in the United States. Like other diasporic groups who have maintained many traditional cultural attributes, the Irish have always retained some of their social behaviors and institutions (Meagher 2001; Shannon 1963). For example, Meagher (2001:69) quotes a first-generation Irish American priest, Father John J. McCoy, who in 1895 stated, "We are Americans of the Americans and loyal to the core. We have no land but this land yet a holy heritage is ours in the glory of our father's land" (Meagher 2001:69). The quote is telling because it communicates sentiments of allegiance both to America and to Ireland. What is more, Irish American identity was established in large measure through institutions such as the Catholic Church, which did not figure prominently in the United States until the 1850s.

The Irish increased their stock in American society through their building and support of the Roman Catholic Church. By the last decades of the nineteenth century the church was firmly entrenched in American society, but it was not a viable institution until mid-nineteenth century and certainly did not come of age until the early part of the twentieth century (Shelley 2006:574). Its acceptance in the larger society was brought about by the philosophy of the church, and in essence, that of its Irish and Irish American parishioners—that it must become Americanized (Chudacoff and Smith 2000:124). The process of Americanizing Catholicism began midcentury with church leaders such as Bishop John Hughes, who wanted Irish Catholic immigrants to adopt a new social identity, blending traditional Catholic piety with a love for modern views of American morality and values (Diner 1996:103). Throughout the century, the Catholic Church gained ground in its demand of parishioners to move away from traditional notions of communal bonds and toward modern social practices of individualism, independence, land ownership and private property (Miller 1985:332–333). The church believed that Americans' negative perception of their newly arrived brethren and succeeding generations could change if all were seen as hard-working, sober, and healthy parishioners (Meagher 2001:152).

Although a white-collar Irish American community would not exist until the twentieth century, Irish Americans were creating their own avenue in America, mainly through the social, economic, and cultural capital of the Catholic Church (Whelan 2006:280). In recognition of and reaction to American perceptions of the Irish and Catholicism, the Roman Catholic Church took to looking after its own not only spiritually but also physically, caring for their well-being by building Catholic hospitals and training nurses and doctors (Shannon 1963:114–117; Whelan 2006:278). As early as 1890 there were 154 hospitals run by Catholic orders in the United States (Abell 1960:36). The next generation would provide the skilled, trained, and educated professionals that would further uplift Irish America. In slow increments, the large population, becoming educated and actively engaged in political affairs gave stability to the Irish American communities, pushing them toward incorporation on their own terms into mainstream American society (Foner 1980:153; Towey 1986:151–153).

By century's end, the large numbers of naturalized Irish Americans developed into a key demographic for American politicians. This provided a platform for promoting Irish issues in the United States. Perhaps more important to the Irish cause in Ireland and the United States was the growing number of Irish Americans elected to political office (Emmons 1989:99). In 1880 the people of New York City elected its first Irish Catholic mayor, and soon after, Boston, a staunch anti-Catholic city throughout most of the nineteenth century, also elected its first Irish Catholic mayor (Burchell 1980:7). In slow increments, the large population and active interest in political affairs gave stability to Irish American communities, pushing them toward incorporation on their own terms into mainstream American society (Foner 1980:153; Towey 1986:151–153).

Local Histories of the Irish Proletarian Diaspora

Five Points, Manhattan, 1848–1880

The Five Points emerged as a distinct ethnic neighborhood within New York City's Sixth Ward during the first decade of the nineteenth century. It was named for the intersection of Baxter, Park, and Worth streets (Figure 12). The area was made famous by the writings of Charles Dickens ([1842] 1985) and his descriptions of poverty, crime, and miscegenation.

Prior to being an ethnic enclave, the Five Points was within the wetlands of Collect Pond. Located around the pond were unhealthy and highly toxic industries. By 1810, Collect Pond was filled and industries began moving north of the city. This created much sought-after real estate (Pernicone 1973:39). Open real estate was at a premium in Manhattan,

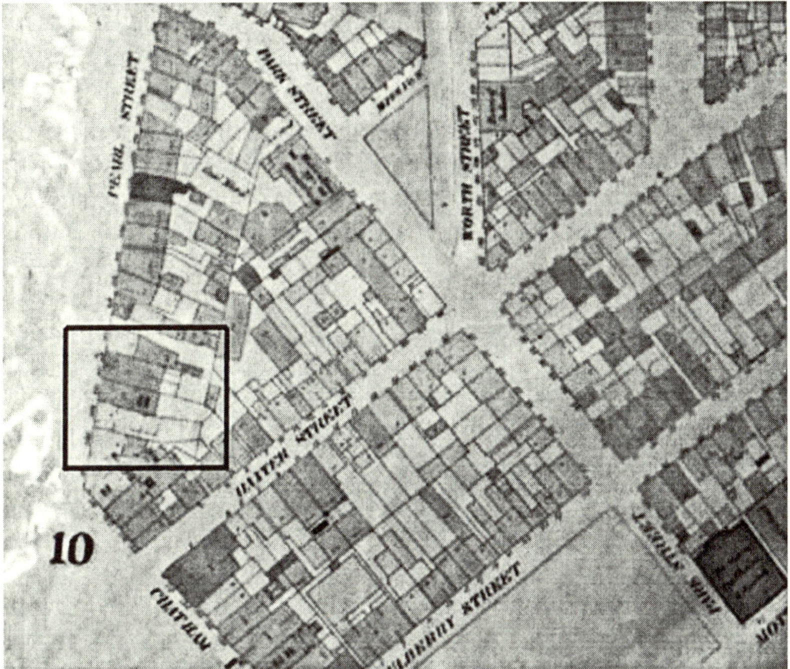

Figure 12. Perris insurance map of the Five Points, Manhattan, in 1857. The tenements along Park Street (*top*) and Pearl Street (*left*) were inhabited mostly by Irish families and boarders. The two tenements in the center of the box are used for this study. The tenements in Anbinder's study are located in the map's center surrounding the triangle park named Paradise Square (Park and Worth Streets).

as post–Revolutionary War America experienced a period of economic and spatial expansion (Blackmar 1989:76; Wilentz 1984:25). American ports were no longer restricted from the lucrative profits of new and exotic ports (Burrows and Wallace 1999:339). Gaining freedom from England, merchants were exposed to and learned a new set of business practices and specialization. As profits were on the rise, the distribution of wealth decreased, thereby generating an increasing inequality in the population and accentuating disparities (Paynter 1988:424).

The growth of inequality and competition prompted the emergence of neighborhoods that distinguished between the propertied and the propertyless. At this time rent began to flow from one to the other, fostering a new structure of class relations within the city's social landscape that changed the principles of land exchange (Blackmar 1989:76; Wall 1994:5). Land, labor, and goods ceased to be tools of social interaction and began to serve as commodities. Property and its ownership fostered a set of complex relations and created antagonistic and unequal forms of interactions in a new ideology that replaced the eighteenth-century idea of the natural right of all men to own property earned by their own labor (Blackmar 1989:73; Wilentz 1984:25).

Throughout the nineteenth century, the area known as the Five Points offered crowded and unsanitary living conditions to the city's poorest, largely immigrant population. Dickens (1985:88–90, 125) described the neighborhood as a "nest of vipers," a "plague spot," and the inhabitants as thieves, prostitutes, and drunkards. To address the influx of Irish immigrants, land owners constructed large, multiple-family brick tenements, and older wood-framed buildings were refitted as tenements to meet the high demand for housing. Tenements were defined as "any house occupied as the home or residence of three families or more, living independently of each other, and doing their cooking on the premises" (DeForest and Veiller 1970:37). Many of the structures were substandard, as there were no legal guidelines governing their upkeep. The lack of safety measures and the unsanitary conditions are reflected in the names the inhabitants gave to the tenements, such as "Gates of Hell."

Brick tenements replaced many of the wood-framed structures at the Five Points. The buildings were generally four to five stories and intended to house 8 to 10 families, although many ended up sheltering as many as 22 families (Ingle et al. 1990:60). The tenements reportedly housed on average 132 people, but in truth most had twice this number of occupants in the form of unrecorded boarders and basement dwellers. The apartments consisted of two to three rooms, the main room no bigger than 10 by 12 feet and the remaining rooms being small sleeping chambers measuring 7 by 7 feet (DeForest and Veiller 1970:81). The sleeping quarters were usually placed in the middle of the building and had no windows, light, or ventilation. The larger room had the only window in the apartment and the only access to ventilation. Contemporary descriptions of the hallways indicate they were extremely dark and dirty. Missionaries described tenement hallways as being "so dark that faces could not be distinguished," making the negotiation of stairways very dangerous (Ladies of the Mission 1854). By the 1860s, the Five Points population had increased exponentially. The large brick tenements were filled to capacity. Absentee landlords sought to further their rental profits by tacking on additional structures in the rear courtyards (Fitts 2000:69).

Wood-framed dwellings were originally meant to house a single family. These houses were built between 1780 and 1790, and at the time of the Famine they were converted into multifamily tenements. The first floor usually consisted of a business in the front section with an apartment in the rear. The basement and garret space were converted into small apartments (Ingle et al. 1990:57). The sleeping quarters usually faced the rear courtyard. In 1866 the Citizen's Association (1866:78–79) remarked that the sleeping quarters looked "upon dismal and fetid well-hole areas that are lined with privies where 350 persons attend calls of nature."

The rear courtyards were meant to be open spaces, but they were crowded with large privies, school sinks, wells, and cesspools. Although sewer systems were introduced to lower Manhattan as early as 1842, it was up to individual landlords to pay for their properties to be connected. This was a cost many absentee landlords did not want to pay (Moehring 1981:46). The Five Points tenements were not connected to the municipal sewer system until well after 1880.

Privy vaults were the sole means of sanitation for human waste. The vaults were mere wells without proper drainage. As a result, they commonly overflowed into the rear courtyards and basement apartments (Warring 1889:586). Privies were in use up to the end of the nineteenth century. According to De Forest and Veiller (1970:xvii–xviii), New York City health investigators commonly reported on the condition of tenement privies in the last decades of the nineteenth century:

> The condition in which they are kept is indescribable. They are seldom flushed [cleaned], as the process is fraught with difficulty and is most unpleasant. They are, moreover, a serious and potent source of contagion and a means of spreading disease. Located in the yards [the privies] are of easy access to the street, and are often abused and rendered most foul by disorderly persons and casual passers by. The inaccessibility of these yard privies to the tenants on the fourth and fifth stories of the tenements house, and the inconvenience of using them at night and in sickness, must have a very considerable influence upon the health and habits of the tenement house dwellers.

Disease was rampant at the Five Points. In 1848 and 1864 there were outbreaks of typhus, or "Irish fever." According to the newly formed Sixth Ward Sanitary District, typhus was the leading cause of death. At the Five Points, it was responsible for 92 deaths on Mulberry Street, 53 on Baxter Street, 27 on Park Street, and 13 on Pearl Street within a 10-month period in 1864 (Citizen's Association of New York 1870:73–74).

Cholera was also prevalent. There were outbreaks in 1849, 1854, and 1866. In 1849, the source of the contagion was reportedly Mr. James Gilligan of the Five Points. Gilligan lived with four women in a basement apartment in the rear of the tenement at 20 Orange Street (now Baxter Street), located within a block of the tenements under study. He died, along with the women, within a few days of contracting the disease (Rosenberg 1987:105–106).

Federal and state census data for the Five Points reveal that Irish families and individual boarders congregated in five-story brick and smaller wood-framed tenements along Park and Pearl streets. Most of the Irish were from Kerry, Cork, Galway, Mayo, Roscommon, Sligo, and Clare. Anbinder (2002) studied forced emigration from the Landesdown Estate in Kerry to the Five Points and found that most of the people who were evicted from their villages upon coming to New York lived in tenement clusters along Anthony (Worth) and Little Water (Park) streets. It is unknown at this time if there was regional continuity for the two tenements under study. Based on the variety of names in the census data, it appears that not all of the tenants hailed from the same county.

472 Pearl Street

The residence at 472 Pearl Street was a large five-story brick tenement constructed in 1848 by then-landlord Peter McLoughlin (Yamin 2000a:98). In 1864 he sold the property to William Clinton. Sometime after Clinton's purchase (ca. 1870s), McLoughlin built a second tenement building in the rear lot. The new building reduced the open space in the courtyard to a mere 20 by 50 feet (Yamin 2000a:98).

At midcentury there were 20 households comprising 107 people. All of the tenement dwellers were Irish with the exception of the Finck family, a German-born husband and wife (Appendix B). Families like the Currys, Callahans, Cronins, and McLoughlins had been in the United States for no more than five years. Many, for example, the Sears, Barry, Papard, and Killoran families, had been in the country less than three years.

On average the Irish tenants at 472 Pearl Street had three children. Living with most of the families were at least 2 boarders, making 7 people the average number who lived in the small apartments. The Garvey family was the exception. They had 5 boarders for a total of 10 people. In the Garvey case, it seems that the boarders were relations.

Male employment ranged from semiskilled jobs such as tailor, coach maker, tinsmith, shoemaker, blacksmith, and clerk and unskilled jobs such as laborer, boatman, and porter. Most males were laborers. The occupations for married women were not always listed in census data, but those that were listed were either keeping boarders or laundresses. The most common employment for single women was in the needle trades. Many were milliners, tailoresses, or seamstresses.

By the time the 1855 state census was taken, the tenement contained 12 households containing a total of 58 people. Many of the families listed in the 1850 federal census appear to have remained at this address, but as expected, new families also had moved in.

There were a number of widows listed. Sara Henry had been living in Manhattan for eight years. She may have moved to this address with her daughter shortly after her husband's death. Bridget and Eliza Burns, both widows, had been living in Manhattan for just under 10 years. Bridget Burns and her two daughters were listed as laundresses. Eliza Burns was not listed as being employed; she lived with her son, a mason, and her daughter, a milliner. Elizabeth McCarthy, listed as head of the household and married, had a young daughter and son in the apartment. They had only been living in Manhattan for two years. Although hers was a single-parent household, McCarthy was not listed as widow, indicating that her husband was missing or perhaps had abandoned the family. This situation was common at the Five Points during times of economic downturns.

According to the 1860 federal census, there were 14 households with a total of 74 people. With the exception of the German Lutz household, the tenement housed only Irish families and boarders. There was a high turnover of residents, demonstrating the transience of the Five Points. The census data also illustrate the development of social networks and bonds of family. Eliza Burns was listed as keeping house and remained with her son, Dennis. They shared the small apartment with her daughter Catherine, her husband Timothy Harrison, and their five-year-old son John. The Callaghan family—Maurice, wife Mary, sons Thomas, Daniel, and Morris, and daughter Johanna—resided at 472 Pearl Street for at least 10 years. By 1860, the family had brought in Mary Twoomey, who was Irish born and listed as an "in-law" because she was Mary Callaghan's mother.

Social networks were established among nonfamily members in the tenement. Catherine MacDonald, a widow, had lived at this address since 1850. She was first listed as the head of household in 1850, but 10 years later she was listed as a boarder with the Loftus family. The Loftuses had been in the United States for at least 9 years and may have been acquainted with the MacDonald family. Also boarding with the Loftus family was Catherine Sullivan; she had lived in this tenement with her father since 1850.

What is striking about the 1860 census is the high proportion of widows living in the tenement. Five out of the 14 households were headed by widows, and they maintained an income mainly through keeping boarders, though some also were engaged in other forms of employment. For example, Margaret Barry, along with her boarder Bridget Clinton, was listed as seamstress. They most likely brought in piece-work from the numerous Manhattan garment industries.

Employment for the males and females of the tenement was relatively consistent with the census data a decade earlier. The working age for young males appears to have been 16. Some of the boys were apprentices, such as John Kelly and Edward Morris, both 16 years old, and John Harvey, age 20. John Kelly was a dryer's apprentice, and Edward and John Harvey were both sail makers' apprentices. Many of the single women were employed in the needle trades.

The number of households increased to 18 and totaled 96 individuals in 1870. Fifteen households represented families new to the tenement, although they were not new to America. According to the census, those families had been in the country more than 10 years. There were only three families from the 1860 census, the Curry, Kelly, and Loftus families. Widows were now the heads of the Kelly and Loftus families. John Loftus and Michael Kelly died sometime after 1860 and prior to 1870. John Kelly, the oldest son at age 25, once a dryer's apprentice, became a laborer along with his younger brothers. His father's death might have been the reason for changing occupations, for as the oldest son he was expected to provide a source of income for his family.

Again in 1870, most men had jobs as laborers. The exceptions were Peter McHenry (shoemaker), Jeremiah Loftus (clerk), and Peter McFadden (clerk). It appears that families with semiskilled employment moved out of the tenement and perhaps out of the Five Points altogether. Those families who remained indicate how the city's economic downturns affected some households living at the Five Points. For example, Maurice Callaghan was a fruit dealer and fish vendor prior to 1870. Sometime before 1870, however, he experienced a radical shift in his employment and became a laborer.

474 Pearl Street

At 474 Pearl Street was a two-story wood-framed structure as old as the Five Points itself, having been constructed as early as 1790. A store was always present on the first floor. Two grocers rented the front of the building between 1814 and 1840. After 1840, the store was converted into a porterhouse and oyster saloon (Yamin 2000a:109, 114). Ownership of the saloon changed hands between 1850 until its closure in 1866. Owners included Irishmen James Doyle (1850–1857), John Sullivan (1865–1866), and John Lysaight (1866–1873). Sometime after 1860 a brick tenement was constructed in the rear of the lot.

The rear courtyard also went through a series of changes. At the beginning of the nineteenth century the rear yard housed a stable and cabinetry shop (Yamin 2000a:109). According to the 1857 Perris map of the project area, by midcentury the outbuildings were associated with second-class hazardous businesses. It is unknown what businesses were in the rear courtyard, but they could have been run by printers, book binders, brass founders, coach makers, paper mills, or cotton presses. The hazardous businesses remained until the rear tenement was constructed. The new brick tenement covered most of the open space in the courtyard including the existing privy vault.

In comparison to the large tenement next door, there were far fewer families living at this address. In 1850 there were 3 recorded households totaling 23 people. None of the tenants had been living in the United States for more than five years. All of the household members were Irish born and had at least 2 boarders. The head of household Margaret McColvin had 9 boarders living with her and her 2 small children. She was not listed as widow, and her youngest child was seven months old.

It is possible that her husband was missing or a migrant laborer. Regardless of McColvin's marital status, it is evident that she was running a boardinghouse. The men in the tenement were employed as carpenters, caulkers, tinsmiths, and clerks. James Doyle was listed as a liquor dealer and ran a saloon on the first floor (Yamin 2000a:114).

The population of the small building increased in 1855. There were 5 households that totaled of 24 people; all were Irish. Those who had recently arrived to America included the Sullivan and Hearley families. They had been in the country less than four years. Both male heads were unskilled laborers. The future owner of the property, John Ward and his family, were listed at this address. He was an undertaker and worked out of a storefront at 470 Pearl Street. He moved his business to 474 Pearl Street in 1870. Three male Irish boarders resided with the Ward family. Two were carpenters, while the third was an apprentice. It is probable that all three worked for John Ward making coffins.

The tenement's demographics changed in 1860. The rear tenement was constructed and housed more of the tenants than the street-facing front building. The front building housed the Ward and Worth families, 16 people in all (Appendix C). Twenty households occupied the rear tenement, totaling 98 people (Appendix C).

The front-facing tenement was home to those employed in skilled trades. John Ward was listed as coffin maker and undertaker, while Thomas Worth was listed as a cook. As with the earlier boarders living with the Ward family, one was a carpenter. The other was a carriage driver, presumably for Ward's funeral business.

The rear tenement housed mostly unskilled laborers and those with semiskilled professions such as gas fitter, glass cutter, and shoemaker. Most of the single women in the tenement were seamstresses. With the exception of the Ryan, McAndrew, and O'Connor families, who had been in America well over 20 years, all of the other households had been in the country for no more than 8 years. Some families, such as the Gareys, McGuires, and Linghans, had been in the country less than 4 years. In fact, the Lingham family had arrived sometime in 1860.

The census data for the 1870s seem to be incomplete. Although the front dwelling is recorded, it appears that much of the area between it and 476 Pearl Street, known as Donovan's Lane, had been briefly noticed. The alley consisted of rear tenements associated with 474 and 476 Pearl Street. There seems to have been some confusion in the proper listing of tenants. With that said, those who were listed were almost all recently arrived Italian immigrants. There are no familiar names among those listed for the tenement at either 474 or 476 Pearl Street. The privy vault subject to analysis here was filled prior to the construction of the rear tenement, shortly after 1860.

The Dublin Section, Paterson, New Jersey, 1880–ca. 1910

Paterson, New Jersey, is located 19 miles (30.58 kilometers) west of New York City in the northeastern corner of New Jersey (see Figure 1). In 1791, the quest for American industry prompted Alexander Hamilton, the first secretary of the treasury, and a new organization, the Society for the Establishment of Useful Manufacturers, to harness the power of the Passaic River and the Great Falls (Fries 1975). It was not until the first decade of the nineteenth century that manufacturers set up shop along the Passaic River. By the 1840s, Paterson was the leading cotton-spinning town in New Jersey and a principal supplier of yarn (De Cunzo 1983:10).

Throughout the nineteenth century several successful industries emerged, including machine works, a locomotive works, and silk mills (Yamin 1999:9). Products from Paterson's locomotive industry and iron works were used for building much of America (Gutman 1977:217–218). During the last half of the nineteenth century, Paterson was known as "Silk City," successfully transforming European and Asian silk into sewing silk, ribbons, and broad goods (Goldberg 1989:26–31). By 1880 almost 70 percent of the employees, mostly unskilled or semiskilled, were Irish and first-generation Irish American who lived in the southern portions of the Dublin section of the city (Warring 1886:726–727).

Paterson was incorporated into New Jersey in 1851. At this time there were 11,334 residents. By 1860 the population had nearly doubled to 19,588, most moving into the south end of Dublin. In the Dublin section, there were 4,291 residents in 1855, and over half were foreign born (Quinn 2004:58). The population nearly doubled to 7,841 within 10 years, and by the end of the nineteenth century, the numbers had increased to approximately 31,364. As the name of this section of Paterson suggests, it was home to Irish and Irish Americans.

The original street grid of Dublin was planned around the existing raceways and mill sites in the 1820s. The area became known as Dublin after the influx of Irish laborers, who, completing the Morris Canal in 1830, settled here to work in the surrounding mills and factories (Quinn 2004:58–59). Dublin's Irish population grew throughout the 1850s with the arrival of individuals and families evicted during the Famine period, and the neighborhood expanded southward. The northern section was multiethnic and included American-born, Irish, first-generation Irish American, English, and Scottish individuals and families. The southern section, however, was predominantly Irish or first-generation Irish American and remained so until the turn of the twentieth century (De Cunzo 1983:83).

The Irish in Paterson were generally unskilled laborers and semiskilled mill operatives. Men were day laborers, machinists, boiler makers, or steamfitters. Women, principally young and single, were clothing makers, dyer's and dyer's helpers, silk winders, pattern makers, and ribbon weavers (Goldberg 1989:24–26). The Irish and Irish American laborers were always underpaid in relation to native workers. Throughout the last decades of the nineteenth century, the Irish male made consistently close to $100 less annually than a native working-class male. The difference in pay was usually greater. In 1874 there was a $265 dollar difference between the two groups (Modell 1978:212). Members of the Irish working class in most cases were making just enough to live on. In most cases the income of the male head was supplemented by the efforts of his wife, either through employment in the mills or by taking in boarders.

Housing in Paterson was much different than in Five Points. The Dublin section was not home to large brick tenements. Although there were a few five-story brick tenements constructed to meet the housing need in 1860, for the most part housing consisted of wood-framed rowhouses in the Greek Revival style, averaging two and a half stories (Cotz et al. 1980).

The rear courtyards consisted of open space, gardens, and, of course, privy vaults. Privy construction in the Dublin section differed from that in the Five Points. Rather than all-stone vaults, many were simply wood-framed or -boxed vaults. Conditions in Paterson's rear courtyards were considerably better than at the Five Points, but there were nevertheless many hazards and sanitary issues. The Paterson Board of Health observed that throughout the last half of the nineteenth-century privy construction was faulty and that "few of the privies are water-tight and there were no ordinances regulating their construction. Very few persons have their privy vaults emptied until compelled to do so" (Dr. Charles F. W. Myers quoted in Yamin 1999:93). Leaking privy vaults allowed accumulated liquid wastes to seep into the soil and contaminate underground water supplies drawn from wells and pumps. One of these water sources was the "Dublin Spring" on the corner of Ward and Jersey streets. Throughout the last half of the nineteenth century it was the neighborhood's source of water. It was closed in the 1890s after typhoid outbreaks were linked to the contaminated water source (Yamin 1999:16).

Cholera and typhus were the leading epidemics in Paterson. In 1832, the ad hoc Board of Health was established to respond to a cholera epidemic that killed 140 people (Cunningham 1994:70). The board's main job was to maintain clean streets and during times of outbreaks to provide medical aid. Once the 1832 epidemic abated the board ceased to exist and nothing was done by the city to prevent further outbreaks.

The State Board of Health formed in 1875. Its role was to assist the development of local health committees. Paterson reestablished the Paterson Board of Health in 1887 (Yamin 1999:91). The main role of the board was to monitor outbreaks, prevent further spread of diseases, and ensure care for the sick. The Public Health Department was not active during ordinary times and therefore nothing was done to prevent the causes of illness related to inspecting faulty cesspools and privies (Waring 1889:75).

Paterson had no regulations regarding sanitation and public health. In 1861, city charters attempted to control the construction and placement of new privy vaults. The policy simply stated that privies could not be placed within 10 feet of any street and stipulated that 2 feet of solid earth or masonry work was to separate the waste pits from adjoining lot boundaries. The charters did not address the repair or closure of leaking privy vaults and cesspools already in existence.

Paterson did have a municipal sewer system. The first system was in place between 1852 and 1853. Its function was to drain water and waste from back yards (Yamin 1999:92). The first systematic sewer system with catch basins was in place by 1880. Following the construction of the system, it was illegal to construct or continue to use outdated privies, although archaeological evidence indicates that privies were used by almost all of the residences well into the twentieth century (Cotz et al. 1980; Yamin 1999).

32 Ward Street

The house at 32 Ward Street was a wood-framed two-and-a-half-story structure (Figure 13). In 1866 James Mackel purchased the property. Prior to moving his family to this address. he refitted it to allow for more occupancy space. James Mackel, his wife Sarah, two daughters, and son were born in Ireland. According to the 1870 federal census, the

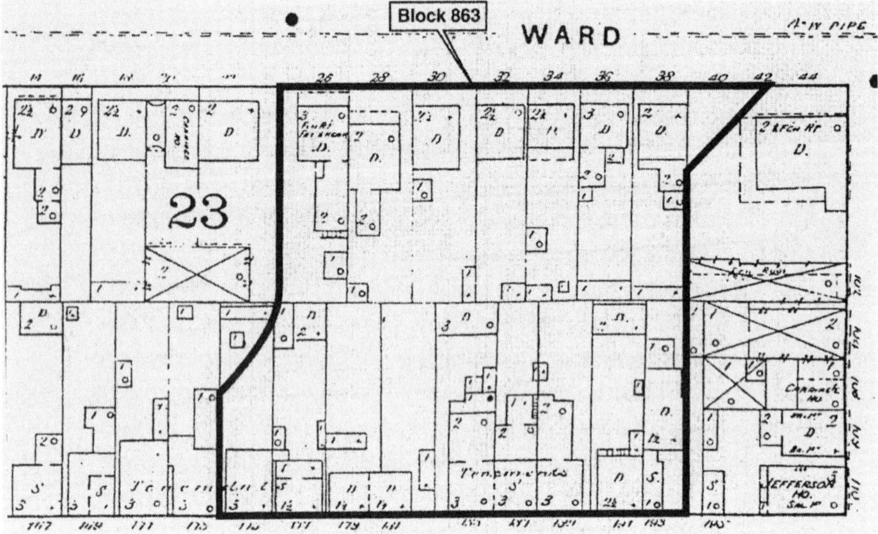

Figure 13. Sanborn atlas map of the Dublin section, Paterson, New Jersey, 1887. The box within the project area of Block 863 is 32 Ward Street. (Courtesy of John Milner Associates.)

Mackels had been in America for less than a year when he purchased the property. James Mackel was a semiskilled machinist in one of the nearby mills (Appendix D).

Family members in the two tenant households were American born, a departure from the pattern established at the Five Points. John Moon and Sarah Moon were born in Massachusetts. The Crowsons' birthplace was New York. Moon's and Crowson's occupations are difficult to decipher. Moon is simply listed as working in a cotton mill. He was most likely a laborer filling various unskilled roles. Crowson was listed as teamster.

Although James Mackel was listed in the 1880 federal census, he died sometime between then and 1888. According to the 1888–1889 city directories, Sarah Mackel was listed as widow. James remained a machinist until his death.

Only one tenant household was listed in 1880. James Minkin, born in Ireland, was listed as a clerk. His wife, Lottie, was American born and from Connecticut. The Minkin family lived in Paterson for about five years and moved out prior to the 1890 census.

By 1890, Sarah Mackel, a widow, and her family were the only residents at 32 Ward Street. They remained there until sometime after

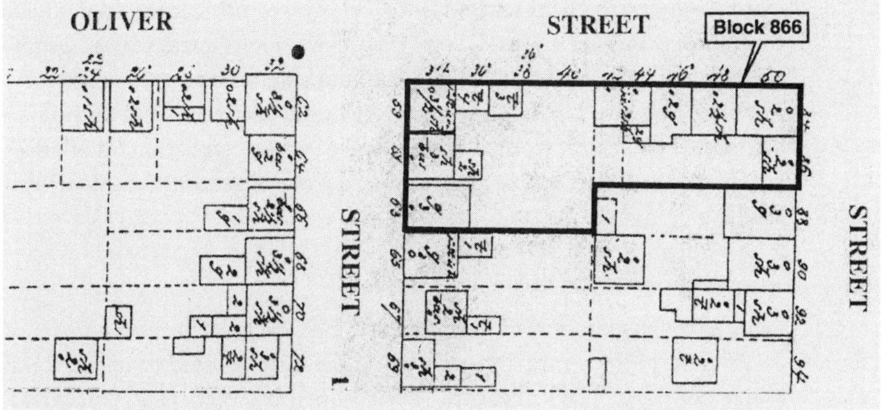

Figure 14. Miller map of Oliver Street, Paterson, New Jersey, 1874. The box within the boundaries of the project area for Block 866 is 46 Oliver Street. (Courtesy of John Milner Associates.)

1895. After 1895, Sarah moved away, but she remained the owner of the property until it was sold in 1909.

46 Oliver Street

Two blocks from the Mackel family, the house at 46 Oliver Street was a two-story, wood-framed rowhouse owned by Thomas and Ann McGill in 1895 (Figure 14). Thomas (firefighter), his wife Mary Ann (housekeeper), and their children Daniel and Richard (attending school) were American born (Appendix E). Thomas and Mary Ann were first-generation American-born citizens of Irish immigrant parents. Like the Mackel family, the McGill children were attending school up to the age of 17. The McGill family continued to live at this address until it was sold to an Italian family in 1911.

The Archaeology of the Irish Proletarian Diaspora in America, 1850–1910

The Five Points, Manhattan, 1850–1870

In 1991, a portion of a city block in lower Manhattan was excavated. The project location formed part of the Five Points. A total of 22 features in 14 rear courtyards were investigated. The courtyards were associated with structures inhabited by American-born artisans as early as the late eighteenth century and with mid- to late-nineteenth-century tenements buildings occupied by predominantly Irish and German immigrants (Yamin 2000a). The excavations focused on shaft features, such as privies, cesspools, wells, and cisterns. Excavators recovered over a million artifacts. The vessels from two privies (Features O and J) in backlots of tenements on Pearl Street (472 and 474 Pearl Street) are used for this study.

472 Pearl Street: Feature J and Feature Z

Prior to the installation of a complex waste system in the rear courtyard at 472 Pearl Street after 1870, a cistern (Feature Z) used to collect rainwater and large privy (Feature J) were open between 1848 and 1850. Two decades later, both features were incorporated into a large waste system known as a school sink. Put succinctly, a school sink is a multiple seat privy created to handle the waste of a large number of people through pipes connected to the municipal sewer system (DeForest and Veiller 1970:307–313). The artifacts from deposits in Features J and Z date between 1850 and 1880.

Feature J was a stone-lined privy vault. It measured 11 feet (3.35 meters) in diameter and was approximately 10 feet (3.05 meters) deep. The subsurface structure was in place by midcentury and was used by tenants at 472 Pearl Street between 1850 and 1870 (Yamin 2000a:A-29). The feature was closed in the 1870s by a brick vault for the school sink (Feature T).

Five analytical strata (AS I, II, III, IV, and V) make up the depositional episodes in Feature J, based on the grouping of distinct soil layers and artifact types located in each deposit. There were two distinct and diagnostic artifact deposits (ASIII and V). The upper most deposit (ASI) was a sandy soil layer that was eventually cut by Feature T. A dark yellow-brown sandy soil (ASII) underlies this deposit. There were no artifacts recovered from either deposit (Yamin 2000a:A-29). Located between deposits III and V (ASIV) was a compact fill of silty sandy soil and ash. Separating this deposit from ASIII was a surface of bluestone slabs. The slabs were placed at this level to compact and stabilize the fill at the bottom end of the feature to underpin the brick structure above (Feature T) (Yamin 2000a:A-29). There were few artifacts recovered from this level.

The two main or primary deposits are ASIII and ASV. The latest deposit (ASIII) is a dark brown sandy soil and ash deposit with a high density of artifacts throughout the fill. Based on the date ranges for the ceramic and glass vessels recovered from this layer the *terminus post quem* (TPQ) is 1870. The lowest and earliest deposit (ASV) (TPQ 1860) is a black, dark gray, and brown silty, sandy soil. The deposit had the largest number of artifacts in the feature.

Feature Z was a brick-lined cistern used to collect rainwater and converted into a cesspool after 1870. Feature Z measured 8 feet (2.44 meters) in diameter and was approximately 10 feet (3.05 meters) deep. The feature comprised four analytical strata, although two of the four are related to the main depositional episodes. Blue sandstone slabs divide the depositional episodes (ASI and II). The slabs are the same type used in Feature J (Yamin 2000a:A-31). The uppermost deposit (ASI) consists of a black soil with charcoal and plaster overlaying yellowish brown sand. It has a TPQ of 1870. The lower deposit (ASII), below the stone slabs, is yellowish brown sand mixed with stone rubble. Directly beneath this layer and positioned at the very bottom of the feature was a black claylike sediment containing a dense deposit of artifacts. There were no diagnostic artifacts recovered from the upper analytical stratum of Feature Z, but the lower deposit (ASII) underneath the bluestone slabs are quantified and described in the tables presenting the data from the analytical stratum of Feature J (ASV). The artifacts are of the same types as those in Feature J, and some ceramic and glass sherds cross-mend between features (Yamin 2000a:A-31). Since there were cross-mends between Features J and Z, the artifacts represent a single assemblage and the data concerning both features will be discussed together.

Artifacts from the Lower Deposit of Feature J and Feature Z (ca. 1850–ca. 1860)

The majority of refined earthenware vessels are in the Teaware (n = 113), Tableware (n = 77), and Serving (n = 21) categories (Appendix B). The date range for the ceramics in the deposit is from ca. 1820 to 1855. The common vessel forms are 10-inch plates (n = 26), 8-inch plates (n = 15), and soup plates (n = 12). Most were decorated with blue transfer-print patterns (n = 35) with almost half in the Willow pattern (n = 15). The remaining printed vessels were in various patterns dating from 1818 to 1855 (1843–1855) (Williams 1978:237–238, 249, 268). The shell-edged vessels have unscalloped rims with blue straight lines (1830–1860). The forms include 10-inch (n = 9) and 8-inch (n = 5) plates. White granite is present in small numbers (n = 13). The white granite vessels are either undecorated (n = 5) or in the *Gothic* pattern (n = 8) (1840–ca. 1860) (Wetherbee 1980:38).

Like the majority of tableware vessels, the 21 serving pieces have transfer-printed patterns. Matching patterns on both tableware and serving pieces include a serving dish in Garden Scenery and a serving platter and 2 dishes in the Willow pattern (Figure 15). The remaining serving dish is decorated with a nonmatching transfer-printed pattern titled Alleghany (1828–1859) (Williams 1978:183). The remaining serving pieces include blue shell-edged dishes (n = 4) (ca. 1830–1860) and white granite platters molded in the pattern Sydenham (n = 2) (1853–ca. 1860).

The 113 tea-related forms consist of teacups (n = 51), saucers (n = 53), teapots (n = 2), slop bowls (n = 9), and sugar bowls (n = 2). Blue transfer-printed vessels comprise a majority of the data set (n = 57) and include patterns such as Rustic (1834–1860), Belvoir (1845–1853), Tyrolean (1834–1854), Florentine (1834–1859), Canova (1826–1848), Lucerne (1839–1864), Friburg (1834–ca. 1860), and Iso Bella II (1818–1864) (Williams 1978:197, 214–215, 261–262, 320, 405, 437; Williams and Weber 1986:203, 582, 597). Most of the transfer-printed saucers (n = 19) are either in the Rustic or Tyrolean patterns. White granite is present in smaller numbers (n = 20). The plain white granite vessels consist of teacups (n = 5), saucers (n = 2), a teapot, and a slop bowl. The molded

Figure 15. Transfer-printed vessels recovered from Features J and Z, the Five Points, including Alleghany (*far left*) and Garden Scenery (*center*). (Courtesy of the General Services Administration and John Milner Associates.)

shapes include Gothic (1840–ca. 1860) (teacups, n = 2; saucers, n = 4; slop bowl, n = 1), Primary (ca. 1840–ca. 1860) (cups, n = 2; saucer, n = 1), and President (ca. 1855–ca. 1860) (saucer, n = 1) (Wetherbee 1980:52–53).

There are 104 glass vessels used for this study. The Medicinal (n = 77) and Tableware (n = 27) functional categories make up most of the assemblage (Appendix B). Twenty-seven vessels make up the Tableware category. Most of the vessels are plain or paneled tumblers (n = 21). Six of the vessels are undecorated wine glasses (n = 5) and goblets (n = 1). The total number of medicinal vessels is 77, including small cylindrical vials (n = 45) obtained from a doctor or dispensary and embossed proprietary (n = 27) and mineral water bottles (n = 5).

Most of the proprietary bottles contained WOLFE'S AROMATIC SCHNAPPS. Its ingredients were a gin tonic, diuretic, antidyspeptic, and invigorator (Fike 1987:187). Also included in the proprietary medicines were MEXICAN MUSTANG LINIMENT, RADWAY'S READY REMEDY, A. J. STAFFORD'S OLIVE TAR, HYATT'S BALSAM OF LIFE, DR. J. HOSTETTLERS STOMACH BITTERS, and HEGEMEN & CO. COD LIVER OIL. The Mustang liniment cure-all was supposed to aid in the healing of burns, sprains, and sore throats (Fike 1987:135). Radway's concoction was meant as a painkiller and nerve tonic. Olive tar was marketed for the treatment of respiratory ailments, as well as cholera, worms, syphilis, and cancers. Hostettlers was promoted as an effective medicine for dyspepsia and dysentery, and liver oil was for ailments such as constipation.

The total number of clay smoking pipes is 52. Two of the pipes are molded with American and Irish symbolism. A single pipe has an American eagle with the American crest or shield across its chest on the left side of the pipe bowl (Figure 16). The other pipe has a molded Celtic harp with the word IRELAND arching above the harp (Figure 17). The Celtic harp dates far back in Irish history. In more modern Irish history, the Celtic harp was the symbol of the United Irishmen. After their failed uprising in 1798, the symbol was banned in Ireland. The Irish Republican Brotherhood resurrected the symbol in the 1850s, and it was commonly used in the flags of both Union and Confederate Irish brigades and regiments during the American Civil War.

Artifacts from the Upper Deposit of Feature J and Z (ca. 1860–ca. 1880)

The majority of refined earthenware vessels are in the Teaware category (n = 68), with smaller numbers in the Tableware (n = 41) and Serving

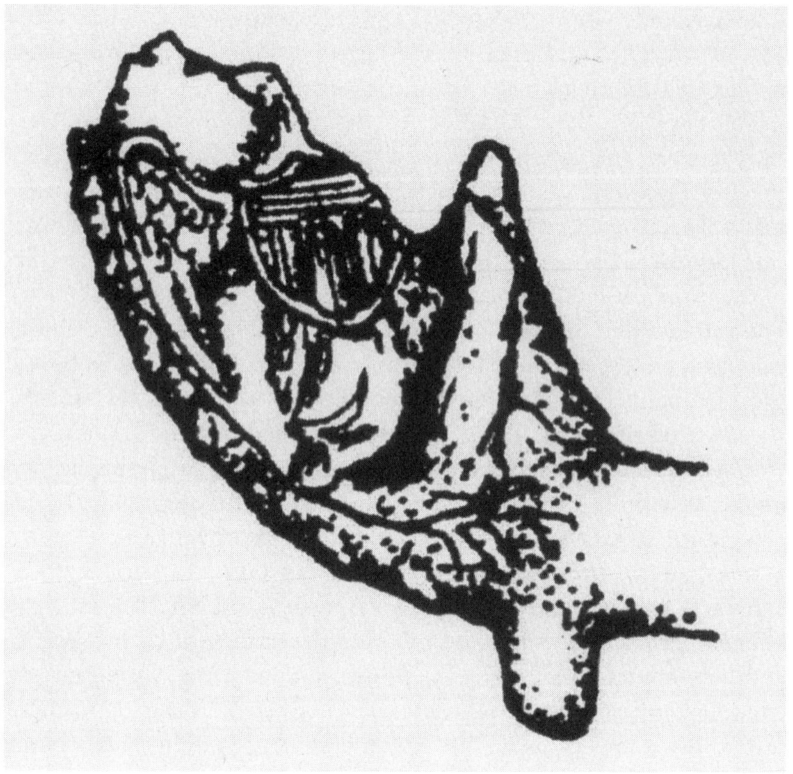

Figure 16. White clay smoking pipe with an American eagle design molded on the bowl of the pipe. (Courtesy of the General Services Administration and John Milner Associates.)

(n = 14) categories (Appendix B). The date range for the ceramic assemblage is 1820–1860. Forty-one vessels comprise the Tableware category. Although there were a few undecorated white granite plates (n = 5), molded white granite plates were the most numerous (n = 16). The molded patterns varied but include common paneled patterns, such as Gothic (ca. 1840–ca. 1860), President (ca. 1855–ca. 1860), and Sydenham (1853–ca. 1860). The molded patterns match 5 out of the 14 serving pieces. The molded white granite serving pieces are dishes. The rest of the molded decorated plates are in the shapes of Wheat (ca. 1859–ca. 1900) and Acanthus (1870–1880) (Wetherbee 1980:72–73; Sussman 1985:7) (Figure 18).

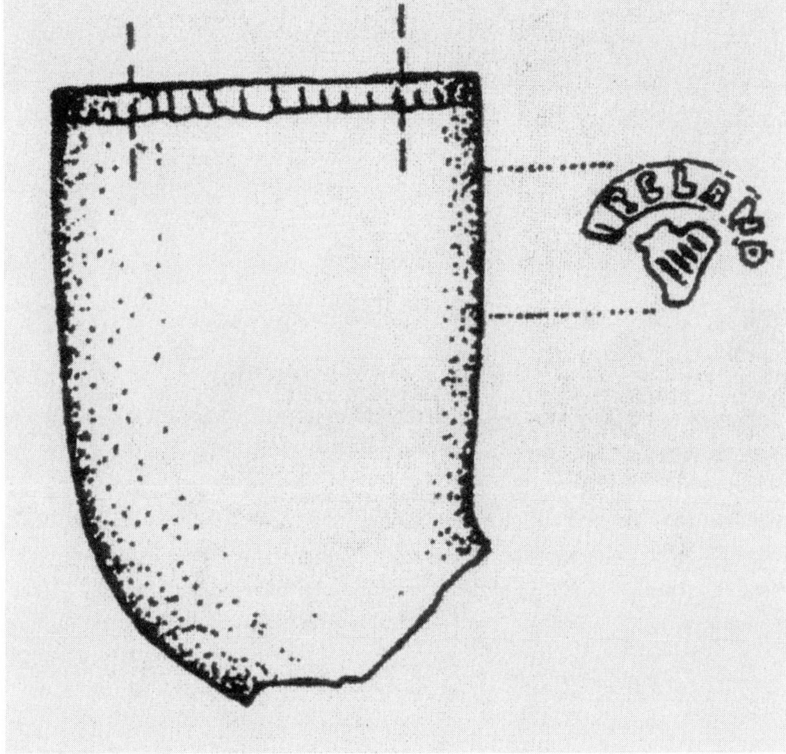

Figure 17. White clay smoking pipe with IRELAND and a Celtic harp stamped on the bowl. (Courtesy of the General Services Administration and John Milner Associates.)

The remaining tableware is either decorated with blue transfer-printed (n = 11) or blue shell-edged patterns (n = 3). The shell-edged decoration dates from the mid- to late nineteenth century and has 2 matching serving dishes. With the exception of the Willow pattern, the plates are in nonmatching patterns such as Aladdin and Florentine. The latter pattern has a matching serving dish.

The 68 teaware vessels are molded white granite (n = 28), blue transfer-printed (n = 17), polychrome painted (n = 6), or undecorated (n = 7). Teacups and saucers in white granite have molded patterns dating between 1850 and 1860. The patterns include Wheat, Primary, Gothic, and Sydenham. New molded shapes include President (1855–ca. 1860),

Figure 18. White granite teaware and tableware. The Wheat pattern is pictured second row, first on the left. (Courtesy of the General Services Administration and John Milner Associates.)

Trent (1854–ca. 1860), and Scalloped Decagon (1856–ca. 1860). Also in the collection are two white granite teapots in the Gothic and President shape. The transfer-printed teacups and saucers are in the patterns Aladdin, Friburg, Florentine, and Siam (1839–1864).

The glass vessel assemblage contains medicinal bottles (n = 80), tableware (n = 25), and serving vessels (n = 2) (Appendix B). The Medicinal category consists of 33 proprietary medicine bottles, 28 mineral water bottles, and 19 dispensary vials. Aside from the embossed medicines mentioned from the lower deposit, there were also commercial medicines such as HUNTS SOVEREIGN OINTMENT and DR. KIERSTED'S JULUP FOR DIARROEA.

The Tableware and Serving categories have 27 vessels. Like those in the lower analytical stratum of this feature, they are plain or undecorated tumblers (n = 20) and plain or undecorated stemware (n = 5). Two paneled salts make up the Serving category.

Three of the 40 white ball clay smoking pipes bear American and Irish symbolism. Similar in design to the pipes in the lower deposit, one has the molded form of an American eagle clutching a crest or shield.

Another pipe bowl is molded in the shape of a male head with a beard and mustache and wearing a turban. Thirteen stars (symbolizing the original colonies) encircle the turban with and the words UNITED STATES OF AMERICA (Figure 19). The Irish pipe is also similar to the one from the lower deposit. Located on the left side of the pipe bowl is a Celtic harp with a female figurehead (Figure 20). On the right side there is an arrangement of three shamrocks.

Artifacts from Feature O at 474 Pearl Street (ca. 1850–1860)

The privy at 474 Pearl Street (Feature O) is stone lined and measures approximately 4 feet (1.22 meters) in diameter and is 10 feet (3.05

Figure 19. White clay smoking pipe molded into the head of a man wearing a turban decorated with thirteen stars. (Courtesy of the General Services Administration and John Milner Associates.)

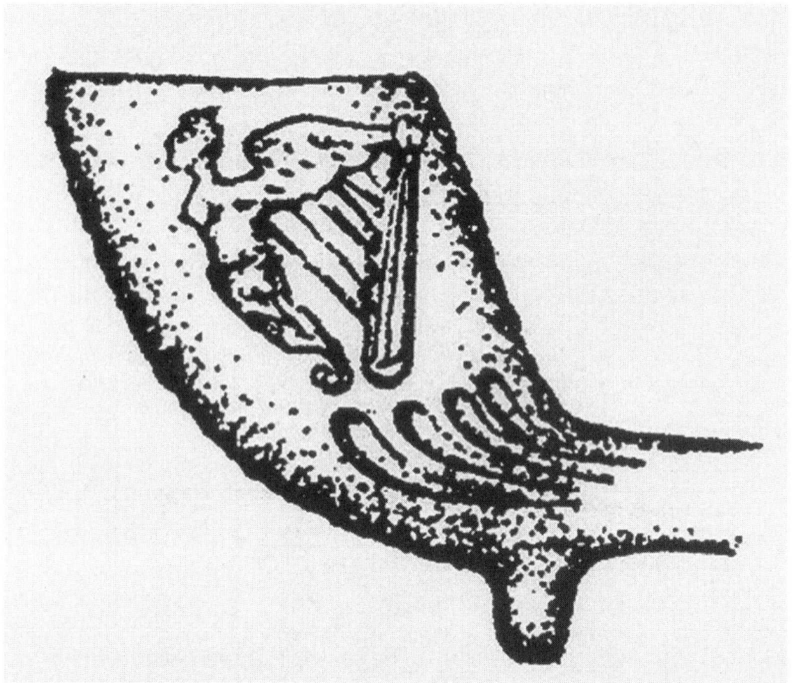

Figure 20. White clay smoking pipe molded with the Celtic harp. (Courtesy of the General Services Administration and John Milner Associates.)

meters) deep. It was closed and filled sometime after 1870 by the construction of rear brick tenement. Six deposits comprised the fill of Feature O (AS I–VI). The fill matrix contained various shades of brown loam with additives of cobble, shell, ash, coal, and brick. Post-excavation analysis indicated that the artifacts from each stratum were deposited in a single filling episode, as there were cross-mending sherds throughout the feature (Yamin 2000a:A-57). The TPQ is 1860.

A majority of vessels are in the Teaware (n = 54) and Tableware (n = 38) categories, with a small amount in the Serving category (n = 6) (Appendix C). Comparable to the lower deposits of Feature J (ASV) and Z (ASII) the decorative types on refined earthenware are transfer-printed (n = 40), white granite molded shapes (n = 12), plain (n = 7), shell-edged (n = 7), and painted (n = 27).

The 38 tableware forms consist mostly of transfer-printed plates (6–10 in). The printed motifs are scenic landscapes such as Alleghany (1828–1859) (n = 17) and the Willow pattern (n = 3) (Williams 1978:183).

The blue shell-edged plates include patterns such as unscalloped rim with impressed lines (1830–1860) and simple painted lines on unscalloped rims (1860–1890). Vessels in white granite are either plain (n = 3) or have various molded shapes (n = 5). Patterns include Gothic and Primary, both common in the assemblages. There is a new shape in this assemblage, Bootes Octagon (1851–ca. 1860) (Wetherbee 1980:48). All of the white granite shapes have matching vessels in the teacups and saucers, but not serving pieces. The 6 serving pieces include dishes (n = 4), a tureen, and a platter. The dishes are decorated in various blue transfer-printed scenic landscape patterns and a molded pattern, Union (1842–1867) (Williams 1978:439).

Unlike the large number of transfer-printed teaware from the deposits at 472 Pearl Street, half of the 54 teaware vessels from the privy at 474 Pearl Street consist of polychrome painted teacups (n = 27). The painted cups have stylized floral and sprig patterns and date from 1830 to 1860. Transfer-printed vessels (n = 18) consist of teacups, a teapot, a slop bowl, and a sugar bowl. The blue transfer-printed patterns were nonmatching, but scenic landscape patterns include Alleghany and Amoy (1830–1834) (Williams 1978:90). Seven of the white granite vessels have matching molded patterns. The forms include a teacup and 3 saucers in the Primary shape, 2 teapots and 3 saucers in the Gothic pattern, and 4 teacups in Bootes Octagon and Sydenham.

As with the tenement at 472 Pearl Street, most of the vessels are medicinal bottles (Appendix C). Proprietary bottles comprise most of the assemblage (n = 27); the rest of the category includes ethical medicine vials (n = 16) and mineral water bottles (n = 7). The commercial medicines are embossed with companies such as F. BROWN'S AROMATIC ESSENCE OF JAMAICA GINGER, LIQUID OPODELDOC, and TURLINGTON'S BASALM OF LIFE. Brown's medicine purported to cure rheumatism, cholera, dyspepsia, and fever. Liquid opodeldoc was used to soothe bruises, sprains, and burns, and as a cure for rheumatism and stiffness of joints. Turlington's medicine was advertised to "enliven the spirit, strengthens and vivifies" (McKearin and Wilson 1978:291). As at the neighboring tenement, Feature O has bottles that contained Radway's commercial medicine.

Twelve vessels make up the Tableware and Serving categories. The 11 tableware forms are either undecorated tumblers (n = 8) or undecorated wine glasses (n = 3). A single undecorated salt dish makes up the serving vessels.

Although 16 white ball clay pipes are in the assemblage, none bear any molded symbols or slogans.

Dublin Section, Paterson

In 1989, John Milner Associates conducted excavations of two city blocks (Block 863 and 866) in Paterson's Dublin section and subsequently undertook post-excavation analysis. The project was part of a data-recovery project prior to the construction of a highway connector scheduled to run through the area (Yamin 1999:28). The initial survey consisted of shovel tests across an established grid to locate any potential historical features. Subsequent to testing, excavation units were placed in areas that potentially contained cultural resources. Features were given numerical designations, and soil layers within the features were designated alphabetically (Yamin 2000:28). Fourteen house lots were investigated (n = 9 on Block 863 and n = 6 on Block 866). A total of 258 features were identified (n = 126 on Block 863 and n = 132 on Block 866). Features consisted of postholes demarcating property boundaries and gardens, privies, and late-nineteenth- and early-twentieth-century waste disposal systems (Yamin 1999:i). The features chosen for this study are associated with Irish and Irish Americans living in single-family structures (Feature 10, Block 866, and Feature 63, Block 863).

Artifacts from Feature 63 at 32 Ward Street (ca. 1890–ca. 1900)

Feature 63 is a wood-lined or "crate"-style privy. The feature was set into an oval hole measuring 7 feet (2.13 meters) in diameter. The crate measured 5 feet (1.52 meters) by 5 feet (1.52 meters) by 8 feet (2.44 meters) deep (Yamin 2000a:59). Thirteen layers were categorized into 3 analytical strata. The uppermost deposit (ASI) was a matrix of soil consisting of yellowish brown sandy silt with stones, ash, and coal. ASII (Levels 5–13) was located inside the feature and consisted of 8 layers of brownish gray sandy silt with cinder, ash, and coal. The bottom of the feature consisted of a black organic layer (Level 9). This organic layer was human waste, also known as night soil. Below the night soil was a level of gravel and brick fragments thought to have been deposited deliberately to facilitate drainage of the privy's contents (Yamin 1999:59–60). ASIII (Levels 6 and 7) is a fill layer surrounding the outside of the crate. Cross-mending between the deposits indicates that the feature was filled in a single episode sometime after 1890.

Forty-three vessels make up the total refined earthenware assemblage. In the functional categories assessed here, white granite makes up Teaware (n = 23), Tableware (n = 17), and Serving (n = 3) categories

(Appendix D). The tableware consists of white granite molded plates with simple panels. The shapes were common throughout the 1850s (Wetherbee 1980:106–107, 135). The plates have matching serving bowls (n = 2). The remaining vessel is an undecorated serving platter. The platter is marked by the American pottery company of J. H. Baum of Wellsville, Ohio (1888–1896) (Gates and Ormond 1982:14). With the exception of a single eggcup, the vessels are plates ranging in size from 8 (n = 2) to 10 in (n = 14) and are marked either by English or American potteries. American manufacturers include the Trenton, New Jersey, potteries of Fell and Thropp Company. (1880–1893) and the Mercer Pottery Company (1868–1930) (DeBolt 1994:48, 96). Mercer Pottery was well known for making white granite dinner sets and was considered one of the leading potteries in the 1880s and 1890s (DeBolt 1994:96–97; Lehner 1988:293). Also present is the mark of William Brunt, Son, and Company from East Liverpool, Ohio (1879–1894) (Gates and Ormond 1982:19; Lehner 1988:60–61).

The 23 tea-related ceramics are predominantly teacups (n = 14). The rest of the assemblage consists of saucers (n = 8) and a teapot. With the exception of a teacup molded with vertical ribs on the exterior and a saucer with curved panels along the rim, all of the teacups and saucers are plain. One of the saucers is marked by the Staffordshire pottery company of Henry Alcock (1891–1900) (Godden 1991:27).

Most glass vessels are in the Medicinal category (n = 34), with small amounts in Tableware (n = 8) and Serving (n = 2) categories (Appendix D) (Figure 21). The 8 tableware vessels consist of stemware (n = 3) and tumblers (n = 5). The stemware is decorated in the molded honeycomb pattern. The tumblers vary in patterns with 3 vessels in the ribbed pattern and 2 paneled. The serving vessels include a handled bowl and a plain cruet. The handled bowl is pressed with paneled decoration matching the decorative type on the paneled tumblers.

The 30 medicinal bottles were of the ethical variety. They were cylindrical in shape and of various sizes. Unlike the Five Points, there were no commercial medicines. The 4 mineral water bottles were similar to those found elsewhere in the Dublin section and include manufacturers such as WM. ALLEN, WM. S. KINCH, GEORGE SPREITZER AND COMPANY, and TIFFANY AND ALLEN.

Although there are 19 white ball clay smoking pipes, only a single pipe is directly related to the Irish American transnationalism. The pipe is stamped GLADSTONE along the stem and refers to William Ewert Gladstone, a member of England's Liberal Party and a strong proponent

Figure 21. Glass forms recovered from the Dublin section of Paterson exemplify the types of forms recovered from Feature 63. (Courtesy of John Milner Associates.)

of Irish self-government. Gladstone was one of the key English figures pushing for Irish self-government, education, disestablishing the Church of Ireland, and tackling the serious issues of agrarian violence and inequalities through the creation of more secure land tenures and ownership (Dewey 1974; Goodlad 1989; Loughlin 1986; Lubenow 1985; O'Day 1986; Parry 1982). In 1881, Gladstone pushed through a land act that established laws for tenants' rights, including fixity of tenure, fair rents, and free sale. He also passed an arrears act to restore many evicted tenants and include them the land act. Furthermore, he was one of the key figures bringing the Home Rule bill to a vote in 1886 (Hachey et al. 1989:120–121), providing for the establishment of an Irish assembly and the restoration of Irish representation at Westminster.

Artifacts from Feature 10 at 46 Oliver Street (ca. 1880–ca. 1910)

Feature 10 is a rectangular stone-lined privy vault in the rear lot of 46 Oliver Street. The privy measured 6 feet (1.83 meters) by 3 feet (.91

Figure 22. A white granite dinner plate in the Moss Rose pattern. (Courtesy of John Milner Associates.)

meters) and was approximately 5 feet deep (Yamin 1999:43). There were 9 soil layers comprising the feature's fill. Post-excavation analysis concluded that the layers made up 3 deposits. ASI (Levels 1–3) is the uppermost deposit consisting of a dark brown to yellowish brown sandy silt with slag fragments, ash, and organic matter. Most of the artifacts came from Level 2 (Yamin 1999:111). The TPQ for this deposit is 1906.

The lower primary deposit (ASII, Levels 4–7) consists of yellowish brown sandy silt containing numerous artifacts (Yamin 1999:111,120). The TPQ for ASII is 1890. The bottommost layers (ASIII, Levels 8–9) were brown sandy silt mixed with rocks. The tight date range of the artifacts suggests that the feature was filled in a single episode over a short period of time after 1906. The artifacts from both strata are considered to constitute a single assemblage.

Most refined earthenware vessels are in the Teaware category (n = 26), with smaller amounts in Tableware (n = 10) and Serving (n = 4) (Appendix E). Almost all of the vessels are plain white granite. The TPQ is 1906 and is based on the manufacturer's mark of John Madock & Sons on a white granite dinner plate (Godden 1991:406). Ten vessels comprise the tableware assemblage. All of the vessels are white granite and either undecorated (n = 3) or transfer-printed in the pattern titled Moss Rose (n = 7) (Figure 22). The plain set consists of 2 dinner plates. The mark of Staffordshire potter of John Maddock and Sons is present on the back of one of the plates (1906+). Another plate has the mark of the American Crescent Pottery Company (1881–1907). The Crescent Pottery Company was located in Trenton, New Jersey and was established by Charles Cook and W. S. Hancock in 1881 (DeBolt 1994:37; Lehner 1988:473). The plates have 4 matching serving pieces (2 bowls, a platter, and a tureen). The tureen is marked by L. B. Beerbower and Company of Elizabeth, New Jersey (1879–1904). The company in 1816 began manufacturing utilitarian stoneware crocks and bottles; by 1893 it was making white granite tea, table, and serving pieces. The company closed by 1902 (DeBolt 1994:20; Lehner 1988:41). The Moss Rose set consists of 5 dinner plates, and the decorative pattern is an underglaze transfer print with a gilded band around the rim. It was a very popular pattern in the United States as part of series of wild rose motifs beginning in 1860 (Wetherbee 1980:91).

Like the tableware and serving pieces, all of the 26 tea-related vessels are white granite. The assemblage includes teacups (n = 17), saucers

Figure 23. A variety of glass forms recovered from Feature 10, Dublin Section. (Courtesy of John Milner Associates.)

(n = 6), slop bowls (n = 2), and teapots (n = 2). The white granite teacups and saucers were undecorated, with the exception of a teacup and saucer in the Wheat pattern. Three of the 6 plain or undecorated saucers were marked by Trenton, New Jersey, pottery companies of Fell and Thropp Company (1879–1893) and the Crescent Pottery Company (1890–1906). Fell and Thropp was manufacturing white granite in the 1890s before becoming Thropp and Brewer in 1901 (Lehner 1988:474). The two teapots are made of refined yellow ware. The pots are decorated with a brown mottled glaze in the molded pattern titled Rebecca at the Well, which was very popular throughout the last half of the nineteenth century. It was produced by a number of American pottery firms between 1860 and 1890 (Ketchum 1983:138).

Most of the 77 vessels are in the Alcohol/Beverage category (n = 48); the remaining are in the Tableware (n = 15), Medicinal (n = 14), and Serving (n = 2) categories (Appendix E) (Figure 23). Seventeen vessels represent the Glass Tableware and Serving categories. Fifteen tumblers molded in various patterns comprise glass tableware vessels. The patterns on the tumblers include simple panels, the arch pattern, the honeycomb pattern, and the sunburst pattern. The single piece of stemware is a wine glass, the bowl of which has a pressed paneled decoration. Two plain dish lid fragments make up the serving assemblage.

Unlike the Five Points, most of the medicinal bottles at Dublin were unlabeled ethical medicinal bottles (n = 9). The single embossed commercial bottle is too fragmentary to permit identification of the manufacturer or the contents. The remaining are mineral water bottles (n = 4) from companies such as PETER RICE'S CELEBRATED MINERAL WATERS, TIFFANY AND ALLEN'S MINERAL WATER, GEORGE SPREITZER AND COMPANY and RICHARD WARREN AND COMPANY.

Twenty-three clay pipes are in the assemblage. Five of the pipes were molded with Irish symbols and slogans and 4 were stamped with the slogan HOME RULE. The slogan is positioned on the inner side of the bowl facing the smoker. The home rule campaign was a nationalist movement throughout the last decades of the nineteenth century in Ireland. Pipes bearing the slogan signify the push for political and economic freedom and self-government in Ireland, as the country had become officially part of Great Britain after the 1801 Act of Union. The slogan was popular throughout the nineteenth century and had been used by Irish nationalist factions since the development of the Fenian movement by midcentury (Dooley 2003). The remaining pipe was molded with the symbol of the Red Hand of Ulster. The motif is the form of a hand with palm side out

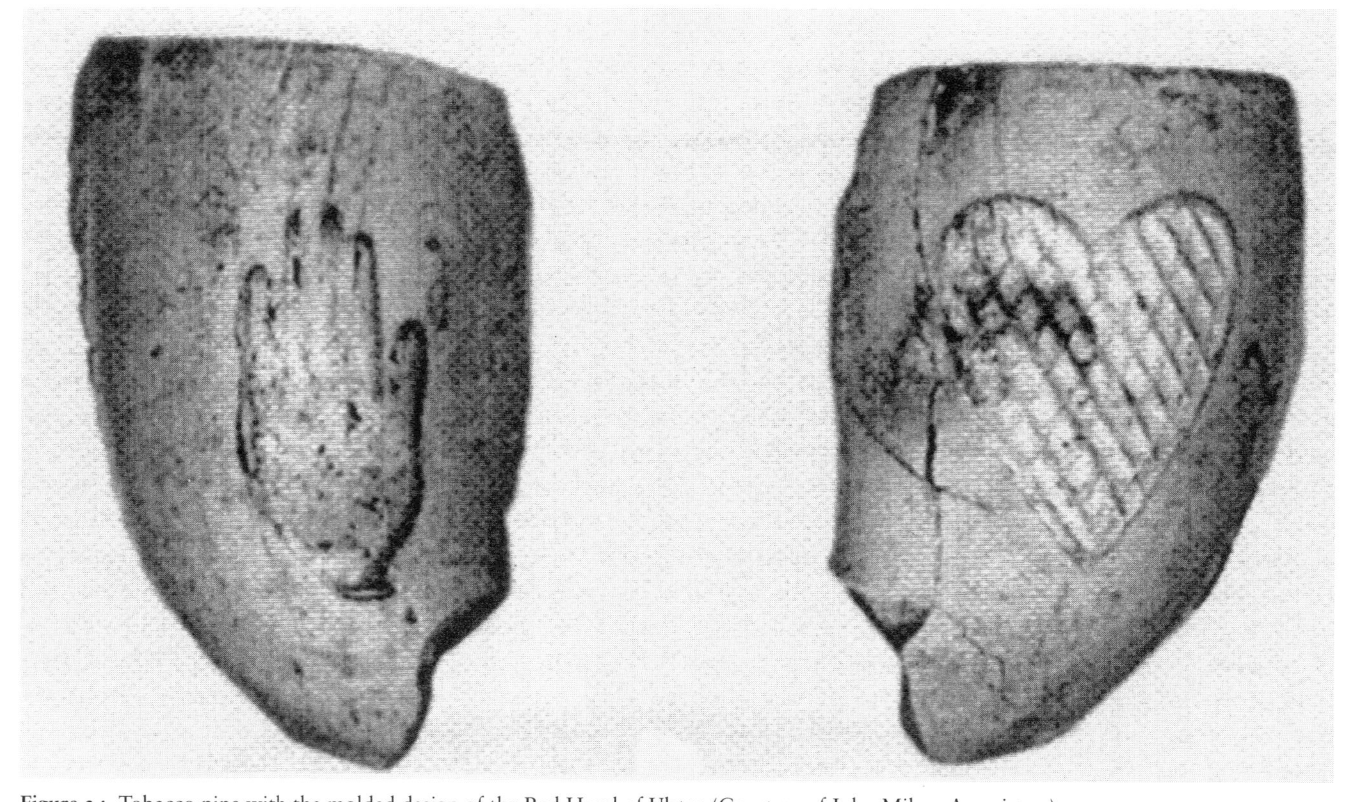

Figure 24. Tobacco pipe with the molded design of the Red Hand of Ulster. (Courtesy of John Milner Associates.)

on the left and a cross-thatched heart on the right face of the pipe bowl (Figure 24). The Red Hand of Ulster, which dates back to the original king of the province, symbolizes many things, among them Irish Protestant ascendancy in the seventeenth century.

The overarching goal is to begin a dialogue moving from site-specific interpretations to a broader narrative shedding light on the important role of material culture reflecting the varied social relations of conflict and negotiation leading to the formation of Irish American identities. The social history of the sites chosen for this study and the material assemblage fit well into the broader history of the Irish diasporic experience. The Irish proletariat faced alienation in America. Negative stereotypes followed the Irish poor across the Atlantic and served to segregate them into neglected urban areas such as the Five Points. Traditionally, it was thought that the Irish chose to live in such disease-ridden and poverty stricken enclaves because it was inherent in their culture. In actuality it became a defense mechanism to confront and negotiate their tenuous position in American society. Throughout a social discourse of conflict and struggle, Irish immigrants and American-born Irish continually reinterpreted what it meant to be Irish.

This research program sheds light on the shifting experiences of alienation and incorporation that were tempered by changing positions of Irish national identity in the United States. The extensive social history combined with the mute and mundane objects of daily life must be situated within the larger structure of social life in Ireland and the United States. The heritage of Irish immigrants to America was maintained through strong connections to Ireland. Over time their collective memories were balanced with their desires to be accepted in their adopted homeland. The shift in how they outwardly communicated their transnational consciousness led to a gradual process of incorporation. Those making up the Irish proletarian diaspora in the United States had little or no capital—except to sell their own, and often unskilled, labor. That governed the fields within which the larger collective moved and lived out their daily lives. As a result, social and economic success or failure was predicated by and reflected through the material culture.

6
The Material Manifestations of the Irish Proletarian Diaspora

Historians of Irish America argue that 1880 marks the beginning of an identity shift from Irish immigrant to Irish American. It was a slow process, blending values and behaviors from pre-Famine and Famine Ireland while concurrently adopting new patterns of thinking and acting from industrial American society. Material culture forms an important part of that history, and it provides the physical evidence of the social relations influencing identity construction and experiences of the everyday world. Continuities may evoke a shared heritage reinforcing traditional social behaviors and values, while change reflects the introduction and acceptance of new sociocultural identities. The material evidence presented here forms the crucial aspect of the analytical discourses of alienation, incorporation, and transnationalism through objects reflecting conflict and desire. The types of objects recovered from Irish immigrant and Irish American sites form an important database illustrating the materialization of an Irish nationality and heritage connecting political and social issues both at home and abroad.

Symbolism found on various objects, such as nationalist symbols on smoking pipes, express a collective identity, reflecting the larger history or collective social relations and experiences. According to Fredrick Barth (2000:31), material culture and its associated symbolism reflect a multiplicity of operations and social processes as a group categorizes and is categorized based on difference. The objects themselves do not give meaning to identities but in fact are given relevance by the group as they reflect the social processes of reconstructing social identity and social position through contact with different groups.

Material and symbolic differences shape group identities and diversity that can spark communal conflict. Strife, mistrust, and alienation occur at the arena of convergence where two groups have competing interests and express their social positions by strict adherence to cultural differences used to identify themselves from others, and cultural baggage that presents a certain degree of discontinuity. Material signs provide the physical expression of identity as categorization through cultural differences; continuities may evoke a shared heritage, whereas differences suggest changes and the creation of new sociocultural identities.

In a diasporic context, material culture can be employed to mobilize subordinate peoples against external social and political conflicts (Brah 1996:91). Meaning rests in its reference to common social identities in reaction to communal differences. Objects are given meaning that is rooted between what is considered real and ideal (McCracken 1988). The context of the ideal is a romantic social concept acting as a bonding agent because it creates a reassurance of a better time or a "golden age" (McCracken 1988:106–108). This age may be fictional, but its importance rests in its ability to promote sociocultural ideals in the present to bring together the disparate people of a diasporic group.

The archeological study linking objects, specific decorative types, and symbols is especially significant in sociohistorical contexts that involve the international movement, exile from a homeland, and alienation in the new place of settlement. The structure of group formation consists of the memory (real or imaginary) of the homeland, a world view, and current experiences of injustice. The symbolism is used to convey the meaning of injustice and hope.

It is not the intention to represent Irish immigrant and Irish American communities as "whole cultures" that are static and unchanging through time and space; rather, the aim is to bring together the localized contexts to look at temporal changes in the archaeological record. I recognize that in any ethnic and class group there is diversity creating tensions as individuals negotiate competing and conflicting ideals, however, such individual spaces and actions are beyond the scope of mute, mass-produced objects. Archaeologists of the modern world must look beyond the individual actors and move their localized patterns to bear in the larger relations and networks of racialization and racialized spaces in which such individuals acted (Brighton 2005; Mullins 1999a, 1999b; Orser 2004, 2007).

There are basic principles underlying this chapter. First, any social archaeological study of the nineteenth century is a practice in understanding the impacts of a world system, industrialism, social stratification, institutional racialization, and modern capitalism. Therefore, studies of material culture must include the realities of inequality and alienation from the economic, political, and social structure. The varying levels of inequalities are built upon values of difference (real or imaginary) fostering social and economic divisions, and one's position in the social hierarchy dictates the degree of advantages or depravations in the quality of life (Lodziak 2002:4–5; Orser 2003:319).

Second, the social history of the nineteenth century consisted of an ideology defining daily life and social value through mass consumerism. The acquisition of material wealth increasingly became a condition of existence and reinforced the ideology of accumulation enriching a person's life. For archaeologists studying this period, what is important is not necessarily that goods express wealth or something akin to a classless society, rather, archaeologists need to identify the social, political, and economic realities of the social (de)valuation, stratification, and marginalization of various cohorts that it attempts to mask (Althusser 1979:112–113, 205; Castells 1977:83–86, 445; Lodziak 2002:viii; Merrifield 2002:115–116).

Finally, objects have value. In the preindustrial and industrial period, exchange value or the commodification of objects reflect the larger social relations of class and the ideology of unfettered access to the marketplace (Orser 1996a:114–115; 2004:158–164). It is therefore possible to identify and track shifts in social and economic positions through changes in the material record. Based on the principles above, the argument presented here is that the degree of alienation and incorporation of Irish and Irish American communities are reflected materially in changes in the types of decorative ceramic and glass vessels at the sites.

To provide a meaningful interpretation of the material from this period, the recovered ceramic and glass vessels are viewed as commodities with use, exchange, and aesthetic values that reflect broader social and economic relations between the various classes of Irish immigrants and native-born Americans. Archaeologists of the modern world convincingly illustrate that differing types of material culture are the physical evidence of social stratification and inequalities and are shrouded in the social pressures brought about by the ideology of mass consumerism and its promise of social aspirations and gratification (Leone 1995, 1999, 2003; Orser 1996a, 1999; Paynter 1988; Shackel 1996, 1998). Charles Orser (1996a:234–235) contends that objects have imbued in them a set of "social attributes" that relate to an individual's social and economic position and thus opportunities or limitations in everyday life. By the end of the eighteenth century and increasingly throughout the nineteenth century, American consumer culture was based on material wealth as symbolic of publicly shared social expectations, tangible examples of improved standards of living, and the outward expression of an individual's social worthiness (Mullins 1999a:178). To illustrate this point, Henri Lefebvre (1982:84) contends that being deprived of objects would be to deprive an individual or group social existence. In short, it is this complex and often contradictory relational network between objects and people, and the interconnections between individuals and group membership, that needs to be the focus of material culture studies.

The material culture presented here includes objects used in the daily lives of Ireland's rural poor, Irish immigrants, and Irish Americans and is actively situated in the analytical discourses of alienation, transnationalism, and incorporation. Understanding exclusion requires that one understand incorporation and class and ethnic struggle, all three of which involve the study of the everyday lives as a starting point because it is at the micro-level where meaning is given to social resistance and through this recognition it is possible to expand and begin to grasp the whole structure of social life (Lefebvre 1991).

Teacups, plates, tumblers, platters, and smoking pipes are physical evidence of social relationships and the social processes at the "area of convergence" between Irish immigrants, Irish Americans, and Americans. These items form and dictate such relationships and processes between daily practice and the broader social and historical economic, political, and social forces. It is the materialization of the daily experiences of inequality, dominance, subordination, conflict, desire, and the gradual process of heritage creation (Brumfield 2004:225; DeMarrais et al. 2004:1–2; Rowlands 2004:199). The timing of incorporation is directly related to the degree of alienation from the host society. What is more, each discourse is tempered by the dual consciousness of the diasporic group. A transnational discourse is fostered by the group's "in between" status of immigrant and citizen. It involves conceptions of cultural retentions amid social and cultural transformation. Transnationalism is the impetus for incorporation, as it expresses first and foremost loyalties to the adopted country, but at times it fosters alienation whereby the group retains a notion of its former cultural self. Incorporation, alienation, and transnationalism are interdependent discourses that ebb and flow in relation to external pressures from the dominant society and provide the structure with which to illustrate the material culture of identity creation and transformation in the negotiation and struggle to become Irish American citizens.

Negotiating Identities through Continuity and Change

The ceramic assemblage from Ireland illustrates the types and forms of refined earthenware available to some pre-Famine classes of the rural poor. The date range for the data is 1820 to ca. 1830. It is difficult to provide concrete evidence as to when the vessels were purchased. The end date for the Ballykilcline is the time of eviction, between 1847 and 1848. Based on specific manufacturer date ranges, it can be argued that at the time of eviction, the Nary family had refined earthenware that was relatively new (Appendix A).

Based on the types of ceramic vessels in both assemblages, it can be argued that Strokestown and the outlying areas had a certain amount of access to relatively contemporary mass-produced refined earthenware. Little is known about how English ceramics were distributed in the Republic of Ireland, including in Ballykilcline; it is known, however, that refined English earthenware first came through Irish ports and market towns such as Dublin, Galway, Westport, Clifden, and Belfast. From the larger market towns the items were shipped via canal or land routes to smaller hinterland market towns (Brighton and Levon-White 2005).

Strokestown was one such town; its market center is nearly 4.97 miles (8 kilometers) away from Ballykilcline, and it had set market days on which goods were sold. Fair days and market days were either annual or monthly (Inglis 1835:16). According to *I. Slater's National Commercial Directory of Ireland* (1846:249), the Strokestown market was held on Fridays and the fairs on May 18, June 15, October 19, and November 16; these were well attended by the local inhabitants. The *National Commercial Directory of Ireland* (1846:141) also lists Edward Conroy and Nicholas Gilleran, both located in Church Street, as earthenware dealers in Strokestown throughout the year. Because of the distance it may have made purchase of ceramics on a frequent basis difficult. Therefore it is possible that a good portion of the vessels from both cabin assemblages were purchased from traveling or itinerant merchants.

Whether the vessels were purchased during market or fair days or acquired during an annual visit from an itinerant traveler, the assemblages from the north and south Nary cabins were purchased piece-meal or over time rather than as a complete set. The lack of any substantial matching patterns, such as shell edged, reflects this. This is not surprising given rural Ireland's high rents and the poor economic conditions for most tenant families. Small farmers, cottiers, and landless laborers and their families were forced to live at or below the subsistence level; this raises the interest regarding the presence and use of refined earthenware at tenant farmer sites.

The rural landless Irish were active participants in the modern economy. Examples from *Slater's Commercial Directory* (1846) illustrate that the rural Irish were constantly exposed to the advertisement of refined earthenware. One advertisement specifically appealed to aspirations of respectability and economic freedom, boasting that the store carried everything "the modern consumer needed" (Slater 1846:268). Brand consumption of refined earthenware suggests that the rural Irish strove for respect.

The objects recovered are used as a comparative sample to understand the formation of an Irish immigrant and Irish American consumer culture. There is a distinct pattern between ceramic functional vessels and decorative types. With the exception of the transfer printed Willow pattern tableware and the Lucano serving piece, in the Nary assemblages all of the transfer-printed vessels are teacups. At this time in nineteenth-century Ireland, transfer printing would have been the most costly decoration on refined earthenware (Brighton and Levon-White 2005). Although painted teacups and saucers are considerably less expensive than transfer-printed teaware, the expenditure on at least some form of decorative teaware still emphasizes the social importance of tea drinking.

Based on the archaeological assemblages in Ireland, it is evident that tea was consumed by the rural poor classes beginning as early as the first decade of the nineteenth century. Economic historians, however, consider tea to be a luxury item with limited consumption at that time, if it was consumed at all (Mokyr and Ó Gráda 1988:217). Nevertheless, the teacups and saucers in each assemblage indicate that the rural classes were drinking tea. Its importance is reflected by the emphasis on the vessels' contemporary decorative styles. Jane Gray (1993:251) argues that all classes of the rural poor were drinking tea by the first decade of the nineteenth century. Drinking tea was recognized by the tenant farmers and laborers as a luxury and leisure activity, and because of its social context, it became a cultural symbol of a collective consciousness (Gray 1993; Harlow 1997; McGowan 2001). Tea drinking remains an important part of social activities in many areas of rural Ireland and has been noted by both folklorists and anthropologists (Arensberg 1988; Arensberg and Kimball 1940; Glassie 1975).

Based upon the available accounts and historical research into the daily diet of the rural classes in nineteenth-century Ireland, potatoes were part, if not all, of the daily family meals. Therefore, the acquisition and cost of decorative dinner forms would not have been a prudent expense for families living at or below the subsistence level. The Nary assemblage differs in that there is transfer-printed tableware, specifically a Staffordshire serving piece, suggesting that dining was a more important ceremony in the household, especially during social occasions and holidays. Perhaps small farmers like the Nary family owned such ceramics to emphasize their social status among the other rural classes. Small and middling farmers throughout the west of Ireland did consume meat, and in some regions fish, more often than the cottier and laboring classes (Kennedy et al. 1999:70; Langan-Egan 1999:21). The meaning of the occasions is emphasized not only from the break of the daily diet of potatoes and the inclusion of meat, but signified by the use of the expensive ceramic plates. The Nary assemblage contained two different sets of decorative tableware. Drawing from historical accounts and descriptions, the size and variety of the Nary assemblage is surprising. Nevertheless, research on nineteenth-century rural communities reveals that refined earthenware was a feature in most tenant farming cabins, not only in Ireland but also on the far-off islands in Scotland (Grant 1961; Thorton 1978).

Jane Webster (1999) studied nineteenth-century refined earthenware (both Scottish and Staffordshire) from poor tenant sites on the marginal island of South Uist in the Outer Hebrides (a chain of islands off the northwest coast of Scotland). Conditions of poverty, famine, and ultimately eviction on South Uist were similar to the conditions in rural Ireland during the first half of the nineteenth century. Webster (1999:59) discovered that it was not uncommon, in fact, it was a point of pride, for poor tenants living in small thatched cabins similar to those in Ireland to own dressers with three or four shelves for displaying plates, bowls, and teacups.

The cabin assemblages range in date between 1820 to the end of the 1830s. It can be said with some degree of certainty that both Nary families did have two sets of dishes, one for everyday use and a smaller one for display on shelves or atop a chest of drawers (Brighton and Levon-White 2005). The refined earthenware illuminates and to an extent contradicts the historical record. The contradiction lies in the late-eighteenth- and nineteenth-century travelers' accounts of the rural Irish living conditions; most if not all reported on the lack of refinement of the cabins and furniture and the outdatedness of refined earthenware ceramics. Arthur Young (1780) in his travels wrote that

> the cottages of the Irish, which are called cabins, are the most miserable looking hovels that can well be conceived. The furniture of the cabins is as bad as the architecture; in very many, consisting only of a spot for boiling their potatoes, earthenware, a bit of a table, and 1 or 2 broken stools; beds are not found universally, the family lying on straw, equally

> partook of by the cows, calves, and pigs. I very generally found that these acquisitions were all made within the last 10 years. . . . I think the bad cabins and furniture are the greatest instances of Irish poverty.

Young's remarks are revealing. First, he somewhat begrudgingly acknowledges the presence of material culture in many of the cabins visited, even though the condition of the items are not to his level of satisfaction and comfort. Second, Young's dating of the material culture is close to accurate. The ceramic vessels in both cabin assemblages were at least 10 years old at the time of the Narys' eviction in 1847 (with some exceptions, most of the vessels date to the 1820s). Young viewed the lack of contemporary material culture as a sign of Irish poverty, which is indicated and reflected by the piece-meal purchasing patterns of each of the three assemblages. Furthermore, the fact that the most recent ceramic vessels are from the 1830s is also indicative of the turbulent early years of the 1840s and ultimately the clearances between 1847 and 1848.

Comparing the patterns of continuities and changes in decorative types and vessel complexity in the ceramics and glass assemblages with the Irish data marks the starting point for illustrating the physical manifestation of an Irish American identity and consumer culture. Irish and Irish American tenement dwellers and living in single-family homes were part of or descended from the Irish proletarian diaspora, and their discarded ceramic and glass vessels and food remains provide the earliest evidence of the formations of an Irish American identity (Brighton 2005; Brighton and Orser 2006a). Nineteenth-century refined earthenware was mass produced and reached, to varying degrees, all levels of society (Blaszczyk 1994:126; Majewski and Schiffer 2001:34). The main point here is that the ideology imbued in these mass-produced items instilled a need in the owner to be recognized as civilized, prosperous, and, ultimately, as having the right to citizenship. To own the proper types of forms gives the impression, real or imaginary, that you are a contributing member of society. Changes in this material culture over time suggest new routines and practices brought about by capitalism and the measure to which a household is integrated into the larger social, political, and economical processes of society (Leone 1999; Orser 1996a, 1996b; 2004; Shackel 1996, 1998).

Pertinent to the focus here is the change in ceramic and glass vessel complexity. Vessel complexity is employed and defined as those forms not considered necessary in the everyday routines of eating or drinking. Serving pieces such as platters, large deep dishes, and gravy and soup tureens have implications regarding socially learned and accepted eating styles and behaviors (Brighton 2005; Groover 2003; Lucas 1994; Wall

1994, 2001). More complex vessel forms are function specific in the way food is prepared, eaten, and served. In American assemblages, vessel complexity and the variation in tableware and serving pieces increased as the nineteenth century progressed. The number of different forms is part of the larger social transformation and new formed ritual of eating associated with the industrial age (Mullins 1999b:181; Shackel 1996:122).

Vessel complexity also includes the number of glass tableware and serving forms. When trying to discern patterns in table settings, historical archaeologists tend to ignore glass tableware such as tumblers, wine glasses (stemware), and dishes and focus only on refined earthenware vessels. This fails to capture the complexity and total pattern of the types and forms of table settings (Lucas 1994:84; Wall 2001:110–111). Like ceramic forms, significant numbers of glass tumblers, wine glasses, decanters, serving dishes, bowls, and cruet sets provide further insights into consumer patterns and the meaning of such vessels in the context of nineteenth-century American social values of moral citizenship and respectability. It is argued and demonstrated here that what is more revealing are the differences between the types of ceramic and glass forms acquired by Irish immigrants and Irish Americans—differences that reflect new consumption patterns and identities.

Studies influencing this work vary in context, but all agree that alterations to forms and decorative types over time are interconnected with social transformations associated with emerging industrialization and the ideology of collective consumerism. Michael Lucas (1994:80) posits that the degree of vessel complexity, or the number of vessel forms having specific functions, is indicative of social inclusion or exclusion. Through the nineteenth century, objects such as variously sized plates, bowls, and platters in concert gave value to the individual and increasingly defined one's position and respectability in American society because their presence illustrated adherence to and acceptance of the collective social organization (Lucas 1994:80).

Mark Leone (1995, 1999) identified the formation of that ideology and its material manifestation. Leone (1999:210–212, 2003:xv) argues that greater numbers of matching decorative vessel forms and vessel complexity reveal access to the market place. Furthermore, the accompanying aesthetic value (or esteem value) along with the changes in form and decoration represent a change in the social position and respectability in the American social and economic system.

In the same theoretical parameters of Leone, Paul Shackel (1996) highlights the changing esteem values of new ceramic decorative patterns and forms of the romantic period's new social order. The emerging American consumer pattern calling for the accumulation of mass-produced nonessentials and luxury items was physical evidence of the philosophical fusion of increasing technological advancements and the ideology of respectability, modernity, and citizenship (Shackel 1996:111). Mass consumerism at this point became an activity of individual indulgence moving beyond acquiring basic needs. The study's relevance rests with bringing to the forefront one of the many contradictions of capitalism. Shackel (1996:122–123) is very astute to point out that individuals were not necessarily seeking satisfaction from the products consumed but were buying into the "self-illusory experiences" created by the objects, which symbolically expressed social aspirations and individuality. The contradiction becomes lost on consumers in that rather than creating the individual, mass consumerism solidified social groups through ownership of identical mass-produced objects, thereby perpetuating institutionalized inequalities drawn on differences of material wealth.

Paul Mullins (1999a, 1999b, 1999c, 2001, 2004) focuses on mass consumption as a means to convey a person's expectations to the fundamental rights of American citizenship, as well as an optimistic indication of improved personal circumstances. Mullins's study differs from the previous work in that he incorporates the social construct of racism and the inequalities of racialized consumer space. Although Mullins employs various artifact types to illustrate his point, his interpretation of the types of ceramic forms and decorative styles is more relevant to this study. The presence of forms reflecting material wealth through the setting of an orderly table, he argues, is the outward expression of the desire and struggle for acceptance in a highly racialized society (Mullins 1999a:182). The construction of an African American consumer culture was a complex negotiative process within a highly charged racialized content that limited privileges of personal worth and citizenship (Mullins 1999a:170–172). The results of that uneven negotiation are evidenced in the changes to the material culture. Specific to the case presented here, movements in identity reformation and tolerance in the larger, mainstream (white) society can be seen by changes in ceramic vessel forms and increased complexity.

The studies by Leone, Shackel, Lucas, and Mullins provide a basic example of the archaeology of consumerism, social inequality, and racialized space to build upon in this study. It is apparent that interpreting social relations through material culture is complex and often contradictory. To attempt to shed some light onto the social context of Irish experiences and social relations with mainstream Americans, it becomes necessary to understand the formation of the American middle class and its influence on how people were considered part of or alienated from American society.

Material culture reflects broader social behaviors and value judgments. Some scholars have argued that the driving force of consumer patterns in America was the middle classes (Praetzellis et al.1988:192–193). Therefore, any interpretation of the archaeological manifestations of identity and consumption among Irish immigrants and Irish Americans must be compared with the larger structure of American consumer culture.

Mass consumerism in the nineteenth century was formed by the emerging American, Protestant middle class and predicated on the belief that material goods dictated social position and morality (Kasson 1990), a notion drawn from the consumer habits of the middle classes. The new consumer culture of the middle classes was the result of changing attitudes in American Protestantism after the Second Great Awakening (1800–1830). Religious ideology changed from the belief in predetermined salvation to the belief that morality and piety was the responsibility of each individual. The outward expression of this was through the necessary material culture. As a consequence, those who could not obtain the material signs of Christian piety were judged immoral and thus un-American (Bushman 1993; Clark 1988; Green 1983; Grier 1988; McLoughlin 1978; Rosenberg 1971; Ryan 1981).

Archaeological evidence of the middle classes dating throughout the last half of the nineteenth century demonstrates the meaning and importance of material culture symbolizing the ideologies of respectability and morality. Matching ceramic tea, tableware, and serving forms in the prescribed numbers, as well as the incorporation of religious piety and naturalism, galvanized a consumer demand in forms such as Christian-inspired pattern names and forms (Fitts 1999, 2000; Fitts and Yamin 1996; Praetzellis and Praetzellis 1992; Praetzellis et al. 1988; Wall 1994, 2001). The patterns of change in the assemblages are assessed by comparing the data to contemporary American-born, non-Irish households in Manhattan and Paterson. In order to identify cultural change, it is important understand and interpret the basis of continuities in the Irish immigrant community. From there it is possible to reveal the expression of new behaviors, consumer culture, and desires of respectability and civic citizenship and the transformation of Irish identity in America (Brighton 2001, 2005).

Diana Wall's (1994, 2001) research into the emergence of the middle class and its material correlates ensconced in the "cult of domesticity" is well known. Matching ceramic tea, tableware, and serving forms in the prescribed numbers and the symbolism of religious piety on the forms galvanized consumer demand for goods legitimizing their place and power in the social world (Lucas 1994:p. 81). Robert Fitt's (1999, 2000) research on middle-class identity in Brooklyn, New York, reinforces the ideology of racialized spaces and ownership of material wealth interpreting social relations of inclusion in the dominant ideology. Fitts expressly states that the ideology of respectability was exclusively meant to maintain the social and economic power of American born, white, Anglo-Protestants.

Under the concept of vessel complexity, continuities exist between the Irish immigrant data (Appendix B) and the assemblages in Ireland. Furthermore, the slow process of differences in vessel complexity reveal new behaviors and desires resembling an American, non-Irish, consumer culture. Figure 25 illustrates similarities in the ratio of teaware to tableware;

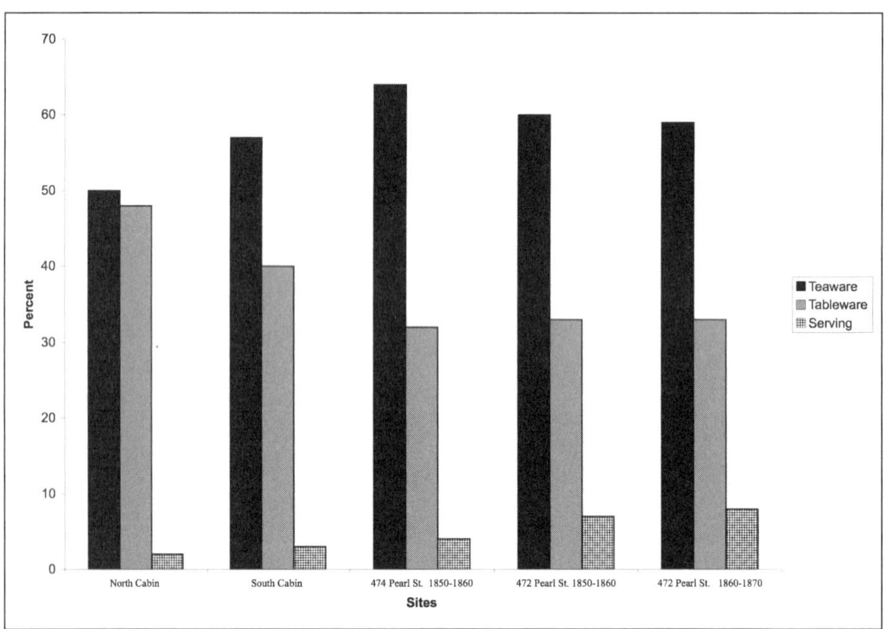

Figure 25. The distribution of ceramic functional categories between the sites in Ireland and the Five Points, Manhattan.

teaware is consistently higher than the proportion of tableware vessels. Furthermore, continuities occur in transfer-printed scenic patterns, or less-expensive polychrome floral patterns, on teaware and inexpensive tableware either in blue shell-edged or Willow pattern. In the Irish and Irish American communities the level of vessel complexity increased as the nineteenth century progressed.

In comparison to the traditional assemblage from Ireland, it appears that serving pieces were a part of the Nary household experience, mainly in the north cabin (Brighton and Levon-White 2005). In America, serving pieces do not factor to a large degree in the material culture of recently arrived Irish immigrants, most of whom would have been tenant farmers in Ireland.

The continuities with Ireland become more prevalent when the Irish immigrant data are compared to a contemporary American-born working-class assemblage from Greenwich Mews in Manhattan (Geismar 1989) (Figure 26). The Greenwich Mews site housed two families, each owning at least 3 serving vessels. In comparison, the percentage of serving

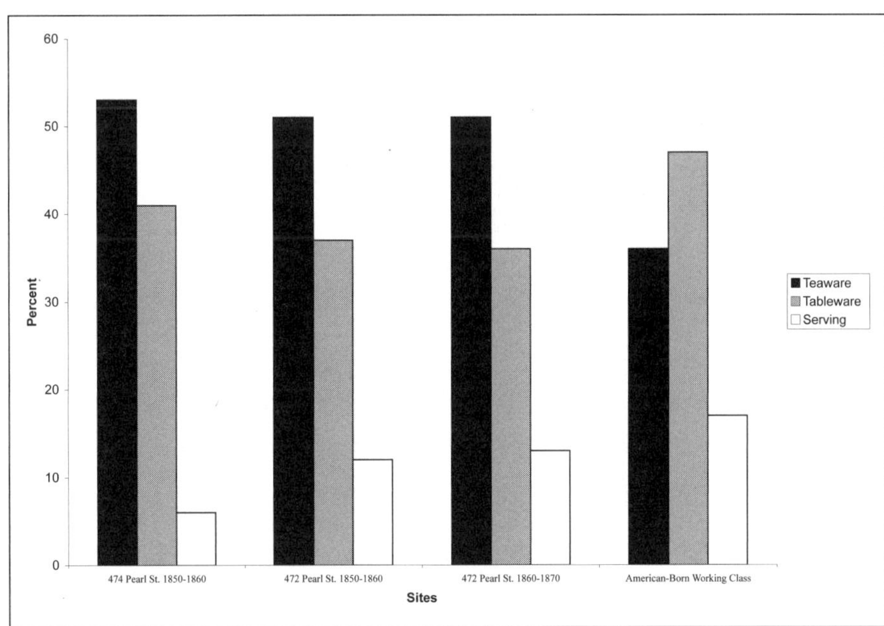

Figure 26. The distribution of ceramic functional categories between the Five Points assemblages and a contemporary American-born working-class household from the Greenwich Mews, Manhattan.

pieces at the Five Points is low considering the number of households living in the tenement. The serving platters and various sized dishes in the data average roughly 1 vessel per household at 472 Pearl Street between 1850 and 1860, approximately 1 serving vessel for every other household between 1860 and 1870, and 1 serving vessel per family at 474 Pearl Street.

This pattern can be explained in two ways. Serving vessels cost much more than other vessel types, and the cost might have been prohibitive to the recently arrived Irish households (Brighton 2001). Families at the Five Points were either semiskilled or unskilled, and in the case of 472 Pearl Street, all of the households by the 1860s consisted of unskilled laborers. Along with cost, the low percentage of vessel complexity at the Five Points might reflect a lack of experience owning and using serving pieces. The Nary assemblages each had a serving piece—a platter and a tureen. Referring back to the daily diet of the rural poor in Ireland, it is not surprising that there was no great demand to acquire these forms,

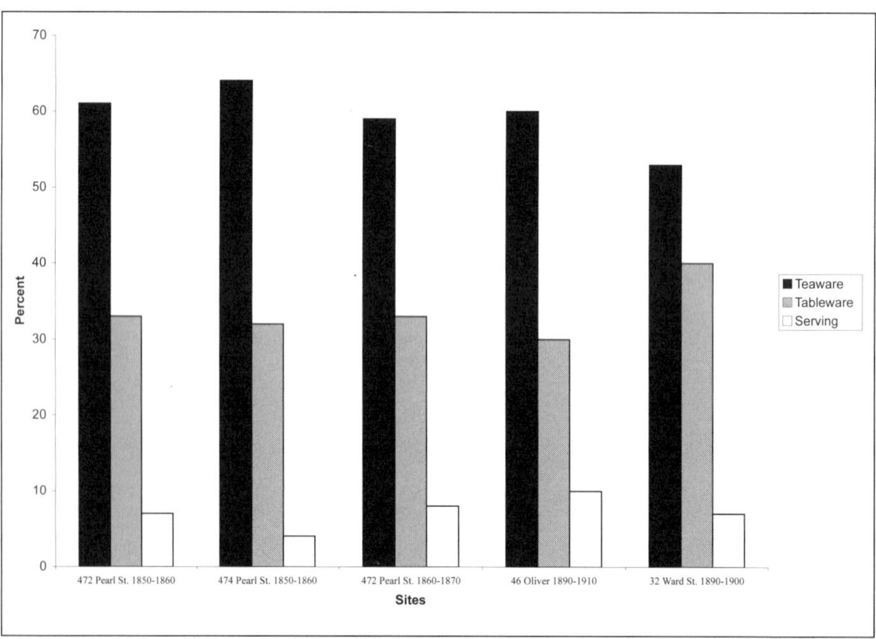

Figure 27. The distribution of ceramic functional categories between the Irish immigrant tenements at the Five Points, Manhattan, and the Irish and Irish American households at the Dublin section, Paterson, New Jersey.

but with the availability of different foods, especially meat, in Manhattan a need to acquire these new ceramic forms was developing.

The increase in vessel complexity over time is directly correlated with the immigrants' length of time in America. An emergence of social dining activities instead of social tea drinking in the 1860s upper deposit at 472 Pearl Street represents the emergence of a new pattern of learned behaviors and practices of a larger group transformation. Unlike the ceramics and glass from the privy's lower deposit associated with families such as the Kellys, Callaghans, Loftuses, Barrys, Morrises, and Flynns, who had recently arrived to America, the tableware and serving forms from the upper deposit belonged to Irish families who had lived in the country for well over 10 years. The overall length of residence suggests that change in vessel complexity was a transgenerational process as a result of negotiation with external social pressures of assimilation (Mintz 1996:112). In order to gain social and economic opportunities after being considered the "foreign other" for nearly 30 years, the Irish were forced

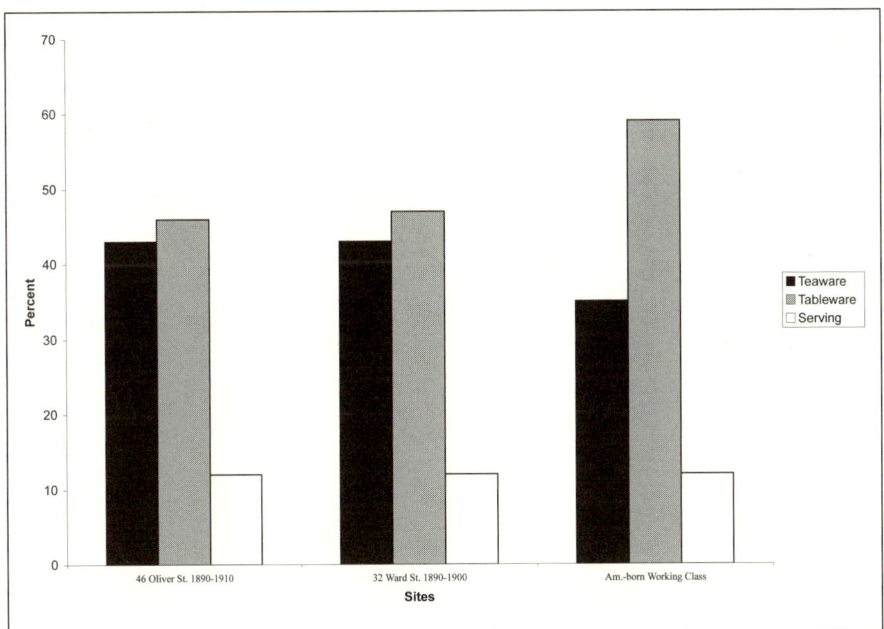

Figure 28. The distribution of ceramic and glass functional categories of Irish and Irish American and a contemporary American-born, non-Irish, working-class household at the Dublin section, Paterson, New Jersey.

to reshape behaviors and world view to acceptance and citizenship in the eyes of American society.

Vessel complexity increases further by the 1890s, and continuities in ceramic form and function between Ireland and the Irish in America cease to exist. At first glance, Figure 27 seems somewhat deceptive because the Serving category in Paterson is only slightly higher than at the Five Points. Again, as with the comparison with the American-born assemblage, each Paterson assemblage represents a single family and contains at least 3 serving vessels per household. This similarity is seen in the American household in New York, also a contemporary non-Irish American-born working-class household from the north end of the Dublin section (Figure 28). The increase in serving pieces represents a change in the consumer culture and dining habits—reflecting what was considered a respectable American form/way of eating (Brighton 2005).

Gradual increases in glass tableware over time provide further evidence of continuity and change. When ceramic functional vessels are

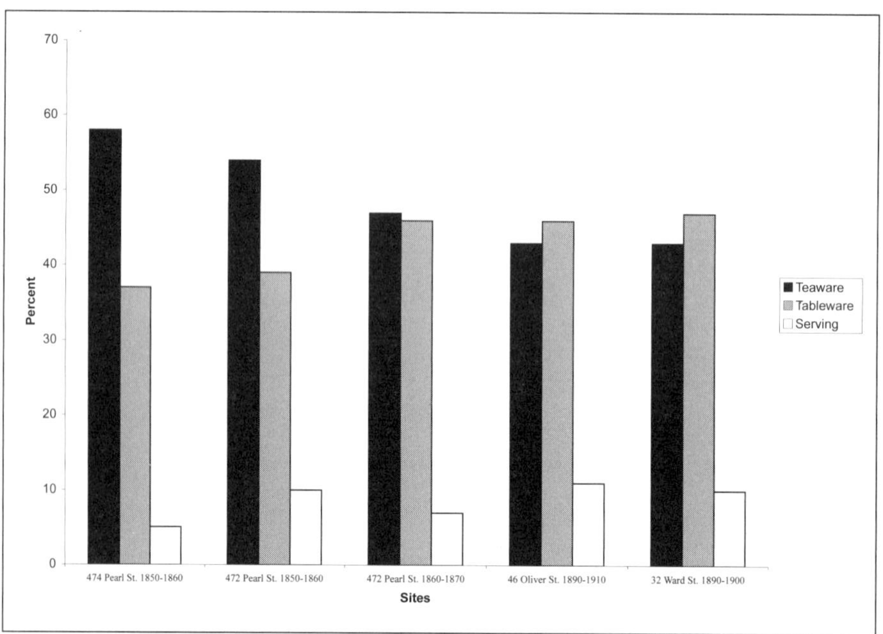

Figure 29. The distribution of both ceramic and glass functional categories between the Irish immigrant tenement assemblages at the Five Points, Manhattan, and the Irish and Irish American assemblages at the Dublin section, Paterson, New Jersey.

evaluated with the addition of glass vessels, a new pattern emerges (Figure 29). When trying to discern patterns in table settings, historical archaeologists tend to ignore glass tableware such as tumblers, wine glasses (stemware), and dishes and focus only on ceramic vessels, but this fails to capture the complexity and total pattern of the types and forms of table settings (Wall 2001:110–111). Like ceramic forms, significant numbers of glass tumblers, wine glasses, decanters, serving dishes, bowls, and cruet sets provide further insights into consumer patterns and the meaning of such vessels in the context of nineteenth-century American social values of moral citizenship and respectability.

The data from Irish immigrant households at both Five Points tenements remains relatively the same; there was an emphasis on owning more decorative teaware in comparison to tableware and serving vessels. This pattern strongly resembles that of the pre-Famine Irish data. However, a shift occurs by the end of the 1860s. The data from the upper privy deposit at 472 Pearl Street is more reflective of a pattern similar to the non-Irish American-born assemblages. This material change is further buttressed by the pattern of both Paterson assemblages, where tableware vessels with the inclusion of glass vessels outnumber teaware. Therefore, with the introduction of glass vessels into the data set, in addition to an increase in vessel complexity, the emergence of an Irish American material assemblage begins as early as 1870 and develops by the 1890s (Brighton 2001, 2005).

While changes in vessel complexity and the increase in glass tableware occurred between 1870 and 1900, a pattern emerges in the numbers of plain and molded white granite vessels. At the time the lower deposit in Feature J at 472 Pearl Street and the deposit in Feature O at 474 Pearl Street were created, sometime after 1860, the Five Points assemblages had a low percentage of white granite vessels, mostly teacups and saucers. The total number of white granite pieces from all functional categories increased in the upper deposit of Feature J, created after 1870. By the end of the nineteenth century, it replaced all ceramic types in the Dublin assemblages. The presence of white granite and its eventual predominance in the Paterson data marks the subtle and gradual social process of incorporation into American consumer culture.

It is not clear whether white granite and glass tableware and serving pieces held the same meaning for Irish-born and Irish American families as they did for non-Irish, American households. White granite vessels are present in very small numbers in the midcentury data. Like the increase in glass and ceramic complexity, the percentage of white granite vessels increases by the 1860s. Three decades later it is the only ware type in the Paterson assemblages. The question then becomes why the change in the material culture between 1860 and 1890?

There are two possible and interdependent reasons late-nineteenth-century Irish households would have goods associated with American ideologies. The first explanation is cost. By the end of the 1860s various patterns of white granite tea and tableware flooded the marketplace, causing a considerable drop in cost, perhaps even for the Irish-born laborer class (G. Miller 1991). By 1890, the Mackel and McGill families, homeowners rather than tenants, were acquiring white granite; by this time, America's ceramic industry stabilized and became a competitive industry. American potteries were mass producing large quantities of white granite at cheaper prices than their English-made counterparts (Gates and Ormerod 1982; Potteries of Trenton Society 2001). Trenton and East Liverpool, both manufacturers with products present in the Paterson data, were producers of inexpensive white granite products that thrived commercially throughout the last decades of the nineteenth century (Gates and Ormerod 1982:128; Potteries of Trenton Society 2001:10).

While affordability is one facet, the other is demographics and the symbolism of respectability and civic citizenship associated with owning these objects. The McGill family was American born, and it is possible that neither Daniel nor his wife were exposed to patterns of traditional Irish material culture. The same could be said for the Mackel family. Although both Sarah and James Mackel were born in Ireland, they had lived in Paterson for over 30 years at the time of the deposit. The white granite vessels may reflect their conscious efforts to acquire objects similar to those owned by their Irish American neighbors. It is most likely that the McGill family, and perhaps the Mackel family, viewed themselves as American citizens first and foremost. Therefore acquiring the objects associated with the American consumer culture would be an expression of their desire for inclusion which separated them from the stigmas and stereotypes of the Irish as the foreign other.

The physical evidence of gradual incorporation between the Five Points and Dublin section is further supported through faunal remains. The changes in the percentages in the variety of animal remains, especially when compared to the non-Irish American-born households, reflect the same pattern of incorporation as the ceramics and glass.

Nineteenth-century American eating habits were stratified, and the meaning of food was a cultural product of the social structure. Choices in diet and how meals were presented and eaten held enormous significance; in one form or another, choices were a declaration of social position

(Mintz 1996:4–6, 13). Throughout the nineteenth century Americans consumption of beef, and then chicken, ranked the highest in relation to other meats such as lamb and salted pork (Davis 1989:202; Rothchild and Balkwill 1993:74). Salted pork was preferred over fresh pork when used for meals. Eschewing fresh pork stemmed from its association with food-born illness and pigs' tendency to live in filth and eat garbage (Davis 1989:202).

The consumption of new types of foods in upper privy deposit at 472 Pearl Street and deposits from the Irish and Irish American households in Paterson indicate learned behaviors and new meanings of food presentation and consumption. Similar to the changes in tableware and serving forms, change takes place in the faunal assemblage once it becomes part of the daily lives of the Irish and Irish American community, and when this happens many of the older patterns seen at the Five Points are replaced by the new ones that resemble non-Irish, American assemblages.

The lower privy deposits for both tenements at the Five Points (ca. 1850–1860s) represent recently arrived Irish immigrants. The percentage of meat in their daily diet presents a new pattern of a consumer culture. Meat did not form the foundation of the Irish rural poor's diet. The potato was a staple in the diet of all classes in Ireland, but for the some of the poor it was the sole means of nutrition (Kennedy et al. 1999:70; Kinealy 1995:87; Scally 1995:123). Potatoes were eaten at two and sometimes three meals, with each person consuming on average 8 to 15 pounds a day. Although potatoes were sometimes accompanied by milk, the common way of eating them was simply to dip them in salt and water with pepper flavoring.

Potatoes were consumed every day in Ireland, but for most of the small farmers and cottiers it was not the only food. They ate oats during the months between potato harvests. Oatmeal was prepared by adding it to boiling water to form a porridge called "stirabout" (Póirtéir 1995:85). It was seldom eaten in the west of Ireland but was common in the diet in counties of Cavan and Longford and west to Donegal (Kennedy et al. 1999:69, 71; Kinealy 1995:87).

Meat was never part of the tenant farming family's daily meals. Meat was a luxury item; only inexpensive cuts of beef and pork were prepared, and even then only for special occasions and holidays (Kennedy et al. 1999:74; Langan-Egan 1999:21). Along the coast, the poor were able to supplement their diet with fish.

The availability of meat had an enormous impact on the immigrant group after the experience of the Famine, and therefore meals and the daily serving of meat had an additional social importance (Mintz 1996:4). Unlike the American meat consumption of beef and chicken, the newly arrived Irish consumed predominantly pork in the form of ham hocks and pigs feet (Milne and Crabtree 2000:181, 188). Beef and sheep are present in the assemblages, but in small numbers and in the cheapest cuts. The sheep remains, for example, are mostly from the shank end of older animals or mutton. There is little difference in the faunal assemblage between the earlier deposits from both tenements and the later dating upper deposit at 472 Pearl Street, with the exception of a slight rise in cuts of beef (Milne and Crabtree 2000:181).

A change in the dietary patterns of Irish and Irish American families occurs by the last decade of the nineteenth century, when there is a shift in the types of meat consumed. This pattern begins to resemble the dietary pattern of non-Irish Americans, specifically in the consumption of beef and chicken. Based on the recovered faunal remains, the Mackel family consumed more beef and lamb, rather than pork and mutton. Pork represents less than 7 percent of the entire faunal assemblage (O'Steen 1999:9). Slightly different, but remaining in the context of American food consumption pattern, is the McGill family. This family had a higher percentage of poultry, predominantly chicken, with less amounts of beef and lamb (O'Steen 1999:9).

The gradual acceptance of new consumer patterns and incorporation is indicative of practice into action. The developing complexity of ceramic and glass forms in conjunction with the introduction of new and different foods is the evidence of learning and accepting of new cultural patterns that replaced many of the traditional patterns (Mintz 1996). It is important to stress that this process has to be negotiated within the larger social structure, and cultural transformations were directly related to the degree of alienation. While the ceramics, glass, and faunal remains point toward a transition from old to new cultural patterns, other artifacts found in the same archaeological context reveal the marginalization of Irish immigrants stemming from moral judgments of class and ethnicity and manifested through hygiene and the public health system.

Medicinal Bottles, Temperance, and Father Mathew

> The tenement house [has formed] practically the only kind of habitation for the great mass of people [and] the tenement house system has become fraught with much danger to the welfare of the community. They are centers of disease, poverty, vice, and crime. From the tenements there comes a stream of sick, helpless people to our hospitals and dispensaries, few of whom are able to afford the luxury of a private

> physician, and some houses are in such bad sanitary condition that few people can be seriously ill in them and get well. The most terrible of all features of the tenement house life in New York however is the indiscriminate herding of all kinds of people in close contact, the fact that mingled with the drunken, dissolute, and improvident, [and] the diseased, dwell the great mass of the respectable working-men of the city and their families. (DeForest and Veiller 1970:10)

The above quote is from Robert DeForest and Lawrence Veiller's 1903 volume *The Tenement House Problem.* Their work as health and housing reformers made a significant contribution to public housing and health reform in New York state. Aside from the vivid description of disease and horrid conditions with which the Irish and other immigrant groups struggled on a daily basis, what is most interesting is that reformers and champions of the marginalized perpetuated American Victorian ideals regarding the desirable and undesirable poor. While the reformers began to look toward the conditions of the tenements and overcrowding, they nevertheless implied that disease equaled a deserved lower status and ignorance and had more to do with a *chosen* life-style than conditions created by absentee landlords and uncaring municipal health officials.

The concept of *agency* is at the center of the argument. Reformers believed that tenement dwellers had a *choice* and that the failure to be healthy was a matter of personal social and moral defect. Agency and the implications of moral and social failing have remained debated topics in the study of health care (Gans 1995). The question remains, if access and knowledge to proper health care practices is a simple matter of choice, why would anyone *choose* to live in abject poverty, in an unsanitary environment exposed daily to fatal diseases? That is the question most reformers and scholars of public health would ask, and the answer is complex in its simplicity: Most people do not have a choice or are denied access to proper health care facilities (Brighton 2005, 2008).

It is obvious that access to sanitation and public health in working-class immigrant neighborhoods was a financial matter and had nothing to do with any choice (Blackmar 1995). The surrounding street conditions were vastly different from those in middle-class enclaves. For years, reporters and reformers describe the streets of immigrant ghettoes as being piled as high as two to three feet with accumulated garbage (Anbinder 2001:83). Municipal policies on street cleaning were not enforced in immigrant communities until the late 1850s, and even then street cleaning was not a regular occurrence, except during cholera outbreaks (Moehring 1981). From the streets and walkways, the filth and the contents of overflowing sewage was carried throughout the hallways and apartments by the inhabitants and visitors, further spreading disease. Because absentee landlords refused to pay to have their tenements fitted for running water and sewage lines, they denied those living in the tenements access to clean water (Condran 1995:35–37). While all back courtyards were outfitted with a well or cistern accessing ground water or rainwater, wells or cisterns often became contaminated by neighboring privies leaking into or overflowing into them, and garbage from backyard industries was sometimes deposited into the tenements' only source of fresh water (Blackmar 1995:53–60).

Although health care and the spread of disease remained class-based issues, ethnicity was also a contentious obstacle for Irish immigrants seeking proper and necessary health care (Brighton 2005). Simply stated, much of the alienation of the Irish by the American public and the medical profession was because they were Irish Catholic (Blackmar 1995; Condran 1995; Kraut 1995, 1996).

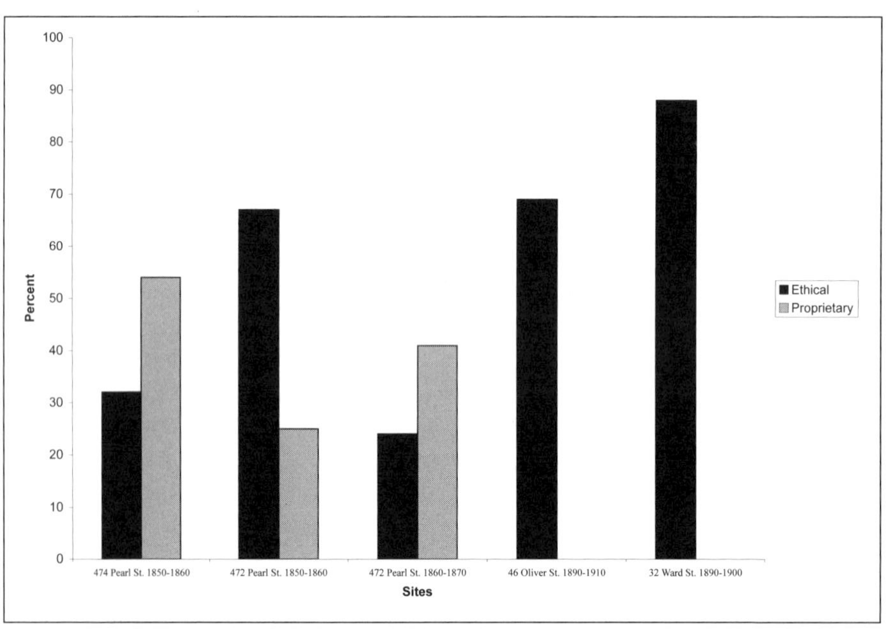

Figure 30. The distribution of ethical and proprietary medicine bottles from the Irish immigrant tenements at the Five Points, Manhattan, and the Irish and Irish American households at the Dublin section, Paterson, New Jersey.

Archaeological studies of public health and hygiene should prioritize the establishment of a historical context, including the social values placed on health care. To date, most historical archaeologists have not followed this direction (with the exception of Beaudry 1993; Milne 2000; Mrozowski et al. 1996). Jean Howson (1992–1993) has concluded in her study of a nineteenth-century middle-class family and working-class tenement that interest in health and hygiene was exclusively the pursuit of the middle and upper classes, or those aspiring to the middle class. Personal cleanliness was found to ward off disease and served as a badge of refinement and gentility, and therefore there is little question that class membership profoundly affected access to basis innovations to sanitation. In short, health care was a matter of financial means (Howson 1992–1993:142–143, 154).

The ethical and proprietary medicinal bottles in the Irish immigrant and Irish American data attest to the struggles each community faced because of the unsanitary housing conditions and the physical stresses of exploitation through manual labor. More important, the differences in percentages between ethical and proprietary bottles in each of the Five Points and Dublin section assemblages reflect the degree of conflict with and alienation from America's health-care professionals (Brighton 2008:143–147). In short, the predominance of proprietary medicines indicates that Irish immigrants were alienated from the health-care system and forced to self-medicate (Figure 30).

In all of the deposits at the Five Points, proprietary cure-alls for cholera were the most common. The most relevant cure-all product, or at least the one marketed to recently arrived Irish immigrants as such, was Dr. Townsend's Sarsaparilla (Fike 1987:135). The product was marketed as "the cure for ship fever associated with the Irish crossing." An ad from the *New York Daily Tribune* (1847) stated,

> That this disease is contagious there can now be no doubt and is spreading throughout the city. It is the duty of everyone as well as the authorities to guard against it. Dr. Townsend's sarsaparilla will prevent ship fever. If the blood is pure and healthy it is impossible to take this fever or any other. Let all such as have impure blood or are in any way debilitated and especially weakly children, take the sarsaparilla and protect them from the pestilence and the hot season before it is too late. (Quoted in Hogan 1999:174)

By the end of the 1860s there was a preponderance of proprietary medicine bottles in comparison to ethical bottles. This is at a time when it appears the presence of different ceramic and glass tea, table, and serving vessels reflect a gradual move toward acceptance and incorporation. The increase in proprietary medicines, however, indicates a departure from American medical institutions.

In theory, Irish tenement dwellers had access to free medical assistance from the local charitable dispensary or voluntary hospital. Unfortunately, the stigma of illness caused by being Irish and Catholic increased after the 1860s. The large number of proprietary bottles from the upper deposit of Feature J at 472 Pearl Street are associated with Irish immigrant families who had been in America for over 10 years and no doubt had experienced alienation from the medical community.

A stirring pattern from Figure 30 is from the earliest deposit from 472 Pearl Street, which has the most ethical bottles in the Five Points data, a pattern matched only in the 1890s data from Paterson. This pattern is also remarkable when compared to a contemporary American-born assemblage (Figure 31). The large number of ethical bottles from the tenement data may rest on a few factors. First, the tenement was inhabited at this time by many families of semiskilled class. Occupations such

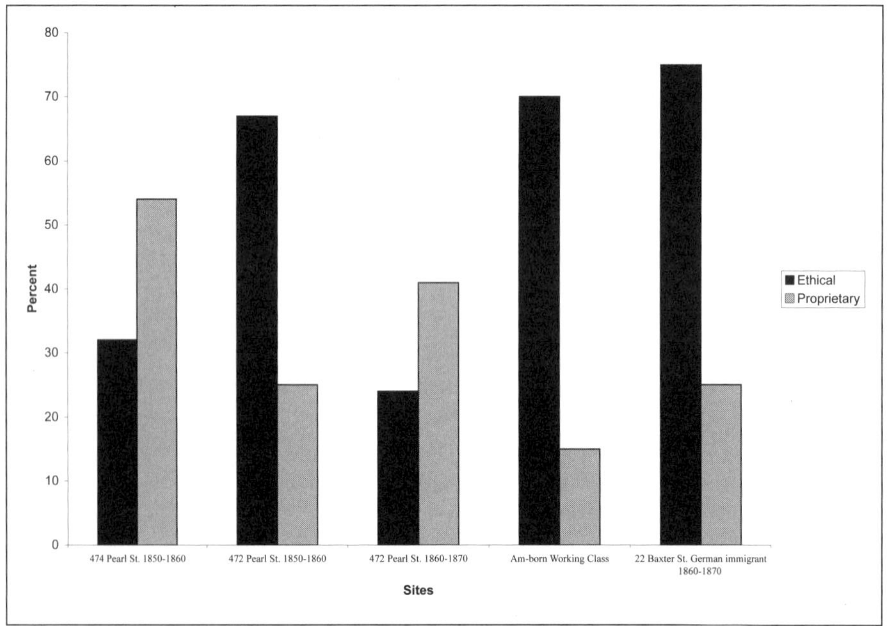

Figure 31. The distribution of ethical and proprietary medicine bottles from the Irish immigrant tenements at the Five Points compared with an American-born household from the Greenwich Mews and a German immigrant household from the Five Points.

as shoemaker, blacksmith, and tinsmith are listed, and these jobs would have been constituted somewhat respectable employment among the working class. It is possible that the recently arrived Irish immigrants sought out the aid of the local dispensary during times of serious illness because they could afford to do so. Second, there were approximately 74 to 107 people living in the tenement between 1850 and 1860; the smaller tenement at 474 Pearl Street averaged 20 to 24 residents. The large population living in close quarters and cramped conditions with no ventilation would have been a breeding ground for disease exposure and transmission.

A report of the committee on immigration to New York in 1852 reported that a great number of Irish immigrants attended a dispensary at least once within four years of their arrival (New York State Assembly Document No. 34 1903:612). Dispensaries treated 28,875 Irish in 1850 (over 50% of the total patients) (New York State Assembly 1925:612). At the time of their arrival, the Irish were not aware of the harsh treatment they would receive from American doctors, who often judged them unworthy of medical attention. American physicians did not help the situation by creating an environment that was "grossly inadequate to handle the large numbers of immigrants arriving . . . [and] was no better at times than Almshouses" (Cassedy 1986:37). Along with treatment for ailments, dispensaries also offered advice on health and hygiene. It is unclear what the advice would entail, but based on the sentiments of the American public and physicians toward the Irish, it assuredly focused on their lack of moral virtues. Those Irish experiencing the process of being labeled worthy or unworthy firsthand may not have wished to repeat the experience.

Stigmas and stereotypes correlating disease with being Irish Catholic increased steadily throughout the 1860s. The large number of commercial bottles from the upper deposit of a large privy at 472 Pearl Street associated with Irish immigrant families living in America for over 10 years reflects this social history (Brighton 2008:145–147). The level of alienation becomes clearer when the medicinal data is compared to the large number of ethical bottles associated with an American-born assemblage at the Greenwich Mews, located northwest of the Five Points, and a German immigrant family located at the Five Points (Geismar 1989; Yamin 2000a, 2000b) (Figure 32). The German data is comparable to that of the American born and a far cry from that of the Irish. The difference is all the more striking when one considers that both groups were living in the same slumlike conditions. Although the number of medicinal bottle is quite low in comparison to other artifact groups recovered from the Five Points, the ratio between ethical and commercially prepared medicines is telling as to the dominant's society's views on ethnicity and religion. As a group, Germans were considered nonthreatening for many reasons, the most important one being that they were Protestant, as a racial or ethnic group they were considered to be thrifty and "more cleanly and orderly in their living habits," and that they arrived to America with skilled professions and a degree of financial stability (Ernst 1994:54; Ward 1989:51). This stark contrast illustrates the social impact of a dominant group's classifications of difference.

The medicinal bottles from the Dublin section reflect a very different relationship with American society in general and the medical profession in particular. Dublin did not offer the best living conditions; outbreaks of disease occurred throughout the last half of the nineteenth century because of contaminated water sources. The residents of Dublin suffered from common issues of fetid standing water and leaking and overflowing privies, whereas in American-born, Protestant, and wealthier parts of the city there was indoor plumbing and running water.

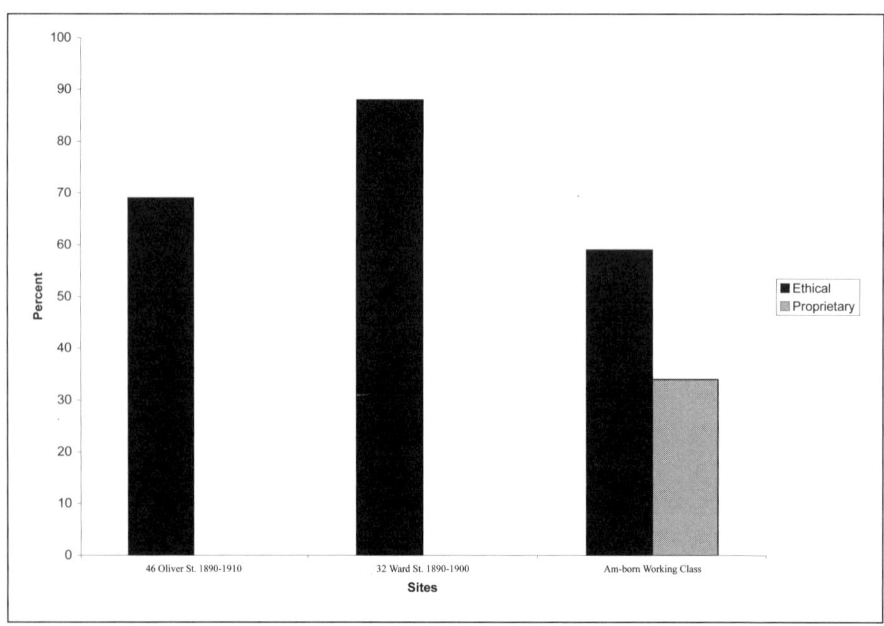

Figure 32. The distribution of ethical and proprietary medicine bottles associated with the McGill and Mackel households and a contemporary American-born working-class household at the Dublin section, Paterson, New Jersey.

Figure 32 shows a high percentage of ethical medicinal bottles. The absence of proprietary bottles in combination with the strong presence of ethical bottles suggests that the Mackel and McGill households relied on the aid of physicians (Brighton 2008:147–150). This shift parallels that of the acquisition of austere white granite tea, table, and serving pieces. The act of visiting a physician may have been an indication and reflection of how these families viewed their social positions in America and an outward communication of inclusion, worthiness, respectability, and citizenship. That they could afford to see a doctor, as well as have some of the material possessions associated with American popular culture, demonstrates their active incorporation into American society.

It is unknown whether they received medical care through a dispensary or a private doctor. The importance of this rests on the fact that neither the Mackel nor McGill families were self-medicating. In a broader historical context, the reason they may have been able to see a doctor reflects the changing policies toward and views of Irish Americans at the close of the century. A major impetus for this shift was the focus of America's prejudice away from the Irish and toward the influx of new immigrant groups, especially Eastern European groups and Chinese. As the focus shifted, the stereotypes of Irish Catholics dissipated (Kraut 1996:167–168).

This process began at the Five Points and was exemplified through the formation of Irish Catholic temperance movements. The most interesting vessel in the Five Points assemblage is a teacup with a transfer-printed pattern depicting Father Mathew (Figure 33). The importance of transfer-printed patterns lies in the specific meaning of the images to those who acquire them. In fact, the meaning be the sole reason for obtaining the item(s). The symbolism on this teacup reflects both a reaction to being alienated from the American health-care system and a transnational consciousness of home and country combined with the social values of temperance, individuality, and hard work, all associated with American Victorian society.

The teacup depicting Father Mathew was recovered from the lower deposit at 472 Pearl Street. The exterior design of the teacup shows Father Theobald Mathew preaching to a flock of devoted followers as part of the larger ritual of "taking the pledge," a simple declaration to abstain from all intoxicating drinks except when dictated by medical necessity (Mathew 1890:35). In 1838, Father Theobald Mathew, an Irish priest of the Capuchin order, accepted the presidency of Cork Total Abstinence Movement in Ireland. His main objective was to eliminate intemperance from the poor and working-class communities and to

Figure 33. Father Mathew teacup recovered from the privy (Feature J) at 472 Pearl Street, Five Points. (Courtesy of the General Services Administration and John Milner Associates.)

help people to better themselves spiritually, emotionally, and physically (Meagher 2001:162). Father Mathew became known as a healer because those who took the pledge, once sick with alcohol poisoning, looked healthier when they stopped drinking (Maguire 1864:113). Mathew's message of abstinence implored people to think of their personal health and the health of their families and to "free themselves from the bondage of a degrading and deadly habit" (Maguire 1864:111). Through his influence, many in Ireland took the pledge. Within a year of his tenure, 230,000 people had pledged sobriety (Quinn 1996:625).

A beehive appears inside the teacup along the upper edge. Busy worker bees fly above the hive, and a shovel, hoe, and rake rests on the ground. The words "Temperance and Industry" appear above the hive, and "Industry Pays Debts" appear below it (Figure 34). The symbolism on this teacup draws from the philosophies and actions of Father Mathew and constitutes a large campaign of the American Catholic Church to combat not only the evils of alcohol but also the associated socially and economically debilitating negative stereotypes of the Irish flourishing in mainstream American society.

Figure 34. Interior of Father Mathew teacup recovered from the privy (Feature J) at 472 Pearl Street, Five Points. (Courtesy of the General Services Administration and John Milner Associates.)

To combat what was considered the moral decay of the country, Protestant members of the middle and upper classes, as early as the 1820s, formed temperance organizations. Although the organizations comprised different Protestant factions, their philosophy was similar in that they all agreed on the prohibition of alcohol to achieve and reinforce their sense of morality, piety, and respectability (Boyer 1978; Goodman 1994; Gusfield 1986; Quinn 1996). The latter was in direct relation to the thousands of Catholic immigrants landing daily on American shores. These organizations were mostly anti-immigrant and anti-Catholic. Contained in their philosophy and public outreach programs, aside from ridding alcohol from immigrant and working poor communities, was to rid themselves of the Catholic presence through conversion. These organizations heightened tensions between Irish Catholic immigrants and native-born, nationalist Americans as it presented a social and economic obstacle for many of the immigrant poor. To combat this prejudicial social movement, the American Roman Catholic Church organized their Catholic immigrant parishioners into their own temperance benevolent organizations.

By 1840, Catholic temperance organizations had formed to counter the highly publicized link between alcohol and the immoral life-style of Irish Catholics. The American Catholic Church perceived this course of action as necessary to break down the social and economic barriers created by the racialized stereotypes of the "drunken paddy" (Quinn 1996:624). The interests of the church rested with the theory that the church's position, power, and influence would grow through the social acceptance of its parishioners in mainstream American society.

The various temperance movements were inspired by the movement in Ireland lead by Father Mathew. In 1840, an Irish-born bishop, Francis Patrick Kenrick, established the first U.S. Irish Catholic temperance society in Philadelphia (Quinn 1996:625). He initiated the work by sending letters to all parishes demanding each establish their own temperance society similar to that created by Father Mathew. Initial temperance meetings in the Philadelphia area attracted 5,000 pledges (Quinn 1996:625). Soon after, Catholic temperance societies quickly emerged in other urban areas, including Washington, DC, Baltimore, Boston, and New York City.

The primary agenda behind the Catholic temperance movement in the United States was to secure a footing for Catholicism in the United States. The Catholic Church thought it vital to present the religion, which was a reflection of its parishioners, as part of mainstream American society. Leaders of the church argued that Catholicism was not different in its philosophy and goals from Protestant denominations and, based on the tenets of the Constitution and religious freedom, should be considered an American institution (Abell 1952:291). By bringing their faith on par with that of American Protestantism, it was argued that all Catholics should have the same rights of citizenship, with the added process that Catholic immigrant parishioners needed to undergo the process and education of "Americanization" (Diner 1996:103).

In order to succeed in its quest for power, the Catholic Church had to socially and culturally reconfigure its flock in order for its parishioners to be viewed from the outside as productive and respectable American citizens. To achieve this goal, the church demanded a shift away from Irish traditional notions of communal bonds and pushed for individualism, independence, and the concepts of land ownership, private property, success through individualism, temperance, and hard work (Miller 1985:332–333). In New York City, Archbishop John Hughes actively discouraged various outward expressions of what he considered traditional Irish behaviors from the newly arrived in order to assuage nativist feelings (Diner 1996:103; Meagher 2001:152). The Catholic Church believed that Americans' negative perception of Irish immigrants could change if the immigrants were seen as sober and healthy parishioners.

At the behest of Bishop Kenrick, Father Mathew came to the United States in 1849. Kenrick's hope was that his presence would provide the momentum to bring Irish Catholic immigrants into the fold and adopt a new identity blending traditional Catholic piety with a love for modern views of American morality (Diner 1996:103). Father Mathew's visit did have an impact on numerous Irish Catholic communities. The movement, however, did not inspire American sentiments; instead it blended Catholic piety with Irish nationalist fervor. Charles Dickens ([1842] 1985:207–208) noted during his tour of the United States that he attended a Father Mathew rally in Cincinnati. He commented that the crowd was "largely Irish immigrants . . . a distinct society among themselves, and mustered very strong with their green scarves; their national Harp and their Portrait of Father Mathew." Upon his departure in 1851, Father Mathew claimed to have administered the pledge to 600,000 individuals (Quinn 1996:627).

At the Five Points, Father Felix Varela created a temperance league at the Transfiguration Church, located a few blocks northeast of 427 Pearl Street. Father Varela was known as the "Vicar-General of the Irish," and his temperance association grew to include 1,000 men, most of whom were Irish Catholics from the Five Points. Father Varela saw it as his responsibility to create the league when he witnessed the "health of his flock diminished due to the ravages of alcohol" (Transfiguration Church 1977:8). Varela invited Father Mathew to visit the Five Points and speak to the parishioners of the Transfiguration Church. He hoped the visit would refresh the people's "personal worth and dignity" (Transfiguration Church 1977:8). Although invited, historians do not know whether Father Mathew actually made the visit. He is recorded to have lectured to a large crowd at City Hall within blocks of the Irish immigrant neighborhood, however (Maguire 1864:462).

At the time of the church's temperance movement and after Father Mathew's visit, only nine tenants associated with the Transfiguration Church were listed at 472 Pearl Street. Church records list tenants such as John Judge and John Herring as parishioners, but these men do not appear in the census data, reflecting the transient demographics of tenement life. The Father Mathew teacup may have belonged to one of the nine parishioners from the tenement, or it is quite possible, given the date range of the maker's mark (ca. 1820–ca. 1840), that it could have been brought from Ireland. Unfortunately, because of the large number of people residing in the tenement, some being transient, any definitive statement as to the ownership of the teacup is problematic. Its presence reflects at least one household's or individual's attempt to communicate self-worth through the ideals of temperance and, more important, to do so through an Irish Catholic organization.

The exact meaning of the beehive, however, is somewhat more complex. William Adams and his factory produced other nontemperance transfer-printed patterns with the same beehive image. Instead of being surrounded by agricultural tools, the beehive was a central element in an idyllic rural landscape (Coysch and Henrywood 1982:37). In this case it seems the beehive is one of Adam's trademark designs and means nothing more but to be aesthetically pleasing. In the context of Father Mathew and other elements such as the agricultural tools, the image has other implications. Throughout history the beehive image has been used as a symbol for industry. The agricultural tools lying beside only serve to reinforce the ideals of hard work. The underlying ideology of the symbols rests with the idea of many bees assigned a different task but coming together for the good of the collective. This is at the core of the ideology espoused by the American Catholic Church. In short, the parishioners involved in the movement were to come together for the common cause of upholding and maintaining the philosophical and ideological foundations of the American Catholic Church, and as such uplift themselves in mainstream America.

The symbolism on this teacup not only reflects a reaction to being alienated from much of mainstream American society but also points toward the sustaining transnational consciousness of Irish immigrants. In order for the Irish to establish themselves in America, they had to come together as a group to struggle against the social stigma of being the foreign other. American newspapers labeled the Famine Irish as "culturally conservative," with a strong need to "clan together content to live together in filth and disorder" (Miller 1985:326). Kerby Miller (1985:134) has argued that the Irish in the mid-nineteenth century were in "a transition between traditional and modern patterns of thinking and behaving" that conflicted with American social behaviors of individualism. The formation of a somewhat cohesive Irish identity in the United States was a complex process bringing together thousands of people connected by a persistent sense of similitude. This was structured around commonalities of ethnicity, religion, and nationalism that were given social relevance through selected symbols, not necessarily looking back to a historical memory so much as forward to the possibilities and existing hard-won benefits in the new place of settlement. It was done on their own terms through the contradiction of blending traditional ways of community along with the new Industrial ideology of individualism

Irish communities in the United States developed a unified heritage through the shared experience of colonialism and exile. At the same time, they sought to combat the prejudice and enforced racialization they encountered as they were marginalized and categorized as inferior to "white" Protestant America (Ignatiev 1995; Roediger 1991). Irish Americans thus created a single Irish identity through the careful use of symbols that served as badges of ethnicity. They used such metaphoric devices to express a civilized and rational heritage to counter demeaning American stereotypes (Ní Bhroiméil 2003:31).

What is particularly relevant here is that continuity of a symbol's meaning may evoke the sense of a shared heritage and so reinforce traditional social behaviors and values. Producers and users of material culture imbue the objects with meanings that are historically, culturally, and even situationally significant. Accordingly, an object's multiple meanings can be contested. According to Fredrick Barth (2000:31), "People use multiple images and perform a multiplicity of operations as they grope for an understanding of the world and fit them to the particular context of events and lives reconstructing their models as they harvest the experiences that ensue." Social groups may assign identity-rich meanings on the basis of what they consider ideal (McCracken 1988:106–108). Consumer goods have the potential to be used to allow people to think nationally. Consumers render the objects meaningful. The objects have no preexisting appeal, but manufacturers can capitalize on their appeal after the assumed meanings have been established (Foster 1999:265). The objects thus become the materialization of a specific sentiment or world view and are used by manufacturers to commercialize ethnic pride and a cultural heritage (Kemper 1993:393; Sissons 1997:184).

Heritage formation is a process of constant reevaluation of meaning, as immigrants collectively experience the new social relations of their locales of resettlement. The invention and management of an ethnic or national heritage constitutes part of fluid, multifaceted, and subjective social process (Brighton and Orser 2006b). Individuals imbue heritage with meaning through the social relations created in reference to shared cultural codes, symbols, and history (Brah 1996:21, 47; Fortier 1998; Hall 1990:223; Panagakos 1998; Panossian 1998a, 1998b). The created heritage can be true or false, justified or illegitimate, and can be manipulated to make sense of the world and to define and reshape values (Barth 2000:31; Mohanty 2000:32, 43). Heritage is thus a form of "self-knowledge" that provides a sense of place and reinforces the emotional significance attached to membership (Ashmore et al. 2001; Bhabha 1994; Comaroff and Comaroff 1992; Payne 2000:2; Tajfel 1981; Woodward 1997).

The life history of the Father Mathew cup did not end at the time of deposition into the privy. The very act of throwing it away offered possible reflections of social relations, and its presence at the privy's depths may be just as revealing as it symbolic meaning during its use. The cup was found at the lowest stratagraphic level, dating to the 1860s. The location in the privy suggests it may have been discarded earlier than the thousands of vessels resting above it. What is more important is that the cup was mended to nearly complete condition, indicating it was most likely thrown away complete as opposed to being discarded fragments of a broken cup. It may never be known who owned the teacup, for what purposes, and how it came to be at the bottom of a privy, but the timing is provocative in that it does coincide with the time of, or really after, Father Mathew's visit to New York City. Could it be related to his possible avoidance of the Five Points and the turmoil of the movement's failure to bring social and economic advancement to those Irish parishioners espousing the Catholic ideology?

Within a decade of Father Mathew's American tour, Irish participation in Catholic temperance societies steadily declined in importance and ceased altogether by 1860. The main reason was that the American Catholic Church lacked the necessary material and economic resources to fulfill the expectations of acceptance and social mobility to its Irish constituents (Abell 1952:299). At the onset of the Civil War, Irish Catholic communities, abstaining from alcohol or not, were not faring much better socially or economically through participation in temperance organizations. It was not until the last decades of the nineteenth century that the American Catholic Church matured and established a firm socioeconomic foothold in which to provide the necessary education, training, and employment opportunities necessary to create an Irish or Irish American middle class (Doyle 2006; Whelan 2006).

The cup's position within the privy speaks this possibility. It may also reflect the reaction to the overall failure of the first Irish Catholic temperance movement and the realization of the uphill battle of intolerance and alienation facing Irish immigrants. The Irish at the Five Points remained at the lowest end of the economic spectrum, as did most Irish Catholics. It was not until the last decades of the nineteenth century that the Catholic Church reached a level of acceptance, prominence, and power in American society, and with that, there was a slow change in the socioeconomic status of Irish and Irish American communities.

By century's end, in areas such as the Dublin section, first-generation Irish Americans were incorporating more American ideals, along with the ideals of education and upward mobility (Shannon 1963:114–117). Opportunities and economic betterment is evident at the Dublin section. It is most likely that both the political clout and the social, cultural, and economic support of the Catholic Church were the most influential factors in bringing about this shift in social position. In Paterson, most Irish American children were enrolled in school well past the age at which Irish immigrant children from the Five Points had typically been sent out to work. Improved living conditions and the extended education available to the children marked a turning point in the history of the Irish in America.

As noted, it is unknown where the Mackels and McGills received medical care. It is likely that both families' health was looked after by the local hospital founded by the Catholic Church. St. John's Church was built in 1867 on Oliver Street, and soon after its construction the Sisters of Charity built St. Joseph's Hospital (Quinn 2004:93, 115). In a broader historical context, the reason the Mackels and McGills may have been able to see a doctor reflects the changing policies toward and views of social and cultural identities Irish Americans and the Catholic Church at the close of the century. A major impetus for this shift was the Irish themselves and their struggle to fit into American society. At the same time, America might have been ready to tolerate the Irish by the last decades of the nineteenth century as its attention moved away from existing immigrants groups and concentrated the new "threats" to America, namely, the influx of the radically different, non-English-speaking immigrant groups from the Mediterranean, Eastern Europe, and Asia. The shift in acceptance by century's end is further evidenced by the waning negative cartoons of and commentary on Irish Catholics in such media as *Harper's Weekly* and *Puck* (Kraut 1996:167–168).

Like the changes happening in the ceramic, glass, and faunal data, the ratio of ethical to proprietary medicinal bottles illustrate the degree of alienation from, and in the case of the Paterson assemblage, a gradual incorporation into American society. Yet at the same time, the Irish combated illness and disease and moral judgments and negotiated their tenuous position as immigrants and eventually citizens without losing a sense of their past. The Father Mathew cup reflects an Irish Catholic discourse on temperance and a double consciousness of being Irish and being involved in issues of American social movements. This transnational identity of being loyal to Ireland through movements and causes in America are further illustrated through ethnic and political symbolism on white ball clay smoking pipes.

Symbols of Immigrant and Citizen

Although the Irish rural poor classes and Irish proletariat immigrants were alienated from most social and economic opportunities, their experience was not altogether negative. Both groups used their low social position strategically to form a cohesive group to negotiate their social and political relations. In pre-Famine Ireland resistance centered on repealing the Penal Laws and the Act of Union and fighting for Catholic emancipation. The fragment of a pipe bowl with the remnants of the stamped slogan REPEAL from the Nary assemblage reflects the longstanding resistance of the small farming tenants. This resistance led ultimately to the rent strike, the assassination of Mahon, and mass evictions.

Individuals in the Irish proletarian diaspora were powerful actors in manipulating and creating Irish organizations in America. An interesting aspect of these diasporic social organizations was their shifting approaches to and sentiment toward their "in between" status as citizen and immigrant (Brighton 2004). The American and Irish symbolism on the clay smoking pipes found within the same archaeological context reveal that the Irish were always conscious of the delicate and subjective positions between their homeland and adopted country. The main organizations expressing their transnationalism were the Fenian movement, the Land League, American Democratic Party, and American labor unions (Brighton 2004).

The major militant organization was the Fenian Brotherhood. The Irish nationalist benevolent organization grew out of the oppression and inequality in Ireland, the Famine, and forced exile (Garvin 1986). The goal of the organizations was to free Ireland through armed conflict. The name, created by John O'Mahony, was meant as a bonding agent, reflecting Ireland's mythical and ancient golden age (Comerford 1998:53; de Nie 2001:215). Its purpose was to inspire Irish immigrants and Irish Americans by instilling a sense of pride in their deep historical roots (Garvin 1986:471). The organization's symbol was the ancient Celtic harp.

The Celtic harp is synonymous with the Republic of Ireland. It was selected as the state emblem upon the establishment of the Irish Free State and became the official Presidential Standard in 1945. The harp's first use as a symbol of freedom was by the United Irishmen in the late

1790s. It formed the centerpiece on the United Irishmen's green flag, without the royal crown, which was flown during the failed rebellion in 1798. Since then, and prior to establishing the Irish Free State, the harp was considered to represent the negative ideas of rebellion and was banned in Ireland. But by midcentury, the symbol was revived and flown in defiance by the Irish Republican Brotherhood and used by the Irish American Fenian Brotherhood (Comerford 1998; Dooley 2003).

The most common symbol recovered from the deposits at the Five Points tenements was the Celtic harp. At the time of the American Civil War, the Fenian Brotherhood formed military regiments in New York to fight for the Union with the plan of eventually liberating Ireland (Miller 1985). Archbishop Hughes was quoted as saying that "many of the enlistees were becoming thoroughly acquainted with the implements of war for the liberation of their homeland" (Spann 1996:194–195). The most notable were the 63rd and 69th New York Regiments; the latter was led by Michael Corcoran, who was one of the leading figures in the Fenian movement (Spann 1996:194). The flag of both regiments incorporated the Celtic harp.

In the nineteenth century Irish nationalism was enmeshed with the Democratic Party and labor unions. The dual nature of transnationalism was an outward expression of a diasporic group's loyalty to its adopted country. American symbolism recovered from the same stratigraphic context as the Irish symbolism suggests the communication of that transnationalism and the developing sense of an American identity (Allen 1993; Kertzer 1988; Knobel 1986; Miller 1985). The American symbolism found on pipe bowls at the Five Points is a direct reflection of the Democratic Party. The sheer numbers of Irish immigrants between 1850 and 1870 at the Five Points created a viable voting force ensuring them a voice in local politics (Anbinder 2001, 2003; Ernst 1994; Gilje 1987; Homeberger 1994; Mushkat 1981; Pitts 2000; Reckner 2000). Archbishop John Hughes, a native of County Tyrone, was one of the first to realize the power of and to organize the Irish vote in New York City (Mushkat 1981:201–203). Although most politically appointed positions for the Irish were at the low end as local ward bosses and aldermen, by the 1870s Irish-born politicians controlled much of the city's voting block.

The symbolism from the Five Points reflects dual loyalties of nationalism within the Irish immigrant community. On one hand the Irish maintained strong ties to Ireland and supported the country's liberation through supporting armed conflict. The militant approach, however, was at odds with popular American sentiment and only furthered mistrust of Irish Catholics. On the other hand, the Irish were emerging as a powerful voting block, and some were moving up the ranks of the Democratic Party. They needed to mobilize symbols of loyalty to America to develop political platforms that reinforced this. The Irish therefore altered the manner in which they presented themselves to the American public. By the1890s, Irish nationalism in America was disassociated with secret societies and was expressed through the Celtic mythology of ancient warriors.

Irish Americans expressed a deeper sense of historical experience and attachment to Ireland by the last decade of the nineteenth century. The symbolism on the smoking pipes reflects the broader sociopolitical history transpiring both in Ireland and America (Brighton 2004). More specifically, pipes with the Red Hand of Ulster symbol are interpreted here as illustrating a new sense of Irish American identity drawing from the mythical origins of Ireland and the golden age of Irish history.

Today, the Red Hand of Ulster is associated with the tensions between loyalists and nationalists in Northern Ireland and commonly associated with the former and more times than not the focal point of Loyalist murals. To Loyalists, the Red Hand stands for Protestant ascendancy and allegiance to Great Britain (Rolston and Shannon 2002; Tanner 2001). The Red Hand became the official symbol for all of Ulster when James I created the Order of Baronets in the seventeenth century (Miller 1985:19). It is usually paired with the symbol of the crown and/or the Star of David. The former symbol represents loyalty to the British monarchy, while the latter is thought to symbolize the six counties of Northern Ireland, each represented by a point of the star.

The Red Hand of Ulster has been and is still being used as a nationalist symbol. It is part of the O'Neill crest and represents all nine counties of Ulster. The O'Neill clan, of all the Gaelic clans, was the most resistant to English invasion. The Red Hand is also on the flag of County Tyrone.

Explanations for the origins of the symbol are numerous, and each story is used to communicate the extensive history of Ireland prior to colonialism. Most histories surround King Hugh O'Neill. The first tells simply of O'Neill adopting the hand as his heraldic symbol after seeing it on a Monasterboice high cross, still standing today in County Louth. The hand on the cross symbolizes the powerful hand of God. The two remaining O'Neill stories are similar in that in each tale the Red Hand of Ulster represents a raised, severed right hand. The stories tell of either Vikings or Scottish clans approaching the coast of Northern Ireland. The land in view is promised to the first man to touch it with his hand or foot. O'Neill is said to have beaten all competition by severing his right hand and throwing it on shore, taking the bloody hand as his heraldic symbol (MacKillop 1998:371).

Pipes with the Red Hand symbol were recovered within the same stratigraphic context as other pipes with Irish nationalist slogans. These include pipes stamped THE GLADSTONE PIPE and HOME RULE (Reckner 1999:148–149). Ethnic solidarities and emotions were especially high among Irish Americans during the Land Wars of 1882. This period marked an upswing in Irish American support for the Irish cause. The Land Wars consisted of both secret societies and violence as well collective social movements such as refusal to pay rents and to shun landlords and land grabbers. Rent strikes and shunning were the most effect tools at this time. Ostracism was such an effective tool in rural Ireland that it was named "boycotting" after Captain Charles Boycott, a land agent of Lord Erne's estate in Mayo (Jordan 1998:165). It was here that the idea of shunning or boycotting was first applied.

The Land League and the Land War created a renewed sense of ethnic identity in America. Drawing from the rural Irish creation of boycott, Irish-dominated labor groups launched successful "labor boycotts" during the 1880s and mixed with them calls for better wages and working conditions in America (McKivigan and Robertson 1996:305). In places such as Worcester, Massachusetts, nationalist spokesmen likened the fight for Irish independence to the ideology of America's struggle for freedom during the American Revolution (Meagher 1986b:79). This phenomenon of strong dual national consciousness began in the late 1880s and emerged in Irish communities throughout the United States, in places such as New York, Philadelphia, St. Louis, San Francisco, and Lowell (Brundage 1996; Clark 1986; Meagher 1986a, 1986b, 2001; Mitchell 1986; Skerret 1986; Towey 1986).

The Irish in Paterson, taking up the Irish nationalist cause and combining it with the struggles for social and political positions in America, were playing an identity game legitimating their position between two different national contexts. Newspapers such as the *Irish World,* one of the first to compare land struggles in Ireland with labor strife in America (Brundage 1996:323), reinforced this concept of dual citizenship. In 1880, Michael Davitt argued in the *Irish World* that fighting for a common cause in Ireland was also an aggressive strike against the feeling of inferiority in America and the Irish in America could gain full status only when Ireland was free (Skerret 1986:127).

At the same time as the Irish ethnic revival in the United States there was a larger revival movement in Ireland, the Gaelic revival, which began in the early 1880s. The goal was to educate the masses and stand for everything that was not English in Ireland in order to rediscover and preserve the true Irish identity. The movement was founded upon the mythology of ancient Celtic heroes. Irish writers such as Douglas Hyde and Eoghan Mac Neil created socially effective myths with moral endings that justified beliefs of and actions toward the advancement of the nationalist movement (Boyce 1996:170; O'Mahony and Delanty 1998:77). Cúchulain, the Celtic warrior-prince, valiant, noble, and willing to sacrifice himself for the good of the people, was resurrected and used as an example of the true Irish nature (MacKillop 1998:373).

The Red Hand of Ulster is a reflection of the Gaelic revival in the nationalist movement and represents a history of creation and belonging to Ireland (Brighton 2004). This theory is supported by another tobacco pipe recovered from an Irish boardinghouse in the Dublin section. The symbolism molded on the pipe bowl is the national symbol of the Isle of Man—the triskelion.

Irish tradition contends that Finn McCool created the Isle of Man by ripping up a huge sod of earth, creating Lough Neagh, then throwing the clod—the Isle of Man—into the Irish Sea (MacKillop 1998:284). Another tale is of Manannán mac Lir, a principle sea deity who by the tenth century portrayed as a merchant and pilot, who was ruler of Irish and Gaelic tradition and appearing in four of the Ulster cycles. In Irish oral tradition he dwells in the otherworldly realm of Emain Ablach, a mythical place off the coast of Scotland in the Irish Sea thought to be the Isle of Man. In the stories he was known to travel between this realm and Ireland by riding a chariot over the waves as if on solid ground. The pattern of the three legs is believed to symbolize Mac Lir's ability to walk over water (MacKillop 1998:284–285). The myths of the settling and true ownership of Ireland and the creation of all things around Ireland represent a deep-rooted history and sense of identity that far surpasses the established English and Anglo-Irish control.

The Gaelic revival provided a sense of empowerment to those at the lower end of the economic and social scale of both Irish and Irish American society. The symbolism associated with this movement pointed squarely to an ideal time, Ireland's "golden age." In America, benevolent organizations took names from Ireland's preconquest past: the Ancient Order of Hibernians, Clan Na Gael, Irish National Land League, St. Patrick Brotherhood, Knights of Tara, and Knights of the Red Feather Branch. These social and political societies expanded during the Land Wars, flourished throughout the 1890s, and raised the awareness of Irish history and struggles in Ireland (Brundage 1996:321). They also created communal interest in the Gaelic language, history, and sports. In Worcester, Massachusetts, the Irish petitioned to have Irish history entered into the pubic school curricula (Meagher 1986b:86). In essence, the revival provided a basis for a renewed sense of self, the ideal of respectability, and cultural strength (O'Mahony and Delanty 1998:77).

Irish Americans created a shared sense of self, history, and a collective world view based not on firsthand experiences of Ireland but from memories handed down through the generations of Irish immigrants. As a collective, they carefully enmeshed romantic notions of their parents' experiences of injustice in Ireland and America with their own experienced struggles in America (Brighton 2004). By the 1890s, Irish American organizations promoting Irish nationalism were less militant and increasingly linked to American labor organizations (Gutman 1977:58). Labor unions, such as the Holy Order of the Knights of Labor, were quite active in bringing individuals of the Irish working class together for the common cause of equal rights both in the homeland and in America (Miller 1985:524; Voss 1993:75–76).

In Paterson, the *Paterson Labor Standard* was largely responsible for bringing together information about exploitation and promoting the cause of Irish home rule and the Land League. At the height of workers' tensions in Paterson and tenant unrest in Ireland, the article "Ireland and America" was published. It conflating the two issues by stating that "the principles for which the Irish Nationalists are contending are practically the same as those held by the labor reformers in their struggle against capitalistic oppression" (*Paterson Labor Standard,* 22 November 1890). Other Irish American newspapers, such as the *Irish World,* equated the inequalities faced both by tenants in Ireland and working-class Irish/Irish Americans with the experience of enslaved Africans (Bodnar 1985:90, 111). Such rhetoric helped raise a nationalist consciousness within the working-class community, fusing the cause of liberation in Ireland and a democratic ideology in America.

The clay smoking pipes in the Paterson assemblage reflect this period of incorporation. Irish American communities at the end of the nineteenth century were on the cusp of formulating their Americanness within their Irish identities. The shift in symbolism on pipes follows a trajectory that parallels changes in ceramic and glass tea, tableware, and serving pieces and faunal data, as well as the ethical and proprietary medicinal bottles. The symbolism communicates the notion of the golden age, the imagined times in Irish history. The material culture in Paterson provides solid evidence of a new era in the Irish proletarian diaspora and of the incorporation of Irish Americans into American society.

Conclusion

Archaeology of the modern world and material culture studies is vital to the analytical discourse of diaspora studies. The archaeological history of the Irish proletarian diaspora covers one of the most dynamic periods in Ireland and America and documents through the material culture how objects were used and thereby how new social behaviors and values were put into practice and expressed changing conceptions of identity and heritage. The archaeological data spanning the nineteenth century from Ballykilcline, Ireland, two tenement privies at the Five Points, Manhattan, and two single-family deposits from two privies from the Dublin section of Paterson, New Jersey, are the physical manifestation of their experiences.

The material culture recovered from the sites in Ireland and America sheds light on the daily lives of some of the Irish who were a part of its history, but who were not a part of its interpretation. The data demonstrate the living conditions and experiences of the tenant farmers prior to the Famine; they also illustrate the material life of Irish immigrants and Irish Americans. Changes in the types and complexity of artifacts reflect periods of conflict within American society and the struggle to maintain a sense of identity and negotiation. The scope for this study was narrowly defined to test material patterns over time and space. To provide a meaningful interpretation of the archaeological data, I focused on ceramic teaware, tableware, and serving forms, glass tableware and medicinal bottles, and the symbolism on white clay smoking pipes because these are the materials that directly pertain to the diasporic experiences of alienation, transnationalism, and incorporation.

The conclusions now need to be further tested through the excavation of other relevant archaeological sites and, more important, the introduction of other artifacts groups. The inclusion of a variety of other material types, such as sewing-related items, objects relating to the experiences of children, buttons, jewelry, and other clothing and personal items, will either enhance the interpretations of incorporation, alienation, and transnationalism presented here or possibly refute the evidence and provide alternate discourses on the Irish experiences of diaspora.

The importance of this study rests in both its transnational approach and critical use of the term *diaspora*. In historical archaeology, little research has been done to create an international comparative material context for studying immigrant groups. The archaeological research of the African diaspora has begun to shift its focus from American plantations toward a variety of historical sites along the West Coast of Africa. That work is beginning to establish an African material database with which to make meaningful interpretations of cultural continuity and change in assemblages linked to enslaved Africans. My research demonstrates the potential for a similar transnational comparative framework toward understanding the creation of an Irish American identity.

Diaspora is defined here as a dispersal of a large group of people, but its deeper meaning reflects victimization and exile. Because of these sweeping and somewhat broad theoretical constructs, many studies do not value the power of the term and its meaning within an international context. It is a societal process of conflict and negotiation by a displaced group as it defines its social position within a new social structure. Diasporic identities differ from immigrant identities because they arise out of the involuntary dispersal of a large number of people due to social, economic, or political conditions. The event(s) are traumatic and form the necessary element for the collective memory of the historic injustices and cannot be cured by external pressures of assimilation.

There can be different groups within a diaspora. The differences between individuals rest on the experiences and reasons for leaving the homeland. A mobilized diaspora is made up of individuals who have social and economic advantages in both the home and host lands. Mobilized diasporic groups enter their new environments with the skills to create opportunities to be upwardly mobile. A proletarian diaspora is made up of individuals at the lower end of the socioeconomic spectrum. Social values of inferiority created by the dominant population legitimize the latter group's social condition and, as a consequence, define sociocultural positions. The importance of diaspora is its definition within a particular social historical context and the conditions of dispersal, the diverse groups leaving the homeland, and how these groups were received in new places of settlement.

The seventeenth century is the beginning of modern Irish history. It is also the beginning of the Irish diaspora. Over its 400-year history, the Irish diaspora encompassed a diverse population—all classes and both Catholics and Protestants. In broad terms, religion dictated access to social and economic capital. The Anglo-Irish, who had better life chances in both Ireland and America, formed the majority of the mobilized diaspora between the seventeenth and early nineteenth century.

The Irish leaving at the time of the Famine formed the Irish proletarian diaspora. Land is central to any study of pre-Famine rural Ireland; it dictated social position based on a complex web of socioeconomic relations with a stratified social structure centered on access to and control of land. Social values differentiated those considered modern and traditional, which equated into dominant and subordinate social relations. Distinctions between the classes of rural poor were based on the amount of land rented and the degree to which individuals were forced to sell their labor to survive. The rural poor in Ireland found themselves at the lowest end of the socioeconomic spectrum. By 1815 and leading up to the Famine, capitalism and large-scale commercial agriculture widened the gap between the land owners and the landless.

The Nary sites exemplify the experiences of tenant farmers forming the Irish proletarian diaspora. Tenant farmers formed a large part of Ireland's rural poor and were at the lowest social and economic position, living at the whim of the landlord. At the time of evictions between 1847 and 1848, most of the evicted families, including the Nary family, emigrated to urban areas of America.

The Irish proletariat faced alienation in America. Negative stereotypes followed the Irish poor across the Atlantic. Social and economic relations in Ireland proved the cornerstone for the constraints that prevented poor people from taking advantage of opportunities for advancement in America. The rural poor were held in perpetual bondage and failed to lose their "traditional" ways, which only widened the social and economic gap between them and mainstream American society. The Famine Irish were considered an invasion of the American way of life. Irish immigrants were racialized as a group because they were deemed naturally inferior, chiefly because of the social and economic deprivations they had suffered in Ireland. To be poor was the fault of the individual, and disease was equated with poverty and ethnicity. Popular opinion blamed Irish immigrants as the cause and transmission of disease.

Between 1850 and 1880, the area known as the Five Points offered crowded and unsanitary living conditions to a mostly Irish population. Federal and state census data for the Five Points reveal that Irish families and individual boarders congregated in five-story brick and smaller wood-framed tenements along Park and Pearl streets. The residence at 472

Pearl was a large five-story brick tenement constructed in 1850. At mid-century, the majority of Irish families and boarders had been in America for no more than 5 years, and some had been in America less than 3 years. By the 1870 many of the Irish families had been in America well over 10 years. The tenement at 474 Pearl Street was a two-story wood-framed structure constructed as early as 1790. In 1850 a 3 recorded households lived in the tenement. None of the tenants had been living in America for more than 5 years, and all of the household members were Irish born. The most common employment in both tenements for single women was in the needle trades. Married women were listed in census as either keeping boarders or as laundresses. Male employment was in a variety of semiskilled and unskilled jobs. By 1870 almost all of the males were listed as laborers.

By the last decades of the nineteenth century there was a change in the conditions and way of life for Irish and Irish Americans. In Paterson, New Jersey, for example, most children were enrolled in school well past the age at which immigrant children had typically been sent out to work. Improved living conditions and extended education for children marked a turning point in the history of the Irish in America. Housing in Paterson was much different than in Five Points. The Dublin section was not home to large brick tenements. Although there were a few brick tenements, most of the housing consisted of wood-framed rowhouses averaging two and a half stories. The house at 32 Ward Street was a wood-framed two-and-a-half story structure purchased by James Mackel, a machinist, in 1866. James Mackel, his wife Sarah, two daughters, and son were born in Ireland and had been in America for less than a year when he purchased the property. By 1890, Sarah Mackel, a widow, and her family were the only residents at 32 Ward Street and remained there until sometime after 1895. The two-story wood-framed rowhouse at 46 Oliver Street was purchased by Thomas McGill, a fireman, in 1895. Thomas and his wife Mary Ann were both American born with parents born in Ireland. The McGill family continued to live at this address until it was sold to an Italian family in 1911.

Throughout a social discourse of conflict and struggle, Irish immigrants and American-born Irish continually interpreted what it meant to be Irish. Over time their collective memories were balanced with their desires to be accepted in their adopted homeland. The shift in how they outwardly communicated their transnational consciousness led to a gradual process of incorporation. Historical documents alone do not provide a satisfactory account for experiences within the Irish proletarian diaspora. Although there are many historical accounts and descriptions of the Irish experience both at home and abroad, little is known about how these people used objects to construct their lives within the contexts of colonialism, eviction, and poverty. The sites examined in this study fit well into the broader history of the Irish diasporic experience. In an archaeological context, the type of diasporic group has a direct impact on the types of material culture recovered. Establishing the material culture of the rural classes in Ireland who formed the Irish proletarian diaspora is vital to understanding the material changes in Irish American communities. Understanding continuities and changes in the material culture between Ireland and America provides a basic comparative foundation for identifying the diachronic material transformations in America.

The ceramic data reveal an interesting pattern. When comparing the Irish assemblage to that of Irish immigrants at the Five Points, there is an overall pattern of continuity in that the newly arrived Irish obtained familiar ceramics similar to those owned by their peers and indeed themselves in Ireland. For instance, there is an emphasis on the importance of tea drinking in both Ireland and America as exemplified by the large numbers of more expensive transfer-printed tea-related vessels in relation to less expensive tableware and serving forms. Furthermore, the level of vessel complexity is low in the Five Points assemblages. In comparison to the traditional assemblage from Ireland, it seems that serving pieces do not factor to a large degree in the material culture of Five Points. This factor is supported by comparing the Irish immigrant data to a contemporary American-born working-class assemblage.

Material commonalities between Ireland and America declined as the nineteenth century progressed. The increase in vessel complexity, resembling non-Irish American assemblages, is directly related to the overall length of residence, suggesting that cultural transformations are a transgenerational process. The developing complexity of ceramic and glass forms in conjunction with the introduction of new and different foods is evidence that Irish immigrants and Irish Americans learned and accepted new cultural patterns in their daily lives. The McGill family was American born, and the Mackel family had lived in Paterson for over 30 years at the time of the deposit. The white granite and glass tableware and serving pieces reflect their efforts to acquire objects that expressed American citizenship.

The archaeological evidence of incorporation during the last decades of the nineteenth century is further supported by diet and faunal remains. A change in dietary patterns, indicative of new and learned behaviors, occurs by the 1890s. Like the ceramic and glass table and serving pieces, the types of meat, mainly beef and chicken, consumed by the Mackel and McGill families reflects the dietary patterns of non-Irish Americans and are the material manifestation of a new Irish American identity.

Continuities and changes in ceramic and glass forms and faunal remains provide only part of the picture of the Irish proletarian diaspora. The negotiation process of incorporation was fraught with obstacles. Ethical and proprietary medicinal bottles reflect the unsanitary conditions and life-threatening illnesses that formed the daily experiences of Irish immigrants. The shift from dispensary to proprietary medicines suggests the degree of alienation and prejudice that existed in American society, which manifest itself through harsh judgment and treatment by the American medical profession.

Reformers placed social values on disease. The poor and unsanitary conditions of immigrant neighborhoods were considered the fault of the inhabitants. Living in such conditions, therefore, was a chosen life-style rather an environment created by absentee landlords and an uncaring health-care system. The presence of ethical medicines in the lower privy deposits at the Five Points indicates that Irish immigrants received some medicines from dispensaries and charitable hospitals but by 1860 had turned to commercially manufactured medicines. The rise in the numbers of proprietary medicines is a reflection of the reactions to the social values placed on health care and alienation from such institutions.

The reemergence of ethical medicines at century's end indicates a change in the perception of Irish and Irish Americans. The ability to access a physician represents the differences in social and economic positions between the Irish and Irish Americans at the Dublin section by 1890 and the newly arrived Irish immigrants at midcentury.

Incorporation, alienation, and transnationalism are interdependent discourses that ebb and flow in relation to external pressures from the dominant society. For example, the timing of acceptance and incorporation is directly related to the degree of a diasporic group's marginalization from social and economic opportunities. Moreover, each discourse is tempered by a dual consciousness fostered within the diasporic group. A transnational discourse negotiates the group's "in between" status of immigrant and citizen. It involves conceptions of cultural retentions amid social and cultural transformation. Transnationalism is the impetus for incorporation, as it expresses first and foremost loyalties to the adopted country but also fosters alienation at times in that the group retains a notion of its former cultural self.

The symbolism on smoking pipes from the Five Points reflects the dual loyalties of nationalism. The Irish immigrant community, drawing from the shared emotional pathos of injustices at the hands of the British Empire, maintained strong ties to Ireland's uprising through armed conflict. This is reflected in the Celtic harp, a symbol originally used by the United Irishmen, which became a metaphor for rebellion for American chapters of the Irish Republican Brotherhood. The militant approach and secret societies, however, were at odds with popular American sentiment. These groups and political philosophy of military uprisings only served to further inflame mistrust of Irish Catholics and gave Americans reasons to keep them in a subordinate and tentative position in America. Concurrently, the sheer number of Irish in American made them into a powerful voting block, and they were pursued rigorously by the Democratic Party. American eagle motifs, a symbol of the Democratic Party, were recovered from the same archaeological context as the Celtic harp. The Irish and American symbols together represent the negotiation of heritage and identity in Ireland and America.

By the last decade of the nineteenth century, Irish nationalism in America moved away from militant societies and embraced the symbolism of Gaelic history. The symbols of the Red Hand of Ulster and the triskelion illustrate the transformation of sociopolitical philosophies into actions against inequalities in Ireland and America. The symbolism on the smoking pipes expressed the beginnings of an Irish American heritage that drew upon the mythical and romantic essence of Irish history.

Timothy Meagher (1986a, 2001) argues that by the 1880s an Irish American identity emerged across America, but little has been done to identify and interpret this important period. Time and memories have an interesting way of romanticizing and creating myths or fantasy about the horrors and injustices of the past. An uncritical focus upon sources that perpetuate misconceptions and stereotypes or deny the wrongs and traumatic events of the past further obfuscates the realities we wish to capture. The daily objects recovered archaeologically demonstrate how the archaeological record documents the physical evidence of that transformation. The Irish did not arrive as cultural blank slates quickly adopting new social values and material culture. Rather, they immigrated with entrenched social dispositions communicated through material signs. Cultural transformation is a slow process that involves learning and accepting practices that are then integrated into daily activities. By comparing the archaeological data to both the rural poor in Ireland prior to emigration and contemporary non-Irish American assemblages, continuities in the Irish immigrant communities and changes in the single-family Irish and Irish American households in Paterson illustrate that by the 1890s families of first-generation Irish Americans employed seemingly mundane objects to express their desire for incorporation as American citizens, and through this process of conflict and struggle, they created a new sense of identity and an Irish American heritage.

There is no "pan-ethnic" way of thinking about the Irish diaspora. It is impossible for an ethnic group to share completely the same thoughts and beliefs. The Irish of the diaspora are no exception. Those leaving Ireland, involuntary or otherwise, were diverse. Each group that departed Ireland, however, had a common outlook based on a collective experience and history. A study of the experience and material culture of the Irish diaspora on a global scale is vital to understanding regional differences of incorporation and degrees of transformation in the Irish identity. In every diaspora there is a web of international networks. As the database in America and Ireland grows, it is important that it be placed in a comparative framework within an international context.

Historians have argued for a more transnational approach to the study of Irish dispersal. To understand the diversity of the Irish diaspora, historians have looked toward places such as the West Indies, Scotland, Argentina, South Africa, and New Zealand. It is hoped that over time archaeological investigations will follow suit. South Africa and the West Indies, for example, should provide interesting perspectives because each contained mobilized, indentured, and proletariat groups. The most interesting aspect would be the material evidence of Irish indentured servitude and transportation between the seventeenth and eighteenth centuries. The archaeology of indentured servitude could have far-reaching applications, not only as it is compared to other transportation colonies, such as Australia, but also in examining the archaeology of slavery. Something that has yet to be done archaeologically but would prove interesting is the study of the similarities and differences between two different yet related diasporas. As more sites are examined and the points of comparison are expanded, we will learn more about the different manifestations of the Irish diasporic experience in tangible, material ways and see that variation within the Irish diaspora in America is only the beginning of understanding the totality of Irish immigration history.

The research presented here is a work in progress. The interpretations mark the beginning of what will become a material culture database of the Irish diaspora. More needs to be done archaeologically in Ireland

and America. In Ireland, data needs to be collected from all counties to interpret and understand regional variations in the material culture of all rural classes. It is hoped that with time, increasing numbers of Irish archaeologists will study nineteenth-century rural sites. An Irish material database is significant to the study of material continuity and change in America through space and time. The database must include not only the rural poor but also the farming class and landed classes, both Catholic and Protestant.

It is not an understatement to declare that more research needs to be conducted covering a wider breadth of the Irish experience in America. More data is always needed and constantly sought after. One of the positive aspects of archaeology is that new data inevitably lead to more questions. The aim of this research was to bring together localized histories concerning the degrees of exclusion and tolerance over time and space. It was not the intention to generate sweeping statements that speak for all Irish and Irish American experiences in America. There are always exceptions to patterns and differing levels of tolerance and exclusion that are context specific. The next step is to test the conclusions drawn here in other locations in which the Irish were one of the first European groups to settle. It will be interesting to see what similarities or differences exist between the various time periods and locations.

The comparative approach should also include other incoming ethnic groups. A comparative discourse with other marginalized groups, such as the Chinese, Italians, and a host of Eastern European groups, while beyond the scope of this study, would serve only to highlight the importance of the physical evidence brought forth by archaeology. The value of comparative studies was demonstrated briefly here in the discussion of Irish and German immigrants. The comparison marks some interesting interpretations of social identity and its impact on a group being worthy or unworthy of American citizenship.

Appendix A

Ceramics from Ballykilcline, County Roscommon, Ireland

Refined Earthenware Vessels from the North Nary Cabin

Decoration	Teaware	Tableware	Serving	Total	Percentage of total
Plain		5		5	8.0
Shell edged		20		20	31.0
Printed patterns	3			3	4.0
Painted	14			14	22.0
Willow pattern		6	1	7	10.0
Chinoiserie	5			5	8.0
Floral pattern	6			6	9.0
Spatterware	5			5	8.0
Total	33	31	1	65	100.0
Percentage of total	51.0	48.0	1.0	100.0	100.0

Refined Earthenware from the South Nary Cabin

Decoration	Teaware	Tableware	Serving	Total	Percentage of total
Plain		1		1	3.0
Shell edged		8		8	27.0
Painted	5			5	17.0
Printed	12		1	13	43.0
Willow pattern		3		3	10.0
Total	17	12	1	30	100.0
Percentage of total	57.0	40.0	3.0		100.0

Appendix B

Artifacts, Ceramics, and Federal Census Data from 472 Pearl Street, Five Points, Manhattan

Refined Earthenware from the Lower Deposits of Feature J (AS V) and Z (ASII)

Ware type	Tea	Table	Serving	Total	Percentage of total
Painted	34	2		36	17.0
Plain		12		12	7.0
Shell edged		15	4	19	9.0
Printed	57	35	15	107	50.0
Sponge/spatter	9			9	4.0
White granite plain	4	5		9	4.0
White granite molded	9	8	2	19	9.0
Total	113	77	21	211	100.0
Percentage of total	54.0	36.0	10.0		100.0

Glass Tableware and Medicinal Bottles from the Lower Deposits of Feature J (ASV) and Z (ASII)

Function	Form	Vessel count	Percentage of total
Tableware	Tumblers	21	20.0
	Goblets	1	1.0
	Wine glasses	5	5.0
Medicinal	Ethical medicines	45	43.0
	Mineral water/soda water	5	5.0
	Proprietary medicines	27	26.0
Total		104	100.0

Refined Earthenware from the Upper Deposit of Feature J (AS III)

Ware type	Tea	Table	Serving	Total	Percentage of total
Plain	7	1	3	11	9.0
Shell edged		4	2	6	5.0
Painted	9			9	7.0
Printed	19	13	4	36	29.0
White granite plain	5	7	1	13	11.0
White granite molded	28	16	4	48	39.0
Total	68	41	14	123	100.0
Percentage of total	55.0	33.0	12.0		100.0

Glass Tableware and Medicinal Bottles from the Upper Deposit of Feature J (AS III)

Function	Form	Vessel count	Percentage of total
Tableware	Tumblers	20	19.0
	Goblets		
	Wine glasses	5	4.0
Serving	Salts	2	2.0
Medicinal	Ethical medicines	19	18.0
	Mineral water/soda water	28	26.0
	Proprietary medicines	33	31.0
Total		107	100.0

1850 Federal Census

Name	Relation	Age	Occupation	Birthplace
Sears, Robert	Head	30	Innkeeper	Ireland
Sears, Sophia	Wife	30		Ireland
Sears, Charles	Son	4		Ireland
Sears, Alfred	Son	6m		New York
Coles, James	Boarder	40	Tailor	New York
Crosby, Ann	Boarder	18		Ireland
Dullinow, Alexander	Boarder	35	Clerk	Massachusetts
Over, John	Head	47	Unknown	New York
Finck, Louis	Head	51	Tobacconist	Germany
Finck, Joana S.	Wife	63		Germany
Burns, Eliza	Head	51		Ireland
Burns, Dennis	Son	24	Marblecutter	Ireland
Burns, John	Son	22	Laborer	Ireland
Burns, Catherine	Daughter	12	Milliner/threads needle	Ireland
Manning, Alexander	Boarder	30	Laborer	Ireland
Garvey, John	Head	40	Porter	Ireland
Garvey, Nancy	Wife	50		Ireland
Garvey, James	Son	19	Soapboiler	Ireland
Garvey, John, Jr.	Son	15		Ireland
Garvey, Catherine	Daughter	11	Seamstress	Ireland
Feeney, Dennis	Boarder	26	Boatman	Ireland
Feeney, Ellen	Boarder	18		Ireland
Feeney, Martin	Boarder	18	Laborer	Ireland
Feeney, Patrick	Boarder	32	Laborer	Ireland
Feeney, Winnifred	Boarder	28		Ireland
Callahan, Maurice	Head	35	Fruit dealer/fish monger	Ireland
Callahan, Thomas	Son	3		New York
Callahan, David	Son	9m		New York
Bernard, Francis	Boarder	20	Tailor	Ireland
Connor, Thomas	Boarder	26	Laborer	Ireland
Johnston, Ann	Mother	50	Widow	Ireland

Name	Relation	Age	Occupation	Birthplace
Johnston, Esther	Daughter	25		Ireland
Johnston, John	Son	23	Silver refiner	Ireland
Johnston, Mary A.	Daughter	20	Widow/grocer	Ireland
Blake, Isabella	Boarder	24		Ireland
Callahan, Mary	Boarder	20		Ireland
Curry, Patrick	Head	18	Laborer	Ireland
Curry, Mary	Wife	18		Ireland
Curry, Ann	Daughter	5		New York
Curry, Michael	Son	1		New York
Gillan, Mary	Boarder	54	Widow	Ireland
Gillan, Mary	Boarder		Capmaker	Ireland
Gillan, Michael	Boarder	22	Cutler	Ireland
McLaughlin, Michael	Head	40	Laborer	Ireland
McLaughlin, Mary	Wife	33		Ireland
McLaughlin, Michael	Son	3		New York
McLaughlin, Mary A.	Daughter	1		New York
Milmore, Patrick	Boarder	45	Mason	Ireland
Taff, Nicholas	Boarder	60	Grocer	Ireland
Hawk, Martin	Boarder	42	Laborer	Ireland
Buckley, James	Head	30	Laborer	Ireland
Buckley, Penny	Wife	30		Ireland
Buckley, John	Son	4		New York
Buckley, Naponyou	Daughter	3		New York
Buckley, Bartholomew	Son	< 1		New York
Jordan, Thomas	Head	31	Porter	Ireland
Jordan, Bridget	Wife	30		Ireland
Flaherty, John	Boarder	18	Coachmaker	Ireland
Nicholason, Thomas	Head	30	Laborer	Ireland
Nicholason, Ann	Wife	25		Ireland
Nicholason, Dominick	Son	4m		New York

Name	Relation	Age	Occupation	Birthplace
Feeney, Patrick	Boarder	22	Tallowchndlr	Ireland
Newman, John	Boarder	22	Tallowchndlr	Ireland
Barry, Margaret	Widow	30	Seamstress	Ireland
Barry, Ellen	Daughter	5		Ireland
Barry, Margaret	Daughter	3		Ireland
Boyle, James	Boarder	32	Clerk	Ireland
Boyle, Mary	Boarder	23		Ireland
McDonald, Catherine	Head	43	Washing	Ireland
Farrell, Honora	Boarder	20		Ireland
Newton, Catherine	Boarder	59		Ireland
Sullivan, Joanna	Boarder	60		Ireland
Turpin, Eliza	Boarder	25		Ireland
Sullivan, Cornelius	Head	68	Porter	Ireland
Sullivan, Catherine	Daughter	25		Ireland
Sullivan, Ellen	Daughter	20		Ireland
Wagner, Ellen	Boarder	28	Tailoress	Ireland
Cronin, Michael	Head	40	Tailor	Ireland
Cronin, Maria	Wife	40		England
Cronin, Catherine	Daughter	9		Mississippi
Sullivan, Florence	Boarder	18	Boatman	Ireland
Wagner, Elizabeth A.	Boarder	8		New York
Lynch, Timothy	Head	26	Tinsmith	Ireland
Lynch, Elizabeth	Wife	25		Ireland
Lynch, Julia	Daughter	5		New York
Lynch, Jeremiah	Son	2		New York
Papard, Thomas	Head	34	Shoemaker	Ireland
Papard, Mary	Wife	33		England
Papard, Thomas	Son	3		England
Papard, Catherine	Daughter	7m		New York
Denny, Timothy	Boarder	40	Blacksmith	Ireland
Dineen, Jeremiah	Boarder	45	Shoemaker	Ireland
Morgan, Robert	Boarder	23	Shoemaker	Ireland
Moriarty, Julia	Boarder	26		Ireland

Name	Relation	Age	Occupation	Birthplace
Killoran, Michael	Head	36	Distiller	Ireland
Killoran, Bridget	Wife	24		Ireland
Killoran, John	Son	4		Ireland
Brennan, Ann	Boarder	22	Seamstress	Ireland
McConnell, Catherine	Boarder	18		Ireland
O'Kelly, Matthias	Head	54	Brass turner	Ireland
O'Kelly, Bridget	Wife	47		Ireland
O'Kelly, Dennis	Son	25	Soda water maker	Ireland
O'Kelly, Michael	Son	23	Soda water maker	Ireland
O'Kelly, Bridget	Daughter	19		Ireland
O'Kelly, James	Son	16	Gilder	Ireland
O'Kelly, Mary Ann	Daughter	13		Ireland
O'Kelly, Patrick	Son	9		Ireland

Appendix C

Artifacts, Ceramics, and Federal Census Data from 474 Pearl Street, Five Points, Manhattan

Refined Earthenware from Feature O

Decorative type	Tea	Table	Serving	Total	Percentage of total
Plain		3	1	4	4.0
Painted	27	0	0	27	28.0
Shell edged	0	7	0	7	7.0
Molded	0	0	1	1	1.0
Printed	18	20	2	40	41.0
White granite plain	2	3	2	7	7.0
White granite molded	7	5	0	12	12.0
Total	54	38	6	98	100.0
Percentage of total	55.0	40.0	5.0		100.0

Glass Tableware and Medicinal Bottles from Feature O

Function	Form	Vessel count	Percentage of total
Tableware	Plates		
	Tumblers	8	13.0
	Shot glasses		
	Goblets		
	Wine glasses	3	5.0
Serving	Salts	1	1.0
Medicinal	Ethical medicines	16	26.0
	Mineral water/soda water	7	11.0
	Proprietary medicines	27	44.0
Total		62	100.0

1860 Federal Census, Front Tenement

Name	Relation	Age	Occupation	Birthplace
Worth, Thomas	Head	27	Cook	England
Worth, Mary	Wife	32		Ireland
Worth, Mary J.	Daughter	2		New York
Coyle, Mary C.	Boarder	14		Ireland
Armstrong, Thomas	Boarder	29	Cooper	Ireland
Armstrong, Anna	Boarder	26		Ireland
Ward, John	Head	35	Undertaker	Ireland
Ward, Catherine	Wife	30		Ireland
Ward, Daniel	Son	8		New York
Ward, John	Son	6		New York
Ward, Catherine	Daughter	1		New York
Ward, Thomas V.	Son	3		New York
Ward, Bridget	Mother	67		Ireland
Harley, Ann	Boarder	16	Servant	Ireland
Clancy, Thomas	Boarder	30	Carpenter	New York
Brown, Abraham	Boarder	21	Carriage driver	New York

1860 Federal Census, Brick Rear Tenement

Name	Relation	Age	Occupation	Birthplace
Mungarvin, Mary	Head	40	Widow	Ireland
Mungarvin, John	Son	14		Ireland
O Connor, Jermiha	Head	59	Watchman	Ireland
O Connor, Levena	Mother	46		New York
O Connor Margaret	Daughter	17	Teacher	New York
O Connor David	Son	14		New York
O Connor Charles	Son	11		New York
Mulloy, John	Head	26	Laborer	Ireland
Mulloy, Bridget	Mother	26		Ireland
Mulloy, Patrick	Son	5		England
Mulloy, Michael	Son	2		New York
McDonell, William	Head	25	Shoemaker	Ireland
McDonell, Ellen	Wife	20		Ireland
Garey, John	Head	60	Laborer	Ireland
Garey, Julia	Wife	40		Ireland
Garey, Jermiha	Son	19	Glasscutter	Ireland
Garey, Patrick	Son	15		Ireland
Garey, Catherine	Daughter	13		Ireland
Garey, James	Son	11		Ireland
Garey, John	Son	8		Ireland
Garey, Mathew	Son	4		Ireland
McNamara, John	Head	30	Laborer	Ireland
McNamara, Margaret	Wife	36		Ireland
McNamara, Ann	Daughter	<1		New York
Flanigan, James	Stepson	19	Cooper	Ireland
Flanigan, John	Stepson	10		Ireland
Maloney, Roger	Head	30	Laborer	Ireland
Maloney, Ann	Wife	26		Ireland
Maloney, Mary	Daughter	1		New York
Maloney, Sarah	Daughter	< 1		New York
Devlin, Arthur	Boarder	36	Laborer	Ireland
Cadock, Catherine	Boarder	19	Seamstress	Ireland

Name	Relation	Age	Occupation	Birthplace
McLoughlin, Mary	Boarder	20	None	Ireland
Ryan, John	Head	50	Laborer	Ireland
Ryan, Mary	Wife	40		Ireland
Ryan, Bridget	Daughter	19	Milliner	New York
Ryan, Mary	Daughter	16	Book folder	New York
Ryan, Ellen	Daughter	12		New York
Ryan, John	Head	24	clerk	New York
Ryan, Margaret	Wife	19		England
Ryan, James	Son	<1		New York
Quin, Bridget	Boarder	50		Ireland
Shea, Thomas	Boarder	21	Bookbinder	Massachusetts
McMahon, Patrick	Boarder	15	None	Scotland
McGuire, Thomas	Head	45	Speculator	Ireland
McGuire, Elizia	Wife	40		Ireland
McGuire, Margaret	Daughter	20	Tailoress	Ireland
Keegan, Gerald	Boarder	22	Tailor	Ireland
Ward, Patrick	Boarder	22	Laborer	Ireland
Smith, Martin	Boarder	19	Gas fitter	Ireland
Turns, Samuel	Boarder	22	Tailor	Ireland
Mulloy, Julia	Head/widow	40	Seamstress	Ireland
Mulloy, William	Son	12		Ireland
Mulloy, Morris	Son	10		Ireland
Wade, Johana	Boarder	60	none	Ireland
McCarthy, Mary	Boarder	50	Laundress	Ireland
Linghan, Jermiha	Head	38	Laborer	Ireland
Linghan, Mary	Wife	33		Ireland
Linghan, Dennis	Son	11		Ireland
Linghan, Morris	Son	7		Ireland
Drurey, Margaret	Boarder	22	Dressmaker	Ireland
Sullivan, Dennis	Head	70	Laborer	Ireland
Sullivan, Catherine	Wife	40		Ireland
Sullivan, Ellen	Daughter	18	Seamstress	Ireland

Name	Relation	Age	Occupation	Birthplace
Sullivan, Mary	Daughter	15	Seamstress	Ireland
Sullivan, Julia	Daughter	8		Ireland
Shea, Mary	Boarder	40	Widow	Ireland
Lane, Julia	Boarder	70	Widow	Ireland
White, John	Head	30	Speculator	Ireland
White, Ellen	Wife	29		Ireland
White, Emelia	Daughter	7		England
White, Margaret	Daughter	4		England
White, James	Son	< 1		New York
McAndrew, Ann	Head/widow	56		Ireland
McAndrew, Charles	Son	24	Metal roofer	New York
Owens, Bridget	Boarder	40	Widow	Ireland
Connoly, Mary	Widow	46		Ireland
Connoly, Michael	Son	22	Cooper	Ireland
Connoly, Mary	Daughter	18	Artificial flower maker	New York
Connoly, John	Son	16	Printer	New York
Connoly, Margaret	Daughter	13		New York
Connoly, David	Son	12		New York
Daley, Bernard	Head	45	Porter	Ireland
Daley, Elizia	Wife	40		Ireland
Hart, John	Head	46	Laborer	Ireland
Hart, Mary	Wife	40		Ireland
Hart, Catherine	Daughter	11		New York
Hart, Mary	Daughter	10		New York
Hart, Margaret	Daughter	8		New York
Hart, Bridget	Daughter	5		New York
Cahill, Richard	Head	40	Laborer	Ireland
Cahill, Margaret	Wife	38		Ireland
Cahill, Morris	Son	16	Clerk	New York
Cahill, Lawrence	Son	14		New York
Cahill, John	Son	12		New York
Cahill, Catherine	Daughter	10		New York
Cahill, Margaret	Daughter	5		New York

Appendix D

Artifacts, Ceramics, and Federal Census Data from 32 Ward Street, Paterson, New Jersey

Refined Earthenware Vessels from Feature 63

Ware Type	Tea	Table	Serving	Total	Percentage of total
White granite plain	20	13	1	34	79.0
White granite molded	3	4	2	9	21.0
Total	23	17	3	43	100.0
Percentage of total	53.0	40.0	7.0		100.0

Glass Tableware and Medicinal Bottles from Feature 63

Function	Form	Vessel count
Tableware	Tumblers	3
	Goblets	1
	Wine glasses	4
Serving	Bowls	1
	Condiment dishes	1
Medicinal	Ethical medicine	30
	Mineral water/soda water	4
	Proprietary medicine	
Total		44

1870 Federal Census

Household	Relation	Age	Occupation	Birthplace
Mackel, James	Head	37	Machinist	Ireland
Mackel, Sarah	Wife	34	Keeps house	Ireland
Mackel, Mary	Daughter	13	At school	Ireland
Mackel, Jennie	Daughter	8	At school	Ireland
Mackel, Charles	Son	4	At home	Ireland
Mackel, Isabella	Daughter	3	At home	New Jersey
Moon, John	Head	43	Works in cotton mill	Massachusetts
Moon, Sarah J.	Wife	33	Keeps house	Massachusetts
Crowson, James	Head	30	Teamster	New York
Crowson, Mary	Wife	22	Keeps house	New York

Appendix E

Artifacts, Ceramics, and Federal Census Data from 46 Oliver Street, Dublin Section, Paterson, New Jersey

Refined Earthenware from Feature 10

Ware type	Tea	Table	Serving	Total	Percentage of total
Painted	2			2	5.0
Printed	6			6	15.0
White granite plain	16	3	3	22	55.0
White granite moss pattern		7		7	18.0
White granite molded	2		1	3	7.0
Total	26	10	4	40	100.0
Percentage of total	65.0	25.0	10.0		100.0

Glass Tableware and Medicinal Bottles from Feature 10

Function	Form	Vessel count	Percentage of total
Tableware	Tumblers	15	48.0
	Goblets		
	Wine Glasses		
Serving	Dishes	2	6.0
Medicinal	Ethical Medicine	9	30.0
	Mineral water/soda water	4	13.0
	Proprietary medicine	1	3.0
Total		31	100.0

1900 Federal Census

Name	Relation	Age	Occupation	Place of birth
McGill, Thomas	Head	41	Fireman	New Jersey
McGill, Mary Ann	Wife	41	Keeps house	New Jersey
McGill, Daniel	Sons	17	School	New Jersey
McGill, Richard	Sons	14	School	New Jersey

References Cited

AALEN, F. H. A., KEVIN WHELAN, AND MATHEW STOUT (EDITORS)

1997 *Atlas of the Rural Irish Landscape.* University of Toronto Press, Toronto.

ABELL, AARON I.

1952 The Catholic Factor in Urban Welfare: The Early Period, 1850–1880. *Review of Politics* 14(3):289–324.

1960 *American Catholicism and Social Action: A Search for Social Justice, 1865–1950.* Hanover House, Garden City, NY.

ADAMS, WILLIAM FORBES

1967 *Ireland and Irish Emigration to the New World, 1815 to the Famine.* Yale University Press, New Haven, CT.

ADDRESS OF THE DELEGATES OF THE NATIVE AMERICAN NATIONAL CONVENTION TO THE CITIZENS OF THE UNITED STATES [JULY 1845]

1925 The "Native American" Declaration of Principles, 1845. In *Historical Aspects of the Immigration Problem: Select Documents,* edited by E. Abbott, pp. 744–746. University of Chicago Press, Chicago.

AKENSON, DONALD H.

1994 *The Irish Diaspora: A Primer.* Institute of Irish Studies, Belfast.

1997 The Historiography of the Irish in the United States. In *The Irish in the New Communities,* edited by Patrick O'Sullivan, pp. 99–127. Leicester University Press, London.

2000 Irish Migration to North America, 1800–1920. In *The Irish Diaspora,* edited by Andy Bielenberg, pp. 111–138. Pearson Education Limited, Edinburgh.

ALLEN, OLIVER E.

1993 *The Tiger: The Rise and Fall of Tammany Hall.* Addison-Wesley, Reading, MA.

ALMQUIST, ERIC L.

1979 Pre-Famine Ireland and the Theory of Proto-Industrialization: Evidence from the 1841 Census. *Journal of Economic History* 39(3):699–718.

ALTHUSSER, LOUIS
1979 *For Marx.* Verso, London.

ANBINDER, TYLER
2001 *Five Points: The 19th-Century New York City Neighborhood that Invented Tap Dance, Stole Elections, and Became the World's Most Notorious Slum.* Free Press, New York.
2002 From Famine to Five Points: Lord Landsdowne's Irish Tenants Encounter North America's Most Notorious Slum. *American Historical Review* 107(2):1–24.
2003 "We Will Dirk Every Mother's Son of You": Five Points and the Irish Conquest of New York Politics. In *New Directions in Irish-American History,* edited by Kevin Kenny, pp. 105–121. University of Wisconsin Press, Madison.

ANTHIAS, FLOYA
1998 Evaluating "Diaspora": Beyond Ethnicity? *Sociology* 32(3):557–580.

ARCHDEACON, THOMAS J.
1983 *Becoming American: An Ethnic History.* Free Press, New York.

ARENSBERG, CONRAD M.
1988 *The Irish Countryman: An Anthropological Study.* Waveland Press, Prospect Heights, IL.

ARENSBERG, CONRAD M., AND SOLON T. KIMBALL
1940 *Family and Community in Ireland.* Harvard University Press, Cambridge, MA.

ARMSTRONG, DOUGLAS V., AND MARK L. FLEISCHMAN
2003 House-Yard Burials of Enslaved Laborers in Eighteenth-Century Jamaica. *International Journal of Historical Archaeology* 7(1):33–66.

ARMSTRONG, JOHN A.
1976 Mobilized and Proletarian Diasporas. *American Political Science Review* 70(2):393–408.

ASHMORE, RICHARD D., LEE JUSSIM, AND DAVID WILDER (EDITORS)
2001 *Social Identity, Intergroup Conflict, and Conflict Reduction.* Oxford University Press, Oxford.

BARNARD, T. C.
1973 Planters and Policies in Cromwellian Ireland. *Past and Present* 61: 31–69.

BARTH, FREDRICK
1994 Enduring and Emerging Issues in the Analysis of Ethnicity. In *The Anthropology of Ethnicity: Beyond "Ethnic Groups and Boundaries,"* edited by Hans Vermeulen and Cora Govers, pp. 11–32. HET SPINHUIS Publishers, Amsterdam.

2000 Boundaries and Distinctions. In *Signifying Identities: Anthropological Perspectives on Boundaries and Contested Values,* edited by A. P. Cohen, pp. 17–36. Routledge, New York.

BARTH, FREDRICK (EDITOR)

1969 *Ethnic Groups and Boundaries: The Social Organization of Cultural Difference.* Waveland Press, Prospect Heights, IL.

BAUGHER, SHERENE

1982 Hoboken Hollow: A 19th Century Factory Worker's Housing Site. *Northeast Historical Archaeology* 11:26–38.

BAUM, DALE

1978 Know-Nothingism and the Republican Majority in Massachusetts: The Political Realignment of the 1850s. *Journal of American History* 64(4):959–986.

BAUMANN, MARTIN

1997 Shangri-La in Exile: Portraying Tibetan Diaspora Studies and Reconsidering Diaspora(s). *Diaspora* 6(3):377–404.

BEAMES, M. R.

1978 Rural Conflict in Pre-Famine Ireland: Peasant Assassinations in Tipperary, 1837–1847. *Past and Present* 81:75–91.

BEAUDRY, MARY C.

1993 Public Aesthetics versus Personal Experience: Worker Health and Well-Being in 19th-Century Lowell, Massachusetts. *Historical Archaeology* 27(2):90–105.

BECKETT, J. C.

1980 *The Making of Modern Ireland, 1603–1923.* Knopf, New York.

BECKLES, HILARY

1990 A "riotous and unruly lot": Irish Indentured Servants and Freemen in the English West Indies, 1644–1713. *William and Mary Quarterly* 47(4):503–522.

BEECHER, CATHERINE, AND HARRIET B. STOWE

1994 [1869] *The American Woman's Home.* Stowe-Day Foundation, Hartford, CT.

BELCHEM, JOHN

1995 Nationalism, Republicanism, and Exile: Irish Emigrants and the Revolutions of 1848. *Past and Present* 146:103–135.

BHABHA, HOMI K.

1994 *The Location of Culture.* Routledge, London.

BLACKMAR, ELIZABETH

1989 *Manhattan for Rent, 1785–1850.* Cornell University Press, Ithaca, NY.

1995 Accountability for Public Health: Regulating the Housing Market in Nineteenth-Century New York City. In *Hives of Sickness: Public Health and Epidemics in New York City,* edited by David Rosner, pp. 42–64. Rutgers University Press, New Brunswick, NJ.

BLASZCZK, REGINA E.

1994 The Aesthetic Moment: China Decorators, Consumer Demand, and Technological Change in the American Pottery Industry, 1865–1900. *Winterthur Portfolio* 29:121–153.

BODNAR, JOHN

1985 *The Transplanted: A History of Immigrants in Urban America.* Indiana University Press, Bloomington.

BOSTON CITY DOCUMENT NO. 66

1925 Cholera in the Boston Slums. Originally published 1849. In *Historical Aspects of the Immigration Problem: Select Documents,* edited by Edith Abbott, pp. 593–596. University of Chicago Press, Chicago.

BOTTIGHEIMER, KARL S.

1967 English Money and Irish Land: The "Adventurers" in the Cromwellian Settlement of Ireland. *Journal of British Studies* 7(1):12–27.

BOURKE, A.

1993 "The Visitation from God"? *The Potato and the Great Irish Famine.* Lilliput Press, Dublin.

BOYCE, D. G.

1996 1916: Interpreting the Rising. In *The Making of Modern Irish History: Revisionism and the Revisionist Controversy,* edited by D. G. Boyce and A. O'Day, pp. 163–187. Routledge, London.

BOYCE, D. G., AND ALAN O'DAY (EDITORS)

1996 *The Making of Modern Irish History: Revisionism and the Revisionist Controversy.* Routledge, London.

BOYER, PAUL

1978 *Urban Masses and Moral Order in America, 1820–1920.* Harvard University Press, Cambridge, MA.

BOYLE, JOHN W.

1983 A Marginal Figure: The Rural Irish Laborer. In *Irish Peasants: Violence and Political Unrest, 1780–1914,* edited by S. Clark and J. S. Donnelly, pp. 311–338. Manchester University Press, Manchester.

BRADSHAW, BRENDAN

1989 Nationalism and Historical Scholarship in Modern Ireland. *Irish Historical Studies* 26(104):329–351.

BRADY, CIARAN (EDITOR)

1994 "Constructive and Instrumental": The Dilemma in Ireland's First "New Historians." In *Interpreting Irish History: The Debate on*

Historical Revisionism, 1938–1944, pp. 3–31. Irish Academic Press, Dublin.

Brady, Ciaran, and Raymond Gillespie (editors)

1986 *Natives and Newcomers: Essays on the Making of Irish Colonial Society, 1534–1641.* Irish Academic Press, Dublin.

Brah, Avtar

1996 *Cartographies of Diaspora: Contesting Identities.* Routledge, London.

Brannon, Nick

1984 Excavations at a Farmyard in the Bonn Townland, County Tyrone. *Ulster Journal of Archaeology* 47:177–181.

1990 Excavations at Brackfield Bawn, County Londonderry. *Ulster Journal of Archaeology* 53:8–14.

Braudel, Fernand

1972 *The Mediterranean and the Mediterranean World in the Age of Phillip II.* HarperCollins, New York.

1980 *On History.* University of Chicago Press, Chicago.

Braziel, Jana E., and Anita Mannur

2003 Nation, Migration, Globalization: Points of Contention in Diaspora Studies. In *Theorizing Diaspora,* edited by Jana E. Braziel and Anita Mannur, pp. 1–22. Blackwell, Oxford.

Brewer, Eileen M.

1987 *Beyond Utility: The Role of the Nun in the Education of American Catholic Girls, 1860–1920.* Loyola University Press, Chicago.

Brighton, Stephen A.

2001 Prices that Suit the Times: Shopping for Ceramics at the Five Points. *Historical Archaeology* 35(3):16–30.

2004 Symbolism, Myth-Making, and Identity: The Red Hand of Ulster in Nineteenth-Century Paterson, New Jersey. *International Journal of Historical Archaeology* 8(2):149–164.

2005 To Begin Again Elsewhere: Archaeology and the Irish Diaspora. In *Unearthing Hidden Ireland: Historical Archaeology in County Roscommon,* edited by Charles E. Orser Jr., pp. 193–216. Wordwell Press, Bray, Ireland.

2008 Degrees of Alienation: The Material Evidence of the Irish and Irish American Experience, 1850–1910. *Historical Archaeology* 42(4):132–153.

Brighton, Stephen A., and Jessica Levon-White

2005 English Ceramic Exports to Ballykilcline. In *Unearthing Hidden Ireland: Historical Archaeology in County Roscommon,* edited by Charles E. Orser Jr., pp. 109–139. Wordwell Press, Bray, Ireland.

BRIGHTON, STEPHEN A., AND CHARLES E. ORSER JR.

2006a Archaeological Investigations at the Barlow's Field Site, County Sligo. Report submitted to the National Museum of Ireland, Dublin.

2006b Irish Images on English Goods in the American Market: The Materialization of a Modern Irish Heritage. In *Images, Representations, and Heritage: Moving Beyond Modern Approaches to Archaeology,* edited by Ian Russell, pp. 61–88. Springer, New York.

BROWN, THOMAS N.

1966 *Irish-American Nationalism, 1870–1890.* J. B. Lippincott, New York.

BRUMFIELD, ELIZABETH M.

2004 Materiality, Feasts, and Figured Worlds in Aztec Mexico. In *Rethinking Materiality: The Engagement of Mind with the Material World,* edited by Elizabeth DeMarrais, Chris Gosden, and Colin Renfrew, pp. 225–238. McDonald Institute for Archaeological Research, Cambridge.

BRUNDAGE, D.

1996 "In Time of Peace, Prepare for War:" Key Themes in the Social Thought of New York's Irish Nationalists, 1890–1916. In *The New York Irish,* edited by R. H. Bayor and Timothy J. Meagher, pp. 321–334. Johns Hopkins University Press, Baltimore.

BURCHELL, R. A.

1980 *The San Francisco Irish, 1848–1880.* University of California Press, Berkeley.

BURLEY, DAVID

1989 Function, Meaning, and Context: Ambiguities in Ceramics Use by the Hivernant Métis of the Northwestern Plains. *Historical Archaeology* 23(1):97–106.

2000 Creolization and Late Nineteenth-Century Métis Vernacular Log Architecture on the South Saskatchewan River. *Historical Archaeology* 34(3):27–35.

BURROWS, EDWIN G., AND MIKE WALLACE

1999 *Gotham: A History of New York City to 1898.* Oxford University Press, New York.

BUSHMAN, RICHARD L.

1993 *The Refinement of America: Persons, Houses, Cities.* Vintage Books, New York.

BUTLER, KIM

2001 Defining Diaspora, Refining a Discourse. *Diaspora* 10(2):189–219.

CABAK, MELANIE A., MARK D. GROOVER, AND SCOTT J. WAGERS

1995 Health Care and the Wayman A.M.E. Church. *Historical Archaeology* 29(2):55–76.

CANNY, NICHOLAS

1973 The Ideology of English Colonization: From Ireland to America. *William and Mary Quarterly* 30(4):575–598.

1982 Formation of the Irish Mind: Religion, Politics, and Gaelic Literature, 1580–1750. *Past and Present* 95:91–104.

CASSEDY, JAMES H.

1986 *Medicine and American Growth, 1800–1860.* Wisconsin Publications in the History of Science and Medicine 5, edited by William Coleman, David C. Lindberg, and Ronald L. Numbers. University of Wisconsin Press, Madison.

CASTELLS, MANUEL

1977 *The Urban Question: A Marxist Approach.* Edward Arnold, London.

CHICKERING, J.

1925 Anxiety about Immigration: A Moderate View, 1848. In *Historical Aspects of the Immigration Problem: Select Documents,* edited by E. Abbott, pp. 758–763. University of Chicago Press, Chicago.

CHOW, R.

1993 *Writing Diaspora: Tactics of Intervention in Contemporary Cultural Studies.* Indiana University Press, Bloomington.

CHUDACOFF, H. P., AND J. E. SMITH

2000 *The Evolution of American Urban Society,* 5th ed. Prentice Hall, Upper Saddle River, NJ.

CITIZEN'S ASSOCIATION OF NEW YORK

1866 Report of Physicians and Citizens Upon the Value and Necessity of Sanitary Improvements and on Health Reform in New York. Miscellaneous Papers of the Citizen's Association of New York. Division of Local History and Genealogy, New York Public Library.

1870 *Report Upon the Condition, Etc., of the Institutions Under Charge of the Commissioners of Public Charities and Correction.* George F. Nesbitt, New York.

CLARK, CLIFFORD E., JR.

1988 Domestic Architecture as an Index to Social History: The Romantic Revival and the Cult of Domesticity in America, 1840–1870. In *Material Life in America, 1600–1860,* edited by Robert B. St. George, pp. 535–549. Northeastern University Press, Boston.

CLARK, DENNIS J.

1973 *Irish in Philadelphia: Ten Generations of Urban Experience.* Temple University Press, Philadelphia.

1986 *Hibernia America: The Irish and Regional Cultures.* Greenwood: New York.

CLARK, SAMUEL
1982 The Importance of Agrarian Classes: Class-Structure and Collective Action in Nineteenth-Century Ireland. In *Ireland: Land, Politics, and People*, edited by P. J. Drudy, pp. 11–36. Cambridge University Press, Cambridge.

CLARK, SAMUEL, AND JAMES S. DONNELLY (EDITORS)
1983 *Irish Peasants: Violence and Political Unrest, 1780–1914*. Manchester University Press, Manchester.

CLIFFORD, J.
1994 Diasporas. *Cultural Anthropology* 9(3):302–338.

COFFEY, MICHAEL, AND TERRY GOLWAY
1997 *The Irish in America*. Hyperion, New York.

COHEN, ROBIN
1994 *Frontiers of Identity: The British and the Rest*. Longman, London.
1997 *Global Diasporas: An Introduction*. University of Washington Press, Seattle.

COLEMAN, ANNE
1999 *Riotous Roscommon: Social Unrest in the 1840s*. Irish Academic Press, Dublin.

COMAROFF, J., AND J. COMAROFF
1992 *Ethnography and the Historical Imagination*. Westview Press, Boulder, CO.

COMBER, MAUREEN (EDITOR)
1985 *Poverty Before the Famine County Clare, 1835: First Report from His Majesty's Commissioners for the Inquiry into the Condition of the Poorer Classes in Ireland*. Clasp Press, Ennis, Ireland.

COMERFORD, R. V.
1985 *The Fenians in Context: Irish Politics and Society, 1848–1882*. Wolfhound Press, Dublin.

CONDRAN, GRETCHEN A.
1995 Changing Patterns of Epidemic Disease in New York City. In *Hives of Sickness: Public Health and Epidemics in New York City*, edited by David Rosner, pp. 27–41. Rutgers University Press, New Brunswick, NJ.

CONNELL, K. H.
1962a The Potato in Ireland. *Past and Present* 23:57–71.
1962b Peasant Marriage in Ireland: Its Structure and Development Since the Famine. *Economic History Review* 14(3):502–523.

CONNER, W.
1986 The Impact of Homelands Upon Diasporas. In *Modern Diasporas in International Politics*, edited by G. Scheffer, pp. 16–45. Croom Helm, London.

CONNOLLY, SEAN J.

1996 Eighteenth-Century Ireland: Colony or *Ancien Régime?* In *The Making of Modern Irish History: Revisionism and the Revisionist Controversy,* edited by D. George Boyce and Alan O'Day, pp. 15–33. Routledge, New York.

COOK, LAUREN

1989a Tobacco-Related Material Culture and the Working Class. In *Interdisciplinary Investigations of Boott Mills, Lowell Massachusetts, Volume 2: The Kirk Street Agents' House,* edited by Mary C. Beaudry and Stephen A. Mrozowski, pp. 29–43. Cultural Resource Management Study 2. Division of Cultural Resources, North Atlantic Regional Office, National Park Service, Boston.

1989b Tobacco-Related Material and the Construction of Working-Class Culture. In *Interdisciplinary Investigations of Boott Mills, Lowell Massachusetts, Volume 3: The Boarding House System as a Way of Life,* edited by Mary C. Beaudry and Stephen A. Mrozowski, pp. 209–230. Cultural Resource Management Study 21. Division of Cultural Resources, North Atlantic Regional Office, National Park Service, Boston.

1997 "Promiscuous Smoking": Interpreting Gender and Tobacco Use in the Archaeological Record. *Northeast Historical Archaeology* 26:23–38.

COOK, LAUREN J., REBECCA YAMIN, AND JOHN P. MCCARTHY

1996 Shopping as Meaningful Action: Toward a Redefinition of Consumption in Historical Archaeology. *Historical Archaeology* 30(4): 50–65.

COTZ, JO ANN

1975 A Study of Ten Houses in Paterson's Dublin Area. *Northeast Historical Archaeology* 4(1–2):44–52.

COTZ, JOANN, MARY JANE RUTSCH, AND CHARLES WILSON

1980 Salvage Archaeology Project, Paterson, New Jersey, 1973–1976. Volume II: Paterson's Dublin: An Interdisciplinary Study of Social Structure. Ms. prepared for Great Falls Development, Inc., and the New Jersey Department of Transportation.

COYSCH, A. W., AND R. K. HENRYWOOD

1982 *The Dictionary of Blue and White Printed Pottery, 1780–1880.* Antique Collectors' Club, Suffolk.

CROKER, THOMAS CROFTON

1824 *Researches in the South of Ireland Illustrative of the Scenery, Architectural Remains, and the Manners and Superstitions of the Peasantry with an Appendix, Containing a Private Narrative of the Rebellion of 1798.* John Murray, London.

CROTTY, RAYMOND D.

1966 *Irish Agricultural Production: Its Volume and Structure.* Cork University Press, Cork, Ireland.

CULLEN, L. M.

1995 The Politics of the Famine and of Famine Historiography. In *The Famine Lectures,* edited by Brendán Ó Conaire, pp. 166–186. Roscommon Herald, Boyle, Ireland.

CULLEN, L. M. (EDITOR)

1969 *Formation of the Irish Economy.* Mercier Press, Cork, Ireland.

CUNNINGHAM, JOHN T.

1994 *This Is New Jersey.* 4th ed. Rutgers University Press, New Brunswick, NJ.

CURTAIN, NANCY J.

1996 "Varieties of Irishness": Historical Revisionism, Irish Style. *Journal of British Studies* 35:195–219.

DALY, MARY E.

1986 *The Famine in Ireland.* Dundalgan Press, Dublin.

1996 Revisionism and Irish History: The Great Famine. In *The Making of Modern Irish History: Revisionism and the Revisionist Controversy,* edited by D. George Boyce and Alan O'Day, pp. 71–89. Routledge, London.

DAULTREY, S. G., D. DICKSON, AND C. Ó GRÁDA

1981 Eighteenth Century Irish Population: New Perspectives from Old Sources. *Journal of Economic History* 41(3):601–628.

DAVIDSON, JAMES M.

2004 Rituals Captured in Context and Time: Charm Use in North Dallas Freedman's Town (1869–1907). *Historical Archaeology* 38(2):22–54.

DAVIS, BARBARA

1989 Faunal Analysis. In *History and Archaeology of the Greenwich Mews Site, Greenwich Village, New York,* edited by Joan H. Geismar, pp. 190–214. Report prepared for Greenwich Mews Associates by Joan H. Geismar, New York.

DAVIS, GARRETT

1925 Opinion in the South. Originally published 1855. In *Historical Aspects of the Immigration Problem: Select Documents,* edited by Edith Abbott, pp. 767–774. University of Chicago Press, Chicago.

DAVIS, GRAHAM

2000a The Irish in Britain, 1815–1939. In *The Irish Diaspora,* edited by Andy Bielenberg, pp. 19–36. Pearson Education, Essex, England.

2000b The Historiography of the Irish Famine. In *The Meaning of the Famine,* Vol. 6, edited by Patrick O'Sullivan, pp. 15–39. Leicester University Press, London.

Deane, Seamus

1994 Wherever Green Is Read. In *Interpreting Irish History: The Debate on Historical Revisionism, 1938–1944,* edited by Ciaran Brady, pp. 234–245. Irish Academic Press, Dublin.

DeBolt, Gerald

1994 *DeBolt's Dictionary of American Pottery Marks: Whiteware and Porcelain.* Collector Books, Paducah, KY.

DeCorse, Christopher

1999 Oceans Apart: Africanist Perspectives of Diaspora Archaeology. In *I Too Am American: Archaeological Studies of African-American Life,* edited by Theresa A. Singleton, pp. 132–155. University of Virginia Press, Charlottesville.

2001 *West Africa During the Atlantic Slave Trade.* Continuum, London.

De Cunzo, LuAnn

1982 Households, Economics, and Ethnicity in Paterson's Dublin, 1829–1915: The Van Houten Street Parking Lot Block. *Northeast Historical Archaeology* 11:9–25.

1983 Economics and Ethnicity: An Archaeological Perspective on Nineteenth-Century Paterson, New Jersey. Unpublished Ph.D. dissertation in American Civilization, University of Pennsylvania, Philadelphia.

1987 Adapting to Factory and City: Illustrations from the Industrialization and Urbanization of Paterson, New Jersey. In *Consumer Choice in Historical Archaeology,* edited by Suzanne Spencer-Wood, pp. 261–295. Plenum Press, New York.

DeForest, Robert, and Lawrence Veiller

1970 *The Tenement Housing Problem.* Originally published 1903. Arno Press, New York.

Degler, Carl N.

1984 *Out of Our Past: The Forces that Shaped Modern America.* 3rd ed. Harper Colophon Books, New York.

Delle, James A.

1999 "A Good and Easy Speculation": Spatial Conflict, Collusion, and Resistance in Late Sixteenth-Century Munster, Ireland. *International Journal of Historical Archaeology* 3(1):11–36.

DeMarrais, Elizabeth

2004 The Materialization of Culture. In *Rethinking Materiality: The Engagement of Mind with the Material World,* edited by Elizabeth

DeMarrais, Chris Gosden, and Colin Renfrew, pp. 11–22. McDonald Institute for Archaeological Research, Cambridge.

DE NIE, MICHAEL
2001 "A Medley Mob of Irish-American Plotters and Irish Dupes: The British Press and Transatlantic Fenianism. *Journal of British Studies* 40(2):213–240.

DE TOCQUEVILLE, ALEXIS
1958 *Journeys to England and Ireland.* Yale University Press, New Haven, CT.

DEWEY, CLIVE
1974 Celtic Agrarian Legislation and the Celtic Revival: Historicist Implications on Gladstone's Irish and Scottish Land Acts, 1870–1886. *Past and Present* 64:30–70.

DICKENS, CHARLES
1985 [1842] *American Notes: A Journey.* Fromm International, New York.

DICKSON, R. J.
1966 *Ulster Emigration to Colonial America, 1718–1775.* Graham Omagh and Sons, London.

DINER, HASIA
1983 *Erin's Daughters in America: Irish Immigrant Women in the Nineteenth Century.* Johns Hopkins University Press, Baltimore.
1996 "The Most Irish City in the Union": The Era of the Great Migration, 1844–1877. In *The New York Irish,* edited by Ronald H. Bayor and Timothy J. Meagher, pp. 87–106. John Hopkins University Press, Baltimore.

DONNELLY, COLM, AND NICK BRANNON
1998 "Troweling Through History": Historical Archaeology and the Study of Early Modern Ireland. *History Ireland* 6(3):22–55.

DONNELLY, COLM J., AND AUDREY J. HORNING
2002 Post-Medieval and Industrial Archaeology in Ireland: An Overview. *Antiquity* 76:557–561.

DONNELLY, JAMES S., JR.
1975 *Land and the People of 19th-Century Cork.* Routledge, London.
2001 *The Great Irish Potato Famine.* Sutton Publishers, Gloucestershire.

DOOLAN, THOMAS
1847 *Practical Suggestions on the Improvement of the Present Condition of the Peasantry of Ireland.* George Barclay, London.

DOOLEY, T.
2003 *The Greatest of the Fenians: John Devoy and Ireland.* Wolfhound Press, Dublin.

Doyle, D. N.
1981 *Ireland, Irishmen, and Revolutionary America, 1760–1820.* Mercier Press, Dublin.

Doyle, David Noel
2006 The Re-Making of Irish America, 1845–1880. In *Making the Irish American: History and Heritage of the Irish in the United States,* edited by J. J. Lee and Marion R. Casey, pp. 213–252. New York University Press, New York.

Drummond, Lee
1980 The Cultural Continuum: A Theory of Intersystems. *Man* 15: 352–374.

Drzewiecka, Jolanta A.
2002 Reinventing and Contesting identities in Constitutive Discourses: Between Diaspora and Its Other. In *Communication Quarterly* 50(1):1–23.

Dublin, Thomas
1979 *Women at Work: The Transformation of Work and Community in Lowell, Massachusetts, 1826–1860.* Columbia University Press, New York.

Durey, Michael
1994 The Dublin Society of United Irishmen and the Politics of the Carey-Drennan Dispute, 1792–1794. *Historical Journal* 37(1):89–111.

Dutton, Hely
1824 *A Statistical and Agricultural Survey of the County of Galway.* R. Graisberry, Dublin.

Edwards, R. D.
1994 An Agenda for Irish History, 1978–2018. In *Interpreting Irish History: The Debate on Historical Revisionism, 1938–1944,* edited by Ciaran Brady, pp. 54–67. Irish Academic Press, Dublin.

Edwards, R. D., and T. Desmond Williams (editors)
1956 *The Great Famine.* Brown and Nolan, Dublin.

Edwards-Ingram, Ywone
2001 African American Medicine and the Social Relations of Slavery. In *Race and the Archaeology of Identity,* edited by Charles E. Orser Jr., pp. 34–53. University of Utah Press, Salt Lake City.

Emerson, Mathew C.
1994 Decorated Clay Tobacco Pipes from the Chesapeake: An African Connection. In *Archaeology of the Chesapeake,* edited by Paul A. Shackel and Barbara J. Little, pp. 35–49. Smithsonian Institution Press, Washington, DC.
1999 African Inspirations in a New World Art and Artifact: Decorated Pipes from the Chesapeake. In *I Too Am American: Archaeological*

Studies of African-American Life, edited by Theresa A. Singleton, pp. 39–46. University of Virginia Press, Charlottesville.

Emmons, David M.

1989 *The Butte Irish: Class and Ethnicity in an American Mining Town, 1875–1925.* University of Illinois Press, Chicago.

Erie, Steven P.

1988 *Rainbow's End: Irish-Americans and the Dilemmas of Urban Machine Politics, 1840–1985.* University of California Press, Berkeley.

Ernst, Robert

1994 *Immigrant Life in New York City, 1825–1863.* 2nd ed. Syracuse University Press, Syracuse, NY.

Everett, A. H.

1925 Difficulties of Assimilation. Originally published 1835. Reprinted in *Historical Aspects of the Immigration Problem: Select Documents,* edited by Edith Abbott, pp. 440–448. University of Chicago Press, Chicago.

Fanning, Charles

2000 Editor's Introduction. In *New Perspectives on the Irish Diaspora,* edited by Charles Fanning, pp. 1–11. Southern Illinois University Press, Carbondale.

Fanning, Ronan

1988 The Meaning of Revisionism. *Irish Review* 4:15–19.

Farnsworth, Paul

1996 The Influence of Trade on Bahamian Slave Culture. *Historical Archaeology* 30(4):1–23.

Faulkner, Alaric, Kim Mark Peters, David P. Sell, and Edwin S. Dethlefsen

1978 Port and Market: Archaeology of the Central Waterfront Newburyport, Massachusetts. Ms. prepared for the National Park Service.

Fennel, Christopher C.

2000 Conjuring Boundaries: Inferring Past Identities from Religious Artifacts. *International Journal of Historical Archaeology* 4(4): 281–313.

2003 Group Identity, Individual Creativity, and Symbolic Generation in a BaKongo Diaspora. *International Journal of Historical Archaeology* 7(1):1–32.

Fennel, Desmond

1988 Against Revisionism. *Irish Review* 4:20–26.

FERGUSON, LELAND

1992 *Uncommon Ground: Archaeology and Early African America, 1650–1800.* Smithsonian Institution Press, Washington DC.

FESLER, GARRETT R.

2004 Living Arrangements among Enslaved Women and Men at an Early-Eighteenth-Century Virginia Quartering Site. In *Engendering African American Archaeology,* edited by Jillian E. Galle and Amy L. Young, pp. 177–236. University of Tennessee Press, Knoxville.

FIKE, RICHARD E.

1987 *The Bottle Book: A Comprehensive Guide to Historic Embossed Medicine Bottles.* Peregrine Smith Books, Salt Lake City.

FITTS, ROBERT K.

1999 The Archaeology of Middle-Class Domesticity and Gentility in Victorian Brooklyn. *Historical Archaeology* 33(1):39–62.

2000 The Five Points Reformed, 1865–1900. In *Tales of the Five Points: Working-Class Life in Nineteenth-Century New York, Volume 1: A Narrative History and Archaeology,* edited by Rebecca Yamin, pp. 67–89. John Milner Associates, Philadelphia.

FITTS, ROBERT K., AND REBECCA YAMIN

1996 *The Archaeology of Domesticity in Victorian Brooklyn.* John Milner Associates, Philadelphia.

FITZGERALD, PATRICK

1997 "Like Crickets to the Crevice of a Brew-house": Poor Irish Migrants in England, 1560–1640. In *Patterns of Migration,* edited by Patrick O'Sullivan, pp. 13–35. Leicester University Press, London.

FITZPATRICK, DAVID

1980 The Disappearance of the Irish Agricultural Laborer, 1841–1912. *Irish Economic and Social History* 7:66–92.

1984 *Irish Emigration 1801–1921.* Economic and Social History Society of Ireland, Dublin.

1987 The Modernization of the Irish Female. In *Rural Ireland, 1600–1900: Modernization and Change,* edited by Patrick O'Flanagan, Paul Ferguson, and Kevin Whelan, pp. 162–180. Cork University Press, Cork, Ireland.

FOGLEMAN, AARON S.

1998 From Slaves, Convicts, and Servants to Free Passengers: The Transformation of Immigration in the Era of the American Revolution. *Journal of American History* 85(1):43–76.

FONER, ERIC

1980 *Politics and Ideology in the Age of the Civil War.* Oxford University Press, New York.

FORD, BENJAMIN

1994 The Health and Sanitation of Postbellum Harpers Ferry. *Historical Archaeology* 28(4):49–61.

FORTIER, A.

1998 The Politics of "Italians Abroad": Nation, Diaspora, and New Geographies of Identity. *Diaspora* 7:197–224.

FOSTER, R. J.

1999 The Commercial Construction of New Nations. *Journal of Material Culture* 4(3):263–282.

FOSTER, ROY F.

1988 *Modern Ireland, 1600–1972.* Penguin Books, New York.

FOSTER, THOMAS CAMPBELL

1846 *Letters on the Condition of the People of Ireland.* Chapman and Hall, London.

FRANKLIN, MARIA

1996 The Material Expressions of Black American Protective Symbolism in Art and Archaeology. Paper presented at the Museum of Early Southern Decorative Arts Conference, Winston-Salem, NC.

2001 The Archaeological Dimensions of Soul Food: Interpreting Race, Culture, and Afro-Virginian Identity. In *Race and the Archaeology of Identity,* edited by Charles E. Orser Jr., pp. 88–107. University of Utah Press, Salt Lake City.

FREEMAN, THOMAS W.

1957 *Prefamine Ireland: A Study in Historical Geography.* Manchester University Press, Manchester.

FRIES, RUSSEL I.

1975 European vs. American Engineering: Pierre Charles L'Enfant and the Water Power System of Paterson, N.J. *Northeast Historical Archaeology* 4(1–2):68–96.

FRY, J. R.

1925 Immigrants and the Dupes of Demagogues. Originally published 1836. In *Historical Aspects of the Immigration Problem: Select Documents,* edited by E. Abbott, pp. 733–738. University of Chicago Press, Chicago.

GAILEY, ALAN

1984 *Rural Houses of the North of Ireland.* HMSO, Belfast.

1987 Changes in Irish Rural Housing, 1600–1900. In *Rural Ireland 1600–1900: Modernization and Change,* edited by Patrick O'Flanagan, Paul Ferguson, and Kevin Whelan, pp. 86–103. Cork University Press, Cork, Ireland.

GALLE, JILLIAN E., AND AMY L. YOUNG (EDITORS)
2004 *Engendering African American Archaeology.* University of Tennessee Press, Knoxville.

GALLMAN, J. M.
2000 *Receiving Erin's Children: Philadelphia, Liverpool, and the Irish Famine Migration, 1845–1855.* University of North Carolina Press, Chapel Hill.

GANS, H. J.
1995 *The War Against the Poor: The Underclass and Antipoverty Policy.* Basic Books, New York.

GARCIA, MARIA C.
1996 *Havana USA: Cuban Exiles and Cuban Americans in South Florida, 1959–1994.* University of California Press, Berkeley.

GARMAN, JAMES
1994 Viewing the Color Line Through the Material Culture of Death. *Historical Archaeology* 28(3):74–93.

GARVIN, TOM
1986 The Anatomy of a Nationalist Revolution: Ireland, 1858–1928. *Comparative Studies in Society and History* 28(3):468–501.

GATES, WILLIAM C., JR., AND DANA E. ORMOND
1982 The East Liverpool, Ohio, Pottery District: Identification of Manufacturers and Marks. *Historical Archaeology* 16(1–2):1–358 (special edition).

GEARY, LAWRENCE H.
1997 "The Living Were Out of Their Feeling": A Socio-cultural Analysis of the Great Famine in Ireland. In *The Famine Lectures,* ed. by Brendán O'Conaire, pp. 308–328. Roscommon Herald, Boyle.

GEISMAR, JOAN H.
1989 *History and Archaeology of the Greenwich Mews Site, Greenwich Village, New York.* Joan H. Geismar, New York.

GIBSON, FLORENCE E.
1951 *The Attitudes of the New York Irish Toward State and National Affairs, 1848–1892.* Columbia University Press, New York.

GILJE, PAUL A.
1987 *The Road to Mobocracy: Popular Disorder in New York City, 1763–1834.* University of North Carolina Press, Chapel Hill.
1997 The Development of an Irish American Community in New York City before the Great Migration. In *The New York Irish,* edited by Ronald H. Baylor and Timothy J. Meagher, pp. 48–69. John Hopkins University Press, Baltimore.

GILLESPIE, RAYMOND
1985 *Colonial Ulster: The Settlement of East Ulster.* Cork University Press, Cork, Ireland.

GILROY, PAUL
1993 *The Black Atlantic.* Harvard University Press, Cambridge, MA.
1997 Diaspora and the Detours of Identity. In *Identity and Difference,* edited by Kathryn Woodward, pp. 299–343. Sage Publications, London.
2003 The Black Atlantic as a Counterculture of Modernity. In *Theorizing Diaspora,* edited by Jana Evans Braziel and Anita Mannur, pp. 49–80. Blackwell, Malden, MA.

GLASSIE, HENRY
1975 *All Silver and No Brass: An Irish Christmas Mumming.* University of Pennsylvania Press, Philadelphia.

GODDEN, GEOFFREY A.
1991 *Encyclopedia of British Pottery and Porcelain Marks.* 11th ed. Barrie and Jenkins, London.

GOLDBERG, DAVID J.
1989 *A Tale of Three Cities: Labor Organization and Protest in Paterson, Passaic, and Lawrence, 1916–1921.* Rutgers University Press, New Brunswick, NJ.

GOLWAY, TERRY
2000 *For the Cause of Liberty: A Thousand Years of Ireland's Heroes.* Simon and Schuster, New York.

GOODFRIEND, JOYCE D.
1997 "Upon a bunch of straw": The Irish in Colonial New York City. In *The New York Irish,* edited by Ronald H. Baylor and Timothy J. Meagher, pp. 35–47. John Hopkins University Press, Baltimore.

GOODLAD, GRAHAM D.
1989 The Liberal Party and Gladstone's Land Purchase Bill of 1886. *Historical Journal* 32(3):627–641.

GORDON, WILLIAM
2003 Setting Sail for America: A Replica of an Irish "Famine Ship" Crosses the Atlantic. *Boston Globe,* 14 January:45–46. Boston.

GORN, ELLIOT J.
1987 "Good-Bye Boys, I Die a True American": Homicide, Nativism, and Working-Class Culture in Antebellum New York City. *Journal of American History* 74(2):388–410.

GRANT, I. F.
1961 *Highland Folkways.* Routledge and Kegan, London.

Gray, Jane
1993 Gender and Plebian Culture in Ulster. *Journal of Interdisciplinary History* 24(2):251–270.

Greeley, Andrew
1973 *That Most Distressful Nation.* Quagdrangle Books, Chicago.

Green, Harvey
1983 *The Light of Home: An Intimate View of the Lives of Women in Victoria America.* Pantheon Books, New York.

Grier, Katherine C.
1988 *Culture and Comfort: Parlor Making and Middle-Class Identity, 1850–1930.* Smithsonian Institution Press, Washington DC.

Groover, Mark D.
2003 *An Archaeological Study of Rural Capitalism and Material Life: The Gibbs Farmstead in Southern Appalachia, 1790–1920.* Kluwer Academic/Plenum Press, New York.

Guinnane, Timothy W.
1994 The Great Irish Famine and Population: The Long View. *American Economic Review* 84(2):303–308.
1997 *The Vanishing Irish: Households, Migration, and the Rural Economy in Ireland, 1850–1914.* Princeton University Press, Princeton, NJ.

Gundaker, Grey
2000 Discussion: Creolization, Complexity, and Time. *Historical Archaeology* 34(3):124–132.

Gusfield, Joseph R.
1986 *Symbolic Crusade: Status Politics and the American Temperance Movement.* University of Illinois Press, Urbana and Chicago.

Gutman, Herbert
1977 *Work, Culture, and Society in Industrializing America.* Vintage Books, New York.

Hachey, Thomas E., Joseph M. Hernon, and Lawrence J. McCaffrey
1989 *The Irish Experience.* Prentice Hall, Englewood Cliffs, NJ.

Hall, Stuart
1990 Culture Identity and Diaspora. In *Identity, Community, and Culture Difference,* edited by Jonathan Rutherford, pp. 222–237. Lawrence and Wishart, London.
1992 The Question of Cultural Identity. In *Modernity and Its Futures,* edited by S. Hall, D. Held, and A. McGrew, pp. 273–316. Polity Press in association with the Open University, Cambridge.

Handler, Jerome
1994 Determining African Birth from Skeletal Remains: A Note on Tooth Mutilation. *Historical Archaeology* 28(3):113–119.

1996 A Prone Burial from a Plantation Slave Cemetery in Barbados, West Indies: Possible Evidence from an African-type Witch or Other Negatively Viewed Person. *Historical Archaeology* 30(3):76–86.

1997 An African-Type Healer/Diviner and His Grave Goods: A Burial from a Plantation Slave Cemetery in Barbados, West Indies. *International Journal of Historical Archaeology* 1(2):91–130.

Handler, Jerome S., and F. W. Lange

1978 *Plantation Slavery in Barbados: An Archaeological and Historical Investigation.* Harvard University Press, Cambridge, MA.

Handlin, Oscar

1949 *Boston's Irish, 1790–1865: A Study in Acculturation.* Harvard University Press, Cambridge, MA.

Harlow, Ilana

1997 Creating Situations: Practical Jokes and the Revival of the Dead in Irish Tradition. *Journal of American Folklore* 110(436):140–168.

Harris, Ruth-Ann

1999 Introduction. In *The Great Famine and the Irish Diaspora in America,* edited by Arthur Gribben, pp. 1–20. University of Massachusetts Press, Boston.

Hartnett, Alexandra

2004 The Politics of the Pipe: Clay Pipes and Tobacco Consumption in Galway, Ireland. *International Journal of Historical Archaeology* 8(2):133–148.

Hauser, Mark W., and Christopher R. DeCorse

2003 Low-Fired Earthenwares in the African Diaspora: Problems and Prospects. *International Journal of Historical Archaeology* 7(1): 67–98.

Hershkowitz, Leo

1997 The Irish and the Emerging City: Settlement to 1844. In *The New York Irish,* edited by Ronald H. Baylor and Timothy J. Meagher, pp. 11–34. John Hopkins University Press, Baltimore.

Herzog, Don

1998 Poisoning the Minds of the Lower Orders. Princeton University Press, Princeton, NJ.

Hetton, Timothy J., and Jeffrey G. Williamson

1993 After the Famine: Emigration from Ireland, 1850–1913. *Journal of Economic History* 53(3):575–600.

Hill, J. Michael

1993 The Origins of the Scottish Plantations in Ulster to 1625: A Reinterpretation. *Journal of British Studies* 32(1):24–43.

Hoffman, E., and J. Mokyr

1983 Peasants, Potatoes, and Poverty: Transactions Costs in Prefamine Ireland. In *Technique, Spirit, and Form in the Making of the Modern*

Economy: Essays in Honor of William N. Parker, edited by G. Saxonhouse and G. Wright, pp. 115–145. JAI Press, Greenwich, CT.

Hogan, N.

1999 The Famine Beat: American Newspaper Coverage of the Great Hunger. In *The Great Famine and the Irish Diaspora in America,* edited by A. Gribben, pp. 155–179. University of Massachusetts Press, Amherst.

Holt, Michael F.

1973 The Politics of Impatience: The Origins of Know-Nothingism. *Journal of America History* 60(2):309–331.

Homeberger, Eric

1994 *Scenes from the Life of a City: Corruption and Conscience in New York.* Yale University Press, New Haven, CT.

Hoppen, K. Theodore

1999 *Ireland Since 1800: Conflict and Conformity.* Longman, London.

House of Commons

1825 *First Report from the Select Committee on the State of Ireland, 1825: Evidence of Colonel John Irwin of Tanregoe, County Sligo.* House of Commons, London.

Houston, C. J., and W. J. Smyth

1993 The Irish Diaspora: Emigration to the New World, 1720–1920. In *An Historical Geography of Ireland,* edited by B. J. Graham and L. J. Proudfoot, pp. 338–365. Academic Press, New York.

Howson, Jean

1991 Social Relations and Material Culture: A Critique of the Archaeology of Plantation Slavery. *Historical Archaeology* 24(4):78–91.

1992–1993 The Archaeology of Nineteenth-Century Health and Hygiene at the Sullivan Street Site in New York City. *Northeast Historical Archaeology* 21–22:137–160.

Hudgins, Carter L.

1999 Backcountry and Lowcountry: Perspectives on Charleston in the Context of Trans-Atlantic Culture, 1700–1850. *Historical Archaeology* 33(3):102–107.

Hughes, T. Jones

1987 Landholding and Settlement in the Counties of Meath and Cavan in the Nineteenth Century. In *Rural Ireland 1600–1900: Modernization and Change,* edited by Patrick O'Flanagan, Paul Ferguson, and Kevin Whelan, pp. 104–141. Cork University Press, Cork, Ireland.

Hull, Katherine L.

2004 Material Correlates of the Pre-Famine Agri-Social Hierarchy: Archaeological Evidence from County Roscommon, Republic of Ireland. Unpublished Ph.D. dissertation, University of Toronto.

HULL, KATHERINE L., AND STEPHEN A. BRIGHTON
2002 *A Report of Investigations for the Fifth Season of Archaeological Research at Ballykilcline Townland, Kilglass Parish, County Roscommon, Ireland.* Illinois State University, Normal.

HUTTON, SÉAN, AND PAUL STEWART (EDITORS)
1991 Introduction: Perspectives on Irish History and Social Studies. In *Ireland's Histories: Aspects of State, Society, and Ideology,* pp. 1–2. Routledge, London.

IGNATIEV, NOEL
1995 *How the Irish Became White.* Routledge, New York.

INGLE, MARJORIE, JEAN HOWSON, AND EDWARD S. RUTSCH
1990 *A Stage IA Cultural Resource Survey of the Proposed Foley Square Project in the Borough of Manhattan, New York, New York.* Historic Conservation and Interpretation, Newton, NJ.

INGLIS, HENRY D.
1835 *Ireland in 1834: A Journey Throughout Ireland, During the Spring, Summer, Autumn of 1834.* Whittaker, London.

JACKSON, JOHN A.
1986 *Migration.* Longman, New York.

JAMIESON, ROSS W.
1995 Material Culture and Social Death: African-American Burial Practices. *Historical Archaeology* 29(4):39–58.

JOHNSON, JAMES H.
1967 Harvest Migration from Nineteenth-Century Ireland. *Transactions of the Institute of British Geographers* 41:97–112.
1990 The Context of Migration: The Example of Ireland in the Nineteenth Century. *Transactions of the Institute of British Geographers* 15(3):259–276.

JONES, DAVID S.
1999 The Transfer of Land and the Emergence of the Graziers during the Famine Period. In *The Great Irish Famine and the Irish Diaspora in America,* edited by Arthur Gribben, pp. 85–103. University of Massachusetts Press, Amherst.

JONES, MALDWYN A.
1960 *American Immigration.* University of Chicago Press, Chicago.

JORDAN, DONALD
1998 The Irish National League and the "Unwritten Law": Rural Protest and Nation-Building in Ireland, 1882–1890. *Past and Present* 158:146–171.

KASSON, JOHN
1990 *Rudeness and Civility: Manners in Nineteenth-Century Urban America.* Hill and Wang, New York.

KEARNEY, M.

1995 The Local and the Global: The Anthropology of Globalization and Transnationalism. *Annual Review of Anthropology* 24:547–565.

KEMPER, S.

1993 The Nation Consumed: Buying and Believing in Sri Lanka. *Popular Culture* 5:377–393.

KENNEDY, LIAM, PAUL S. ELL, E. M. CRAWFORD, AND L. A. CLARKSON

1999 *Mapping the Great Irish Famine: A Survey of the Famine Decades.* Four Courts Press, Dublin.

KENNEDY, LIAM, AND DAVID S. JOHNSON

1997 The Union of Ireland and Britain, 1801–1921. In *The Making of Modern Irish History: Revisionism and The Revisionist Controversy,* edited by D. George Boyce and Alan O'Day, pp. 34–70. Routledge, New York.

KENNY, KEVIN

1998 *Making Sense of the Molly Maguires.* Oxford University Press, New York.

2003 Diaspora and Comparison: The Global Irish a Case Study. *Journal of American History* 90(1):134–162.

KERTZER, DAVID I.

1988 *Ritual, Politics, and Power.* Yale University Press, New Haven, CT.

KETCHUM, WILLIAM C., JR.

1983 *The Knopf Collectors' Guide to American Antiques: Pottery and Porcelain.* Knopf, New York.

KINEALY, CHRISTINE

1995 *This Great Calamity: The Irish Famine, 1845–52.* Roberts Rinehart, Boulder, CO.

1997 Was the Famine Inevitable? The Response of the Government to the Great Famine. In *The Famine Lectures,* edited by Brendán Ó Conaire, pp. 16–27. Roscommon Herald, Boyle, Ireland.

KING, C.

1998 Introduction: Nationalism, Transnationalism, and Postcommunism. In *Nations Abroad: Diaspora Politics and International Relations in the Former Soviet Union,* edited by C. King and N. J. Melvin, pp. 1–26. Westview Press, Boulder, CO.

KLINGELHOFER, ERIC

1992 The Renaissance Fortifications at Dunboy Castle, 1602: A Report of the 1989 Excavations. *Journal of the Cork Historical and Archaeological Society* 117:85–96.

KNOBEL, D. T.

1986 *Paddy and the Republic: Ethnicity and Nationality in Antebellum America.* Wesleyan University Press, Middletown, CT.

KRAUT, ALAN

1982 *The Huddled Masses: The Immigrant in American Society, 1880–1921.* Harlan Davidson, Arlington Heights, IL.

1994 *Silent Travelers: Germs, Genes, and the "Immigrant Menace."* Basic Books, New York.

1995 Plagues and Prejudice: Nativism's Construction of Disease in Nineteenth- and Twentieth-Century New York City. In *Hives of Sickness: Public Health and Epidemics in New York City,* edited by David Rosner, pp. 65–90. Rutgers University Press, New Brunswick, NJ.

1996 Illness and Medical Care Among Irish Immigrants in Antebellum New York. In *The New York Irish,* edited by Ronald H. Bayor and Timothy J. Meagher, pp. 153–168. Johns Hopkins University Press, Baltimore.

LACY, BRIAN

1979 The Archaeology of British Colonization in Ulster and America: A Comparative Approach. *Irish-American Review* 1:1–5.

LADIES OF THE MISSION

1854 *The Old Brewery and the New Mission House at the Five Points.* Stringer and Townsend, New York.

LAL, BRIJ V.

1996 The Odyssey of Indenture: Fragmentation and Reconstitution in the Indian Diaspora. *Diaspora* 5(2):167–188.

LANGAN-EGAN, MAUREEN

1999 *Galway Women in the Nineteenth Century.* Open Air, Dublin.

LARSEN, ERIC L.

1994 A Boardinghouse Madonna—Beyond the Aesthetics of a Portrait Created Through Medicinal Bottles. *Historical Archaeology* 28(4):68–79.

LEE, EVERETT S.

1966 Theory of Migration. *Demography* 3(1):47–57.

LEES, LYNN HOLLEN

1979 *Exiles of Erin: Irish Migrants in Victorian London.* Cornell University Press, Ithaca, NY.

LEFEBVRE, HENRI

1982 *The Sociology of Marx.* Trans. N. Guterman. Columbia University Press, New York.

1991 *The Production of Space.* Blackwell, Oxford.

LEHNER, LOIS

1988 *Lehner's Encyclopedia of U.S. Marks on Pottery, Porcelain, and Clay.* Collector Books, Paducah, KY.

LEONE, MARK P.

1995 A Historical Archaeology of Capitalism. *American Anthropologist* 47(4):251–268.

1999 Ceramics from Annapolis, Maryland: A Measure of Time Routines and Work Discipline. In *Historical Archaeologies of Capitalism,* edited by Mark P. Leone and Parker B. Potter Jr., pp. 195–216. Kluwer Academic/Plenum Press, New York.

2003 Where Is Culture to Be Found by Historical Archaeologists? In *The Recovery of Meaning: Historical Archaeology in the Eastern United States,* edited by Mark P. Leone and Parker B. Potter, pp. v–xxi. Percheron Press, Clinton Corners, NY.

LEVIN, L. C.

1925 The "Native American" in Congress. Originally published in 1847. Reprinted in *Historical Aspects of the Immigration Problem: Select Documents,* edited by Edith Abbott, pp. 755–757. University of Chicago Press, Chicago.

LEVINE, EDWARD M.

1966 *The Irish and Irish-Politicians: A Study of Culture and Social Alienation.* Notre Dame University Press, South Bend, IN.

LEYBURN, J. G.

1962 *The Scotch-Irish: A Social History.* University of North Carolina Press, Chapel Hill.

LILLEY, IAN

2004 Diaspora and Identity in Archaeology: Moving Beyond the Black Atlantic. In *A Companion to Social Archaeology,* edited by Lynn Meskell and Robert W. Preucel, pp. 287–312. Blackwell, Oxford.

LODZIAK, C.

2002 *The Myth of Consumerism.* Pluto Press, London.

LORD, REV. W. H.

1925 A Tract for the Times: National Hospitality. Originally published in 1855. Reprinted in *Historical Aspects of the Immigration Problem: Select Documents,* edited by Edith Abbott, pp. 802–810. University of Chicago Press, Chicago.

LOUGHLIN, JAMES

1986 *Gladstone, Home Rule, and the Ulster Question, 1882–1893.* Humanities Press International, Atlantic Highlands, NJ.

LUBENOW, W. C.

1985 Irish Home Rule and the Social Basis of the Great Separation in the Liberal Party in 1886. *Historical Journal* 28(1):125–142.

LUCAS, MARK T.
1994 A la Russe, à la Pell-Mell, or à la Practical: Ideology and the Compromise at the Late Nineteenth-Century Dinner Table. *Historical Archaeology* 28(4):80–93.

MACCARTHY-MORROGH, MICHAEL
1986 *The Munster Plantation: English Migration to Southern Ireland, 1538–1641*. Clarendon Press, New York.

MAC ÉINRÍ, PIARAS
2000 Introduction. In *The Irish Diaspora,* edited by Andrew Bielenberg, pp. 1–16. Pearson Education, Essex, England.

MACKILLOP, J.
1998 *Dictionary of Celtic Mythology.* Oxford University Press, Oxford.

MAGUIRE, JOHN F.
1864 *Father Mathew: A Biography.* D. & J. Sadlier, Boston.
1968 *The Irish American.* Arno Press, New York.

MAJEWSKI, TERESITA, AND MICHAEL B. SCHIFFER
2001 Beyond Consumption: Toward an Archaeology of Consumerism. In *Archaeologies of the Contemporary Past,* edited by Victor Bucjli and George Lucas, pp. 26–50. Routledge, London.

MANKEKAR, P.
1994 Reflections on Diasporic Identities: A Prolegomenon to an Analysis of Political Bifocality. *Diaspora* 3:349–371.

MARSHALL, W. F.
1979 *Ulster Sails West.* Genealogical Publishing, Baltimore, MD.

MARX, KARL, AND FREDERICK ENGELS
1972 *Ireland and the Irish Question.* International Publishers, New York.

MASSACHUSETTS SENATE REPORT NO. 46
1925 A Demand for the Control of Foreign Pauperism in Massachusetts. Originally published 1848. Reprinted in *Historical Aspects of the Immigration Problem: Select Documents,* edited by Edith Abbott, pp. 584–593. University of Chicago Press, Chicago.

MATHEW, FRANK J.
1890 *Father Mathew: His Life and Times.* Caswell, London.

MCCAFFREY, LAWRENCE J.
1992 *Textures of Irish America.* Syracuse University Press, Syracuse, NY.
1997 *The Irish-Catholic Diaspora in America.* Catholic University Press, Washington, DC.

MCCARTHY, JOHN P., B. R. ROULETTE, AND THOMAS A. J. CRIST
1995 *Phase IB/II and III Archaeological Investigations at the Philadelphia Gateway Development Parcel: An Archaeological Perspective on Philadelphia's Nineteenth-Century Irish-American Community.* Realen Gateway Development, Berwyn, PA

McCarthy, John P., Jeanne A. Ward, and Karl W. Hagglund
1996 *An Archaeological Evaluation and Data Recovery Investigation at the New Federal Building/United States Courthouse, Minneapolis, Minnesota: Material Insights into Working-Class Life in the Late 19th Century.* Institute for Minnesota Archaeology, Minneapolis.

McCauley, James White
2000 Under an Orange Banner: Reflections on the Northern Protestant Experiences of Emigration. In *Religion and Identity,* edited by Patrick O'Sullivan, pp. 43–69. Leicester University Press, London.

McCourt, Malachy
2003 *Danny Boy: The Legend of the Beloved Irish Ballad.* New American Library, New York.

McCracken, Grant
1988 *Culture and Consumption: New Approaches to the Symbolic Character of Consumer Goods and Activities.* Indiana University Press, Bloomington.

McEwan, Janis M.
2003 Archaeology and Ideology in Nineteenth Century Ireland: Nationalism or Neutrality? *British Archaeological Reports* 354 (June 1, 2003). John and Erica Hedges, Oxford.

McGowan, Joe
2001 *Echoes of a Savage Land.* Mercier Press, Cork, Ireland.

McGurk, John
1997 Wild Geese: The Irish in European Armies (Sixteenth to Eighteenth Centuries). In *Patterns of Migration,* Vol. 1, edited by Patrick O'Sullivan, pp. 36–62. Leicester University Press, London.

McKearin, Helen, and Kenneth M. Wilson
1978 *American Bottles and Flak and Their Ancestry.* Crown Publishers, New York.

McKivigan, J. R., and T. J. Robertson
1996 The Irish American Worker in Transition, 1877–1914. In *The New York Irish,* edited by Ronald H. Bayor and Timothy J. Meagher, pp. 301–320. Johns Hopkins University Press, Baltimore.

McLoughlin, Dympna
1997 Superfluous and Unwanted Deadweight: The Emigration of Nineteenth-Century Irish Pauper Women. In *Irish Women and Irish Migration,* edited by Patrick O'Sullivan, pp. 66–88. Leicester University Press, London.

McLoughlin, William
1978 *Revivals, Awakenings, and Reform.* University of Chicago Press, Chicago.

McTernan, John C.
1992 *Memory Harbour, the Port of Sligo: An Outline of Its Growth and Decline and Its Role as an Emigration Port.* Avena Publications, Sligo, Ireland.

Meagher, Timothy J.
2001 *Inventing Irish America: Generation, Class, and Ethnic Identity in a New England City, 1880–1928.* University of Notre Dame Press, South Bend, IN.

Meagher, Timothy J. (editor)
1986a Introduction. In *From Paddy to Studs: Irish-American Communities in the Turn of the Century Era, 1880 to 1920,* by Timothy J. Meagher, pp. 1–25.Greenwood Press, New York.
1986b Irish, American, Catholic: Irish-American Identity in Worcester, Massachusetts, 1880–1920. In *From Paddy to Studs: Irish-American Communities in the Turn of the Century Era, 1880 to 1920,* by Timothy J. Meagher, pp. 75–92.Greenwood Press, New York.
1986c *From Paddy to Studs: Irish-American Communities in the Turn of the Century Era, 1880 to 1920.* Greenwood Press, New York.

Merrifield, A.
2002 *Metromarxism: A Marxist Tale of the City.* Routledge, New York.

Meyers, Allan D.
1999 West African Tradition in the Decoration of Colonial Jamaican Folk Pottery. *International Journal of Historical Archaeology* 3(4):201–224.

Miller, George L.
1991 A Revised Set of CC Index Values for Classification and Economic Scaling of English Ceramics from 1787 to 1880. *Historical Archaeology* 25(1):1–25.

Miller, K., A. Schrier, B. D. Boling, and D. N. Doyle
2003 *Irish Immigrants in the Land of Canaan: Letters and Memoirs from Colonial and Revolutionary America, 1675–1815.* Oxford University Press, New York.

Miller, Kerby A.
1985 *Emigrants and Exiles: Ireland and the Irish Exodus to North America.* Oxford University Press, New York.
2000 Emigrants and Identities in the Old South. In *The Irish Diaspora,* edited by Andy Bielenberg, pp. 139–157. Pearson Education, Essex, England.

Miller, Kerby A., David N. Doyle, and Patricia Kelleher
1997 "For Love and Liberty": Irish Women, Migration, and Domesticity in Ireland and America, 1815–1920. In *Irish Women and Irish*

Migration, edited by Patrick O'Sullivan, pp. 41–65. Leicester University Press, London.

MILLER, ORLOFF

1991 *Archaeological Investigations at Salterstown, Co. Londonderry, Northern Ireland.* Ph.D. dissertation, Department of American Studies, University of Pennsylvania, Philadelphia. University Microfilms, Ann Arbor, MI.

MILNE, CLAUDIA

2000 Unhealthy New York: Sanitation and Health in the Tenements at Five Points. In *Tales of the Five Points: Working-Class Life in Nineteenth-Century New York, Volume 11: An Interpretive Approach to Understanding Working-Class Life,* edited by Rebecca Yamin, pp. 341–370. John Milner Associates, West Chester, PA.

MILNE, CLAUDIA, AND PAMELA CRABTREE

2000 Revealing Meals: Ethnicity, Economic Status, and Diet at the Five Points, 1800–1860. In *Tales of Five Points: Working-Class Life in 19th-Century New York: Volume II: An Interpretive Approach to Understanding Working-Class Life,* edited by Rebecca Yamin, pp. 130–196. John Milner Associates, West Chester, PA.

MINTZ, SIDNEY

1996 *Tasting Food, Tasting Freedom: Excursions into Eating, Culture, and the Past.* Beacon Press, Boston.

MITCHEL, JOHN

1854 *Jail Journal of Five Years in British Prisons.* Irishmen Office, Dublin.

1861 *The Last Conquest of Ireland (Perhaps).* Irishmen Office, Dublin.

MITCHELL, BRIAN C.

1986 "They do not differ greatly": The Pattern of Community Development Among the Irish in Late Nineteenth-Century Lowell, Massachusetts. In *From Paddy to Studs: Irish-American Communities in the Turn of the Century Era, 1880 to 1920,* edited by Timothy J. Meagher, pp. 53–73. Greenwood Press, New York.

MODELL, JOHN

1978 Patterns of Consumption, Acculturation, and Family Income Strategies in Late Nineteenth-Century America. In *Family and Population in Nineteenth-Century America,* edited by T. K. Hareven and M. A. Vinovskis, pp. 206–227. Princeton University Press, Princeton, NJ.

MOEHRING, EUGENE

1981 *Public Works and Patterns of Urban Real Estate Growth in Manhattan, 1834–1894.* Arno Press, New York.

MOHANTY, SATYA P.

2000 The Epistemic Status of Cultural Identity: On *Beloved* and the Post-Colonial Condition. In *Reclaiming Identity: Realist Theory and the*

Predicament of Postmodernism, edited by Paula M. L. Moya and Michael R. Hames-García, pp. 29–66. University of California Press, Berkeley.

MOHL, RAYMOND

1971 *Poverty in New York, 1783–1825.* Oxford University Press, New York.

MOKYR, JOEL

1980 Industrialization and Poverty in Ireland and the Netherlands. *Journal of Interdisciplinary History* 10(3):429–458.

1983 *Why Ireland Starved: A Quantitative and Analytical History of the Irish Economy, 1800–1845.* Allen and Unwin, London.

MOKYR, JOEL, AND CORMAC Ó GRÁDA

1984 New Developments in Irish Population History, 1700–1850. *Economic History Review* 37(4):473–488.

1988 Poor and Getting Poorer? Living Standards in Ireland Before the Famine. *Economic History Review* 41(2):209–235.

MONROE, J. CAMERON, AND SETH MALLIOS

2004 A Seventeenth-Century Colonial Cottage Industry: New Evidence and Dating Formula for Colono Pipes in the Chesapeake. *Historical Archaeology* 38(2):68–82.

MOODY, T. W.

1994 Irish History and Irish Mythology. In *Interpreting Irish History: The Debate on Historical Revisionism, 1938–1944,* edited by Ciaran Brady , pp. 71–86. Irish Academic Press, Dublin.

MOONEY, THOMAS

1850 *Nine Years in America.* J. McGlashan, Dublin.

MORASH, CHRISTOPHER

2000 Making Memories: The Literature of the Irish Famine. In *The Meaning of the Famine,* Vol. 6, edited by Patrick O'Sullivan, pp. 40–55. Leicester University Press, London.

MROZOWSKI, STEPHEN A., GRACE H. ZIESING, AND MARY C. BEAUDRY

1996 *Living on the Boott: Historical Archaeology at the Boott Mills Boardinghouses, Lowell, Massachusetts.* University of Massachusetts Press, Amherst.

MULLINS, PAUL R.

1999a *Race and Affluence: An Archaeology of African-America and Consumer Culture.* Kluwer Academic/Plenum Press, New York.

1999b "A Bold and Gorgeous Front": The Contradictions of African America and Consumer Culture. In *Historical Archaeologies of Capitalism,* edited by Mark P. Leone and Parker B. Potter Jr., pp. 169–193. Kluwer Academic/Plenum Press, New York.

1999c Race and the Genteel Consumer: Class and African-American Consumption, 1850–1930. *Historical Archaeology* 33(1):22–38.

2001 Racializing the Parlor: Race and Victorian Bric-a-Brac Consumption. In *Race and the Archaeology of Identity,* edited by Charles E. Orser Jr., pp. 158–176. University of Utah Press, Salt Lake City.

2004 Ideology, Power, and Capitalism: The Historical Archaeology of Consumption. In *A Companion to Social Archaeology,* edited by Lynne Meskell and Robert W. Preucel, pp. 195–211. Blackwell, Malden, MA.

MURPHY, M.

2000 Bridget and Biddy: Images of the Irish Servant Girl in *Punch* Cartoons, 1880–1890. In *New Perspectives of the Irish Diaspora,* edited by C. Fanning, pp. 152–175. Southern Illinois University Press, Carbondale.

MUSHKAT, JEROME

1981 Tammany: The Evolution of a Political Machine, 1789–1865. Syracuse University Press, Syracuse, NY.

NEAL, FRANK

1997 Black '47: Britain and the Famine Irish. In *The Famine Lectures,* edited by Brendán Ó Conaire, pp. 329–356. Roscommon Herald, Boyle, Ireland.

2000 The Famine Irish in England and Wales. In *The Meaning of the Famine,* Vol. 6, edited by Patrick O'Sullivan, pp. 56–80. Leicester University Press, London.

NEW YORK STATE ASSEMBLY DOCUMENT NO. 34

1925 Destitute Foreigners at the New York Dispensary. 1852. In *Historical Aspects of the Immigration Problem: Select Documents,* edited by Edith Abbott, pp. 611–612. University of Chicago Press, Chicago.

NÍ BHROMÉIL, ÚNA

2003 *Building Irish Identity in America, 1870–1915: The Gaelic Revival.* Four Courts Press, Dublin.

NOONAN, KATHLEEN M.

1998 "The Cruell Pressure of an Enraged, Barbarous People": Irish and English Identity in Seventeenth-Century Policy and Propaganda. *Historical Journal* 41(1):151–177.

O'CALLAGHAN, SEAN

2000 *To Hell or Barbados: The Ethnic Cleansing of Ireland.* Mountain Eagle Publications, Dingle.

Ó CATHAOIR, EVA

1997 The Workhouse During the Great Famine. In *The Famine Lectures,* edited by Brendán Ó Conaire, pp. 218–237. Roscommon Herald, Boyle, Ireland.

Ó Ciosáin, Niall

2001 Famine Memory and the Popular Representation of Scarcity. In *History and Memory in Modern Ireland,* edited by Ian McBride, pp. 95–117. Cambridge University Press, Cambridge.

O'Connor, Thomas H.

1995 *The Boston Irish: A Political History.* Back Bay Books, Boston.

O'Day, Alan

1986 *Parnell and the First Home Rule Episode, 1884–1887.* Gill and MacMillan, Dublin.

1996 Revising the Diaspora. In *The Making of Modern Irish History: Revisionism and Revisionist Controversy,* edited by D. G. Boyce and A. O'Day, pp. 163–187. Routledge, London.

O'Farrell, Patrick

1982 Whose Reality? The Irish Famine in History and Literature. *Historical Studies* 20(78):1–13.

O'Gallagher, Marianna

2000 The Orphans of Grosse Île: Canada and the Adoption of Irish Famine Orphans, 1847–1848. In *The Meaning of the Famine,* edited by Patrick O'Sullivan, pp. 81–111. Leicester University Press, London.

Ó Gráda, Cormac

1988 *Ireland Before and After the Famine: Explorations in Economic History, 1800–1930.* Manchester University Press, Manchester.

1989 *The Great Irish Famine.* MacMillan, Dublin.

1994 *Ireland: A New Economic History, 1780–1939.* Clarendon Press, Oxford.

1995 *The Great Irish Famine.* Cambridge University Press, Cambridge.

O'Grady, Joseph P.

1973 *How the Irish Became Americans.* Twayne, New York.

Ogundiron, Akin O.

2002 Filling a Gap in the Ife-Benin Interaction Field (Thirteenth–Sixteenth Centuries AD): Excavation in Iloyi Settlement, Ijesaland. *African Archaeological Review* 19(1):27–60.

Ohlmeyer, Jane

1999 Seventeenth-Century Ireland and the New British and Atlantic Histories. *American Historical Review* 104(2):446–462.

O'Mahony, Patrick, and Gerard Delanty

1998 *Rethinking Irish History: Nationalism, Identity, and Ideology.* MacMillan Press, London.

O'Neill, Kevin

1984 *Family and Farm in Pre-Famine Ireland: The Parish of Killashandra.* University of Wisconsin Press, Madison.

"One of 'Em" (editor)

1925 "America for Americans" in The Wide-Awake Gift: A Know-Nothing Token for 1855. Originally published 1855. Reprinted in *Historical Aspects of the Immigration Problem: Select Documents,* edited by Edith Abbott, pp. 791–793. University of Chicago Press, Chicago.

Orser, Charles E., Jr.

1994 The Archaeology of African-American Slave Religion in the Antebellum South. *Cambridge Archaeological Journal* 4:33–45.

1996a *A Historical Archaeology of the Modern World.* Plenum Press, New York.

1996b Can There Be an Archaeology of the Great Famine? In *"Fearful Realities": New Perspectives on the Famine,* edited by Chris Morash and Richard Hayes, pp. 77–89. Irish Academic Press, Dublin.

1998a Archaeology of the African Diaspora. *Annual Review of Anthropology* 27:63–82.

1998b *A Report of Investigations for the First Season of Archaeological Research at Ballykilcline Townland, Kilglass Parish, County Roscommon, Ireland.* Illinois State University, Normal.

1999 Archaeology and the Challenges of Capitalist Farm Tenancy in America. In *Historical Archaeology of Capitalism,* edited by Mark P. Leone and Parker B. Potter, pp. 143–167. Kluwer Academic Press, New York.

2000 Why Is There No Archaeology in Irish Studies? *Irish Studies Review* 8(2):157–165.

2001 Vessels of Honor and Dishonor: The Symbolic Character of Irish Earthenware. *New Hibernia Review* 5:83–100.

2003 Towards a Theory of Power for Historical Archaeology: Plantations and Space. In *The Recovery of Meaning: Historical Archaeology in the Eastern United States,* edited by Mark P. Leone and Parker B. Potter, pp. 313–343. Percheron Press, Clinton Corners, NY.

2004 *Race and Practice in Archaeological Interpretation.* University of Pennsylvania Press, Philadelphia.

2007 *The Archaeology of Race and Racialization in Historic America.* University of Florida Press, Gainesville.

Orser, Charles E., Jr., and Katherine L. Hull

1998 *A Report of Investigations for Archaeological Research at Mulliviltrin, County Roscommon, Ireland: A Tenant Village Destroyed During the Mass Evictions of 1847.* Centre for the Study of Rural Ireland, Normal, IL.

2001 *A Report of Investigations for the Third Season of Archaeological Research at Ballykilcline Townland, Kilglass Parish, County Roscommon, Ireland.* Illinois State University, Normal.

Orser, Charles, Jr., David S. Ryder, and Jessica Levon
2000 *A Report of Investigations for the Second Season of Archaeological Research at Ballykilcline Townland, Kilglass Parish, County Roscommon, Ireland.* Illinois State University, Normal.

O'Steen, Lisa
1999 Zooarchaeological Remains from Site 28PA151, Block 866 and Site 28PA152, Block 863: 19th–Early 20th-Century Irish, English, and Italian Immigrant Diet in Paterson, New Jersey. In *With Hope and Labor: Everyday Life in Paterson's Dublin Neighborhood,* Vol. 2, edited by Rebecca Yamin, pp. 1–34. John Milner Associates, West Chester, PA.

O'Sullivan, Patrick
1997a Introduction: Patterns of Migration. In *Patterns of Migration,* edited by Patrick O'Sullivan, pp. 1–12. Leicester University Press, London.
1997b Introduction to Volume 2: The Irish in the New Communities. In *The Irish in the New Communities,* edited by Patrick O'Sullivan, pp. 1–25. Leicester University Press, London.
2000 Introduction. In *The Meaning of the Famine,* edited by Patrick O'Sullivan, pp. 1–14. Leicester University Press, London.

O'Sullivan, Patrick, and A. Lucking
2000 The Famine World Wide: The Irish Famine and the Development of Famine Policy and Famine Theory. In *The Meaning of the Famine,* edited by Patrick O'Sullivan, pp. 195–232. Leicester University Press, London.

Ó Tuathaigh, M. A. G.
1994 Irish Historical "Revisionism": State of the Art or Ideological Project? In *Interpreting Irish History: The Debate on Historical Revisionism, 1938–1944,* edited by Ciaran Brady, pp. 306–326. Irish Academic Press, Dublin.

Panagakos, R.
1998 Citizens of the Trans-Nation: Political Mobilization, Multiculturalism, and Nationalism in the Greek Diaspora. *Diaspora* 7:53–73.

Panossian, R.
1998a The Armenians: Conflicting Identities and the Politics of Division. In *Nations Abroad: Diaspora Politics and International Relations in the Former Soviet Union,* edited by C. King and N. J. Melvin, pp. 79–102. Westview Press, Boulder, CO.
1998b Between Ambivalence and Intrusion: Politics and Identity in Armenian Diaspora Relations. *Diaspora* 7:149–196.

Parry, J. P.
1982 Religion and the Collapse of Gladstone's First Government, 1870–1874. *Historical Journal* 25(1):71–101.

PATERSON LABOR STANDARD.
2000 "Ireland and America." 22 November.

PAYNE, GEOFF (EDITOR)
2000 An Introduction to Social Divisions. In *Social Divisions,* edited by Geoff Payne, pp. 1–19. St. Martin's Press, New York.

PAYNTER, ROBERT
1988 Steps to an Archaeology of Capitalism: Material Change and Class Analysis. In *The Recovery of Meaning: Historical Archaeology in the Eastern United States,* edited by Mark P. Leone and Parker B. Potter, pp. 407–433. Percheron Press, New York.

PERNICONE, CAROL G.
1973 *The "Bloody Ould Sixth": A Social Analysis of a New York City Working-Class Community in the Mid-Nineteenth Century.* Ph.D. dissertation, Department of History, University of Rochester. University Microfilms, Ann Arbor.

PIKIRAYI, INNOCENT, AND GILBERT PWITI
1999 States, Traders, and Colonists: Historical Archaeology in Zimbabwe. *Historical Archaeology* 33(2):73–89.

PITTS, REGINALD H.
2000 "Suckers, Soap-Locks, Irishmen, and Plug-Uglies": Block 160, Municipal Politics, and Local Control. In *Tales of Five Points Working-Class Life in Nineteenth-Century New York, Volume II: An Interpretive Approach to Understanding Working-Class Life,* edited by Rebecca Yamin, pp. 59–85. John Milner Associates, West Chester, PA.

PÓIRTÉIR, CATHAL
1995 *Famine Echoes.* Gill and Macmillan, Dublin.

POSNANSKY, MERRICK
1999 West African Reflections on African-American Archaeology. In *I Too Am American: Archaeological Studies of African-American Life,* edited by Theresa A. Singleton, pp. 21–37. University of Virginia Press, Charlottesville.

POTTERIES OF TRENTON SOCIETY
2001 *From Teacups to Toilets.* Potteries of Trenton Society, Trenton, NJ.

PRAETZELLIS, A., AND S. B. STEWART (EDITORS)
2001 *Block Technical Reports: Historical Archaeology I-880 Cypress Replacement Project, Blocks 4, 5, 6, and 9.* California Department of Transportation, Oakland.

PRAETZELLIS, ADRIAN, AND MARY PRAETZELLIS
1992 Faces and Facades: Victorian Ideology in Early Sacramento. In *The Art and Mystery of Historical Archaeology: Essays in Honor of*

James Deetz, edited by Anne E. Yentsch and Mary C. Beaudry, pp. 75–99. CRC Press, Boca Raton, FL.

PRAETZELLIS, MARY, ADRIAN PRAETZELLIS, AND MARLEY BROWN III

1988 What Happened to the Silent Majority? Research Strategies for Studying Dominant Group Material Culture in the late 19th Century. In *New Directions in Archaeology: Documentary Archaeology in the New World,* edited by Mary C. Beaudry, pp. 192–202. Cambridge University Press, Cambridge.

PRUNTY, JACINTA

1998 *Dublin Slums, 1800–1925: A Study in Urban Geography.* Irish Academic Press, Dublin.

PUCKREIN, GARY A.

1984 *Little England: Plantation Society and Anglo-Barbadian Politics, 1627–1700.* New York University Press, New York.

PUTMAN'S MONTHLY: A MAGAZINE OF AMERICAN LITERATURE, SCIENCE, AND ART

1925 Who Are Americans? Originally published May 1855. In *Historical Aspects of the Immigration Problem: Select Documents,* edited by E. Abbott, pp. 793–799. University of Chicago Press, Chicago.

QUINLAN, TODD B.

1998 Big Whigs in the Mobilization of Irish Peasants: A Historical Sociology of Hegemony in Prefamine Ireland (1750s–1840s). *Sociological Forum* 13(2):247–264.

QUINN, DERMOT

2004 *The Irish in New Jersey: Four Centuries of American Life.* Rutgers University Press, New Brunswick, NJ.

QUINN, JOHN F.

1996 Father Mathew's Disciples: American Catholic Support for Temperance, 1840–1920. *Church History* 65(4):624–640.

RADHAKRISHNAN, R.

2003 Ethinicity in the Age of Diaspora. In *Theorizing Diaspora,* edited by Jana E. Braziel and Anita Mannur, pp. 119–131. Blackwell, Oxford.

RAFFERTY, OLIVER P.

1999 *The Church, the State, and the Fenian Threat, 1861–1875.* St. Martin's Press, New York.

RECKNER, PAUL

1999 Tobacco Pipes as Symbols of Ethnicity, National Identity, and Labor in Late Nineteenth-Century Paterson. In *With Hope and Labor: Everyday Life in Paterson's Dublin Neighborhood,* edited by Rebecca Yamin, pp. 147–153. John Milner Associates, West Chester, PA.

2000 Negotiating Patriotism at Five Points: Clay Tobacco Pipes and Patriotic Imagery among Trade Unionists and Nativists in a

Nineteenth-Century New York Neighborhood. In *Tales of Five Points Working-Class Life in Nineteenth-Century New York, Volume II: An Interpretive Approach to Understanding Working-Class Life,* edited by Rebecca Yamin, pp. 99–129. John Milner Associates, West Chester, PA.

ROEDIGER, DAVID R.

1991 *Wages of Whiteness: Race and the Making of the American Working Class.* Verso, New York.

ROLSTON, BILL, AND MICHAEL SHANNON

2002 *Encounters: How Racism Came to Ireland.* Beyond the Pale Publications, Belfast.

ROSENBERG, CARROLL S.

1971 *Religion and the Rise of the American City: The New York Mission Movement, 1812–1830.* Cornell University Press, Ithaca, NY.

ROSENBERG, CHARLES E.

1987 *The Cholera Years: The United States in 1832, 1849, and 1866.* University of Chicago Press, Chicago.

ROSNER, DAVID

1982 *A Once Charitable Enterprise: Hospitals and Health Care in Brooklyn and New York, 1885–1915.* Cambridge University Press, New York.

ROTHCHILD, NAN A., AND DARLENE BALKWILL

1993 The Meaning of Change in Urban Faunal Deposits. *Historical Archaeology* 27(2):71–89.

ROWLANDS, MICHAEL

2004 The Materiality of Sacred Power. In *Rethinking Materiality: The Engagement of Mind with the Material World,* edited by Elizabeth DeMarrais, Chris Gosden, and Colin Renfrew, pp. 197–204. McDonald Institute for Archaeological Research, Cambridge.

RUANE, J.

1992 Colonialism and the Interpretation of Irish Historical Development. In *Approaching the Past: Historical Anthropology Through Irish Case Studies,* edited by M. Silverman and P. H. Gulliver, pp. 293–323. Columbia University Press, New York.

RUSSELL, AARON E.

1997 Material Culture and African-American Spirituality at the Hermitage. *Historical Archaeology* 31(2):63–80.

RYAN, MARY P.

1981 *Cradle of Middle Class: The Family in Oneida County, New York, 1790–1865.* Cambridge University Press, Cambridge.

SAFRAN, W.

1991 Diasporas in Modern Societies: Myths of Homeland and Return. *Diaspora* 1:83–99.

SAID, EDWARD

1991 *Orientalism.* Vintage, New York.

SCALLY, ROBERT JAMES

1995 *The End of Hidden Ireland: Rebellion, Famine, and Emigration.* Oxford University Press, New York.

SHACKEL, PAUL A.

1996 *Culture Change and the New Technology: An Archaeology of the Early American Industrial Era.* Plenum Press, New York

1998 Classical and Liberal Republicanism and the New Consumer Culture. *International Journal of Historical Archaeology* 2(1):1–20.

SHANIN, TEODOR

1987 *Peasants and Peasant Societies.* Basil Blackwell, Oxford.

SHANNON, WILLIAM

1963 *The American Irish: A Political and Social Portrait.* MacMillan, New York.

SHELLY, THOMAS J.

2006 Twentieth-Century American Catholicism and Irish Americans. In *Making the Irish American: History and Heritage of the Irish in the United States,* edited by J. J. Lee and Marion R. Casey, pp. 574–608. New York University Press, New York.

SHEPARD, JILL

1977 *The "Redlegs" of Barbados: Their Origins and History.* Millwood, New York.

SHEPPERSON, GEORGE

1966 The African Abroad or the African Diaspora. *African Forum: A Quarterly Journal of Contemporary Affairs* 2:76–93.

SHUKLA, SANDHYA

2001 Locations for South Asian Diasporas. *Annual Review of Anthropology* 30:551–572.

SILVERMAN, MARILYN

2001 *Irish Working Class: Explorations in Political Economy and Hegemony, 1800–1950.* University of Toronto, Toronto.

SISSONS, J.

1997 Nation or Desti-Nation? Cook Islands Nationalism since 1965. In *Narratives of Nation in the South Pacific,* edited by T. Otto and N. Thomas, 163–188. Harwood Academia Publishers, Amsterdam.

SKERRET, ELLEN

1986 The Development of Catholic Identity Among Irish Americans in Chicago, 1880 to 1920. In *From Paddy to Studs: Irish-American Communities in the Turn of the Century Era, 1880 to 1920,* edited by Timothy J. Meagher, pp. 117–138. Greenwood Press, New York.

SLATER. I.

1846 *I. Slater's National Commercial Directory of Ireland.* I. Slater, Manchester.

SMITH, ANTHONY D.

1991 *National Identity.* Penguin Books, London.

SOWELL, THOMAS

1981 *Ethnic America: A History.* Basic Books, New York.

SPANN, EDWARD K.

1996 Union Green: The Irish Community and the Civil War. In *The New York Irish,* edited by Ronald H. Bayor and Timothy J. Meagher, pp. 193–209. John Hopkins University Press, Baltimore.

SPIVAK, GAYATRI C.

1988 *In Other Words.* Taylor and Francis, New York.

STAHL, ANN

2004 Making History in Banda: Reflections on the Construction of Africa's Past. *Historical Archaeology* 38(1):50–65.

STEEN, CARL

1999 Pottery, Intercolonial Trade, and Revolution: Domestic Earthenwares and the Development of an American Social Identity. *Historical Archaeology* 33(3):62–72.

STEWART, A. T. Q.

1977 *The Narrow Ground: Aspects of Ulster, 1609–1669.* Faber and Faber, London.

STINE, LINDA F., MELANIE A. CABAK, AND MARK D. GROOVER

1996 Blue Beads as African-American Cultural Symbols. *Historical Archaeology* 30(3):49–75.

STOTT, RICHARD B.

1990 *Worker's in the Metropolis: Class, Ethnicity, and Youth in Antebellum New York City.* Cornell University Press, Ithaca, NY.

SULLIVAN, CATHERINE

1994 Searching for Nineteenth-Century Florida Water Bottles. *Historical Archaeology* 28(1):78–98.

SUSSMAN, LYNNE

1985 *The Wheat Pattern: An Illustrated Survey.* National Historic Parks and Sites, Canadian Parks Service, Ottawa, ONT.

TAJFEL, H.

1981 *Human Groups and Social Categories: Studies in Social Psychology.* Cambridge University Press, Cambridge

TAKAKI, RONALD

1979 *Iron Cages: Race and Culture in Nineteenth-Century America.* Knopf, New York.

TANNER, MARCUS

2001 *Ireland's Holy Wars: The Struggle for a Nation's Soul, 1500–2000.* Yale University Press, New Haven, CT.

THERNSTROM, STEPHEN

1964 *Poverty and Progress: Social Mobility in a Nineteenth Century City.* Harvard University Press, Cambridge, MA.

THOMAS, BRIAN W., AND LARISSA THOMAS

2004 Gender and the Presentation of Self: An Example from the Hermitage. In *Engendering African American Archaeology: A Southern Perspective,* edited by Jillian E. Galle and Amy L. Young, pp. 101–131. University of Tennessee Press, Knoxville.

THORTON, P.

1978 *Seventeenth-Century Interior Decoration in England.* Yale University Press, New Haven, CT.

TÖLÖYAN, K.

1991 The Nation-State and Its Others: In Lieu of a Preface. *Diaspora* 1:3–7.

1996 Rethinking Diaspora(s): Stateless Power in the Transnational Moment. *Diaspora* 5(1):3–36.

TOWEY, MARTIN G.

1986 Kerry Patch Revisited: Irish Americans in St. Louis in the Turn of the Century. In *From Paddy to Studs: Irish-American Communities in the Turn of the Century Era, 1880 to 1920,* edited by Timothy J. Meagher, pp. 139–159. Greenwood Press, New York.

TRANSFIGURATION CHURCH

1977 *Transfiguration Church: A Church of Immigrants.* Park Publishing, New York.

UNITED STATES TWENTY-FIFTH CONGRESS, SECOND SESSION, HOUSE DOCUMENT NO. 70

1925 Dangers of Immigration Suggested: Memorial of 282 Citizens of Sutton and 325 Citizens of Milbury, in the State of Massachusetts, against Foreign Emigration. Originally published 1838. Reprinted in *Historical Aspects of the Immigration Problem: Select Documents,* edited by Edith Abbott, pp. 738–739. University of Chicago Press, Chicago.

VEIT, RICHARD

1996 "A Ray of Sunshine in the Sickroom": Archaeological Insights into Late 19th- and Early 20th-Century Medicine and Anesthesia. *Northeast Historical Archaeology* 25:33–50.

VERTOVEC, STEVEN

1997 Three Meanings of "Diaspora," Exemplified among South Asian Religions. *Diaspora* 6(3):277–299.

VINYARD, JOELLEN

1976 *The Irish on the Urban Frontier: Nineteenth-Century Detroit, 1850–1880.* Arno Press, New York.

VOSS, K.

1993 *The Making of American Exceptionalism: The Knights of Labor and Class Formation in the Nineteenth Century.* Cornell University Press, Ithaca, NY.

WALKER, MARK

2003 Aristocracies of Labor: Craft Unionism, Immigration, and Working-Class Households in West Oakland. Unpublished paper presented at the 36th Annual Conference on Historical and Underwater Archaeology, Providence, RI.

WALL, DIANA

1994 *The Archaeology of Gender: Separating the Spheres in Urban America.* Plenum Press, New York.

2001 Family Meals and Evening Parties: Constructing Domesticity in Nineteenth-Century Middle-Class New York. In *Lines that Divide: Historical Archaeologies of Race, Class, and Gender,* edited by James A. Delle, Stephen A. Mrozowskil, and Robert Paynter, pp. 109–141. University of Tennessee Press, Knoxville.

WALSH, WALTER J.

1996 Religion, Ethnicity, and History: Clues to the Cultural Construction of Law. In *The New York Irish,* edited by Ronald H. Bayor and Timothy J. Meagher, pp. 48–69. Johns Hopkins Press, Baltimore.

WALTER, BRONWEN

2001 *Outsiders Inside: Whiteness, Place, and Irish Women.* Routledge, New York.

WARD, DAVID

1989 *Poverty, Ethnicity, and the American City, 1840–1925.* Cambridge University Press, New York.

WARRING, GEORGE, JR.

1889 *Report of Social Statistics of Cities.* Government Printing Office, Washington, DC.

WATTERS, DAVID R.

1994 Mortuary Patterns at the Harney Site Slave Cemetery, Montserrat, in Caribbean Perspective. *Historical Archaeology* 28(3):56–73.

WEBER, MAX

1976 *The Protestant Work Ethic and the Spirit of Capitalism.* George Allen and Unwin, New York.

WEBSTER, JANE

1999 Resisting Traditions: Ceramics, Identity, and Consumer Choice in the Outer Hebrides from 1800 to the Present. *International Journal of Historical Archaeology* 3(1):53–73.

WEIK, TERRY

1997 The Archaeology of Maroon Societies in the Americas: Resistance, Cultural Continuity, and Transformation in the African Diaspora. *Historical Archaeology* 31(2):81–92.

WETHERBEE, JEAN

1980 *A Look at White Ironstone.* Wallace-Homestead, Des Moines, IA.

WHELAN, IRENE

2006 Religious Rivalry and the Making of Irish-American Identity. In *Making the Irish American: History and Heritage of the Irish in the United States,* edited by J. J. Lee and Marilyn Casey, pp. 271–285. New York University Press, New York.

WHELAN, KEVIN

1996 The Tree of Liberty: Radicalism, Catholicism, and the Construction of Irish Identity, 1760–1830. Cork University Press, Cork, Ireland.

1999 An Underground Gentry?: Catholic Middlemen in Eighteenth-Century Ireland. In *Irish Popular Culture, 1650–1850,* edited by J. A. Donnelly and K. A. Miller, pp. 118–172. Irish Academic Press, Dublin.

WILENTZ, SEAN

1984 *Chants Democratic: New York City and the Rise of the American Working Class, 1788–1850.* Oxford University Press, New York.

WILLIAMS, PETRA

1978 *Staffordshire Romantic Transfer Patterns: Cup Plates and Early Victorian China.* Fountain House East, Jeffersontown, KY.

WILLIAMS, PETRA, AND MARGUERITE R. WEBER

1986 *Staffordshire Romantic Transfer Patterns II: Cup Plates and Early Victorian China.* Fountain House East, Jeffersontown, KY.

WILSON, DAVID A.

1998 *United Irishmen, United States: Immigrant Radicals in the Early Republic.* Cornell University Press, Ithaca, NY.

WOOD-MARTIN, W. G.

1890 *History of Sligo: County and Town from the Close of the Revolution of 1688 to the Present Time.* Hodges, Figgis, Dublin.

WOODWARD, KATHRYN (EDITOR)

1997 *Identity and Difference.* Sage Publications, London.

YAMIN, REBECCA (EDITOR)

1999 *With Hope and Labor: Everyday Life in Paterson's Dublin Neighborhood, Volume 1: Data Recovery on Blocks 863 and 866 within the Route 19 Connector Corridor in Paterson, New Jersey.* John Milner Associates: West Chester, PA.

2000a People and Their Possessions. In *Tales of the Five Points: Working-Class Life in Nineteenth-Century New York, Volume 1: A Narrative History and Archaeology.* John Milner Associates, West Chester, PA.

2000b *Tales of the Five Points: Working-Class Life in Nineteenth-Century New York, Volume 2: A Narrative History and Archaeology.* Report submitted to the United States General Services Administration, New York.

YOUNG, ARTHUR

1780 *A Tour of Ireland with General Observations on the Present State of that Kingdom made in the Years 1776, 1777, and 1778.* T. Cadell and J. Dodsley, London.

YOUNG, LIZ

1996 Spaces for Famine: A Comparative Geographical Analysis of Famine in Ireland and the Highlands in the 1840s. *Transactions of the Institute of British Geographers* 21(4):666–680.

INDEX

Historical Archaeology of the Irish Diaspora was designed and typeset on a Macintosh computer system using InDesign software. The body text is set in 10/13 Sabon and display type is set in Sabon. This book was designed and typeset by Chad Pelton, and manufactured by Thomson-Shore, Inc.